Interesting Bronze Age History Facts

CRAFTED BY SKRIUWER

Copyright © 2025 by Skriuwer.

All rights reserved. No part of this book may be used or reproduced in any form whatsoever without written permission except in the case of brief quotations in critical articles or reviews.

At **Skriuwer**, we're more than just a team—we're a global community of people who love books. In Frisian, "Skriuwer" means "writer," and that's at the heart of what we do: creating and sharing books with readers worldwide. Wherever you are in the world, **Skriuwer** is here to inspire learning.

Frisian is one of the oldest languages in Europe, closely related to English and Dutch, and is spoken by about **500,000 people** in the province of **Friesland** (Fryslân), located in the northern Netherlands. It's the second official language of the Netherlands, but like many minority languages, Frisian faces the challenge of survival in a modern, globalized world.

We're using the money we earn to promote the Frisian language.

For more information, contact : **kontakt@skriuwer.com** (www.skriuwer.com)

Disclaimer:
The images in this book are creative reinterpretations of historical scenes. While every effort was made to accurately capture the essence of the periods depicted, some illustrations may include artistic embellishments or approximations. They are intended to evoke the atmosphere and spirit of the times rather than serve as precise historical records.

TABLE OF CONTENTS

CHAPTER 1: THE DAWN OF THE BRONZE AGE

- Gradual shift from stone to copper and early metal tools
- Origins of settled farming communities and emerging city-states
- Influence of environmental and social conditions on early metal use

CHAPTER 2: THE EMERGENCE OF BRONZE TECHNOLOGY

- Discovery of copper-tin alloy and advances in smelting
- Casting methods and the spread of bronze across regions
- Impact of stronger bronze tools on agriculture, crafts, and warfare

CHAPTER 3: MESOPOTAMIAN BRONZE CIVILIZATIONS

- Rise of city-states like Ur and Babylon
- Temple economies, ziggurats, and cuneiform administration
- Law codes, diplomacy, and mythic traditions in early empires

CHAPTER 4: BRONZE AGE EGYPT

- Pharaohs' divine rule and monumental architecture (pyramids, temples)
- Role of the Nile in agriculture and centralized administration
- Religious beliefs centered on Ma'at, afterlife, and cosmic harmony

CHAPTER 5: THE MINOANS AND THE BRONZE AGE AEGEAN

- Palatial complexes at Knossos, Phaistos, and vibrant fresco art
- Maritime trade, seafaring skills, and cultural exchanges
- Myths of bull-leaping and possible Labyrinth origins

CHAPTER 6: THE MYCENAEANS

- Fortified citadels (Mycenae, Tiryns) with "Cyclopean" walls
- Linear B tablets revealing palace-based economies
- Heroic lore that echoes in later Greek epics (Trojan War traditions)

CHAPTER 7: BRONZE AGE ANATOLIA AND THE HITTITES

- *Expansion of the Hittite Empire from Hattusa*
- *Treaties, vassal states, and the importance of chariot warfare*
- *Stone reliefs, cuneiform, and complex religious ceremonies*

CHAPTER 8: THE INDUS VALLEY CIVILIZATION

- *Urban planning with grid layouts and advanced drainage*
- *Standardized weights, seals, and extensive trade networks*
- *Undeciphered script and subtle artistic styles*

CHAPTER 9: ANCIENT CHINA IN THE BRONZE AGE

- *Xia, Shang, and early dynastic foundations*
- *Elaborate ritual bronzes via piece-mold casting*
- *Oracle bone divination and ancestral worship*

CHAPTER 10: BRONZE AGE EUROPE

- *Diverse tribal societies with hillforts and barrow burials*
- *Metal hoards, megalithic echoes, and regional craft traditions*
- *Connection to Aegean influences and evolving local cultures*

CHAPTER 11: THE TRADE NETWORKS OF THE BRONZE AGE

- *Long-distance exchange of metals (tin, copper) and luxury goods*
- *Maritime and overland routes linking civilizations*
- *Role of merchants, caravans, and diplomatic gift-giving*

CHAPTER 12: RELIGIOUS BELIEFS AND RITUALS

- *Polytheistic worship, temple economies, and priestly hierarchies*
- *Ceremonial practices, sacrifices, and cosmic order*
- *Influence of myth in daily devotion and state authority*

CHAPTER 13: WARFARE AND WEAPONS

- *Advancement of bronze swords, spears, axes, and chariots*
- *Rise of professional armies, fortifications, and siege tactics*
- *Strategic alliances, diplomatic treaties, and the influence of warfare on political power*

CHAPTER 14: DAILY LIFE IN BRONZE AGE SOCIETIES

- Farming, food supply, and the role of bronze tools in agriculture
- Family structures, gender roles, and village organization
- Trade, crafts, leisure, and the rhythms of ordinary existence

CHAPTER 15: ART, ARCHITECTURE, AND CULTURE

- Major monuments: ziggurats, pyramids, palaces, and megalithic sites
- Pottery styles, frescoes, metal casting, and decorative motifs
- Cultural cross-fertilization through shared designs and artistic themes

CHAPTER 16: POLITICAL STRUCTURES AND GOVERNANCE

- Temple-palace economies and scribal bureaucracies
- Dynastic rule, councils, law codes (Hammurabi), and diplomacy
- Empire-building, vassal systems, and the divine legitimation of kings

CHAPTER 17: THE BRONZE AGE COLLAPSE

- Converging factors: invasions, climate stress, and trade disruption
- Destruction of major palaces, end of interregional alliances
- How systems complexity fueled cascading failures across the Mediterranean world

CHAPTER 18: AFTERMATH OF THE BRONZE AGE COLLAPSE

- Survivors' reorganization into smaller polities and new trade networks
- Transition to iron technologies and localized governance
- Rise of Phoenician city-states, Neo-Hittite kingdoms, and early Greek "Dark Age" communities

CHAPTER 19: LEGENDS & MYTHS FROM THE BRONZE AGE

- Epic narratives shaping societal values
- Flood myths, heroic genealogies, and cosmic battles
- Ritual dramas and the endurance of mythic themes post-collapse

CHAPTER 20: LASTING LEGACIES OF THE BRONZE AGE

- Continuities in metallurgy, writing, religious institutions, and political frameworks
- Influence on later Iron Age empires and classical civilizations
- Modern rediscovery of Bronze Age culture and its ongoing significance

CHAPTER 1: THE DAWN OF THE BRONZE AGE

Introduction

The Bronze Age is a period in human history when people began to make widespread use of bronze tools and weapons. It followed the Stone Age and, in some regions, the brief Copper Age or Chalcolithic. The transition from stone to copper to bronze was not immediate or simple. It took many generations for people to learn new methods of mining, metalworking, and metal trade. During this time, societies started to grow beyond small farming villages. New cities emerged, trade routes expanded, and political structures became more organized.

In this chapter, we will explore the early conditions that paved the way for the Bronze Age. We will talk about how people lived before bronze, why the invention of metal tools and weapons mattered, and what changes happened in different parts of the world. While the specific start date of the Bronze Age varies by region, there are common factors that tied all these places together: the need for stronger and more reliable tools, the growth of farming, and the rise of social complexity. This chapter will introduce you to the "dawn" of the Bronze Age and set the stage for the many fascinating developments we will see in later chapters.

---

1. From Stone to Copper: A Gradual Shift

Before bronze tools appeared, people relied on stone, wood, bone, and other natural materials to make their implements. For thousands of years during the Paleolithic and Neolithic periods, humans crafted stone hand-axes, knives, scrapers, and arrowheads. These were effective for hunting, but they had limits. Stones could be sharp but also brittle. They would wear down quickly. They also required a specific kind of craftsmanship to flake them into useful shapes.

As time passed, some communities discovered native copper, which sometimes occurs in pure forms in nature. This led to what is sometimes called the Chalcolithic or Copper Age. Working with copper was not simple at first because it needed to be heated and hammered into shape. Unlike stone, copper could be reshaped by heating and then pounding, though it was still quite soft. This gave it advantages for certain tasks like cutting or drilling, but it also meant it was not as durable as later bronze items.

Yet even copper represented a major leap in technology. People who had reliable access to copper ore or native copper lumps were able to trade these metal items to other groups. These early steps set the foundation for a bigger shift, which occurred when people learned to mix copper with other metals, especially tin, to produce bronze. But for many communities, that knowledge was still in the future. The dawn of the Bronze Age, therefore, was not like flipping a switch. It was more of a slow process of exploration, trial, and error involving multiple cultural groups who realized that metal could change their lives.

2. Environmental and Social Conditions

One reason why the Bronze Age took hold in certain areas first has to do with environmental and social factors. Around the time the world transitioned from the Neolithic to the age of metals, there were shifts in climate patterns that affected agriculture. People began to settle in regions where the soil was fertile, rivers provided irrigation, and raw materials were within reach. River valleys, like those of the Tigris and Euphrates in Mesopotamia, the Nile in Egypt, the Indus in South Asia, and the Yellow River in China, became cradles of early civilization.

The availability of resources such as water for crops, fish, and game allowed communities to grow larger. With bigger populations, people started to specialize in different tasks. Some would farm, while others would weave baskets, build boats, or make pottery. This specialization eventually opened the door to metalworking as a distinct craft. Skilled individuals focused on learning the secrets of smelting copper ore, shaping copper tools, and then later exploring how to create stronger alloys.

In many places, the climate was somewhat stable, which helped predict harvest cycles. Steady harvests led to food surpluses. Surpluses supported craftsmen and traders, who did not need to spend all their time farming. This environment and social organization planted the seeds for the breakthroughs that would define the Bronze Age.

3. Early Mining and Metal Sources

The dawn of the Bronze Age was closely tied to the discovery and control of metal ore deposits. Copper was often the first metal that people learned to extract from the earth, through mining. Sometimes, lumps of native copper could be found on the ground, but more often, people had to dig into hillsides or deeper into the earth to locate copper veins. These early mining activities required considerable effort. Miners used stone hammers and antler picks to chip away at rock. These tunnels were dark, and the work was dangerous. Some of the earliest known mines date back thousands of years, indicating that metal procurement was a critical pursuit for many communities.

Over time, as copper supplies were mined and smelted, people realized that not all copper was the same. Sometimes, certain sources of copper naturally contained small amounts of other metals like arsenic or tin. When these ores were smelted, the resulting metal had different properties—often harder or more durable. This accidental discovery foreshadowed the intentional mixing of copper with tin to create bronze. But at the dawn of the Bronze Age, most metalworkers were still in a phase of discovery, testing various ores, learning to identify them, and experimenting with different techniques for heating and alloying.

Trade networks soon formed around these mines, since not every region had copper or tin deposits. The high demand for metal created a system of exchange where finished metal goods, or raw metal ingots, traveled across long distances. This growing network of trade contributed to the rise of powerful city-states and kingdoms, each eager to control the flow of metals and the prestige that came from them.

---

4. Shifts in Settlement Patterns

As metal tools gained importance, settlement patterns changed in many parts of the world. Rather than living in small, scattered farming communities, people started to form larger towns. Some of these towns were near rivers, crucial for transport and irrigation, while others developed around or near mineral deposits. With metals becoming increasingly important, controlling these mines could bring wealth and political power to local rulers or elites.

In Mesopotamia, for example, farming communities grew into city-states such as Uruk, Ur, and later Babylon. Along the Nile in Egypt, smaller settlements unified under powerful kings, eventually leading to a mighty empire. In the Indus Valley region, cities like Mohenjo-daro and Harappa emerged with advanced urban planning, drainage systems, and trade networks. These expansions did not happen overnight. They were slow, collective processes fueled by population growth, agricultural surplus, emerging trade, and the promise of metal-based technology.

Another factor shaping settlement patterns was defense. Metal weapons began to alter warfare, giving those who had them a military edge. For protection, communities built walls around their towns. As we move further into the Bronze Age, we see more evidence of planned fortifications, towers, and sometimes moats or ditches. But in this early phase, societies were only beginning to explore the ways metal could transform both attack and defense.

5. Early Beliefs and Religious Practices

While religion and spirituality in the Bronze Age varied from one culture to another, there were some shared ideas about the connection between metals and the divine or supernatural. The process of turning raw ore into shiny metal seemed almost magical. Metalworkers might be seen as special, possibly possessing secret knowledge or even magic. In many cultures, temples and religious centers played a role in collecting and redistributing surplus goods, including metals.

In Mesopotamia, temples served as economic hubs, storing grain and resources, and they might have sponsored or overseen workshops for craft specialists. In Egypt, the pharaoh was often considered a living god, and the resources of the state, including metal production, were controlled by royal authority. Across these regions, the idea that precious materials were gifts from gods or spirits helped reinforce the social power of rulers and priests who controlled them. While these beliefs would later become more complex, even in this early stage, people already saw a link between metals, religious life, and the structure of society.

6. Early Communication and Writing

Although writing systems are not strictly part of making bronze, the dawn of the Bronze Age in some regions was also tied to the development or expansion of early writing. In Mesopotamia, for instance, the earliest forms of writing (cuneiform) emerged to keep track of goods, trade, and temple offerings. This writing system used wedge-shaped marks pressed into clay tablets. As trade networks grew, the need to record transactions, shipments, and inventories rose. This need might have been partly driven by the increasing value of metal resources and other items.

Similarly, in Egypt, hieroglyphics developed and were often used on temple walls, monuments, and scrolls. Writing served many purposes—religious, administrative, and political. Though not every Bronze Age culture had a script, those that did found it helpful for governing larger populations and complex economies.

At the dawn of the Bronze Age, many of these writing systems were still taking shape. Yet the ability to record information about resources, including metals, gave certain societies a significant edge. This edge would become more apparent over time, as written laws, contracts, and treaties started to influence how societies organized themselves.

---

7. Cultural Exchanges and Migration

The early Bronze Age was also a time of migration and cultural exchange. Groups of people seeking better lands, more resources, or fleeing climate change sometimes traveled far. These movements put them in contact with other communities, leading to shared ideas and technologies. For example, the knowledge of how to smelt copper could spread through interactions between neighboring regions. Over time, people realized that some metals were rarer than others. The hunt for tin, which was necessary to create bronze of a higher quality, caused traders and explorers to set out on long-distance journeys.

Nomadic groups moved across the steppes of Eurasia, bringing with them horses and different forms of warfare. In some regions, conflict arose as settled farming communities clashed with newcomers. In other cases, peaceful exchanges took place, leading to intermarriage, trade agreements, and alliances. Such interactions fueled the spread of bronze technology, pushing it beyond its original heartlands into many parts of Europe, Asia, and North Africa.

---

8. Timeline Differences Across Regions

It's important to note that the Bronze Age did not start at the same time everywhere. The earliest evidence of copper smelting appears in places like the Near East, in regions that would later become home to Mesopotamian civilizations. Over time, the knowledge spread to other areas. In some parts of the world, like sub-Saharan Africa or the Americas, the transition to a Bronze Age took a different path or happened much later—or did not follow the same pattern at all.

For instance, the earliest forms of bronze technology in the Near East date to around 3300–3000 BCE. In Egypt, bronze came into common use slightly later. In the Indus Valley, the Bronze Age culture is traced back to around 3300–2600 BCE, but it had its own unique characteristics. In China, the Bronze Age is often linked with the rise of the Shang Dynasty around 1600 BCE, though early bronze casting in China might date somewhat earlier. Europe's Bronze Age varied from region to region, but it generally kicked off around 3200–2000 BCE in different parts.

Because of these varied timelines, we can't say there was a single, global dawn of the Bronze Age. Instead, each region had its own journey, shaped by local resources, trade, social structures, and possibly even random chance. Still, the overall pattern is clear: once people realized the power of bronze, it quickly became a prized material, fueling social changes that would reshape civilizations.

---

9. Growing Importance of Trade

Even at this early stage, trade began to knit different regions together. Merchants or traders who saw the opportunity to profit from copper and tin traveled to distant lands. They came back with metals, precious stones, or exotic goods. Over land, trade caravans used donkeys, horses, and sometimes early wheeled vehicles to move goods. Over water, people built rafts, reed boats, or early wooden ships to transport cargo along rivers or across coastlines.

Trade routes helped spread not only metals but also ideas and cultural practices. Pottery styles, religious symbols, and artistic motifs might travel with merchants. In port towns and along caravan stops, people from different places would meet, exchange stories, talk about their gods, and show off their products. It was in these melting pots of trade that new ideas often took root and spread.

---

10. The Role of Elites and Emerging Leadership

At the dawn of the Bronze Age, as societies grew, leadership structures became more formal. In smaller farming communities, decisions were often made by elders or local chiefs. But as metals, trade, and agriculture allowed populations to expand, more complex leadership emerged. Some leaders gained power by claiming religious authority—saying they spoke for the gods or that they were divine themselves. Others took power through military strength, organizing warriors to protect the settlement or to raid neighbors.

These leaders, whether kings, chiefs, or priestly rulers, recognized the importance of controlling metal resources. They might sponsor mining expeditions or form alliances with regions that had vital resources. Over time, controlling the production and distribution of bronze tools and weapons became a way to solidify power. Early city-states and kingdoms often boasted of their wealth in metal, building grand structures or tombs to show off their prosperity.

---

11. Agricultural Developments and Metal Tools

The shift to metal tools did more than just improve weaponry. In many areas, metal plowshares, sickles, and other farming implements made agriculture more efficient. Fields could be turned over faster with sturdy bronze plows than with wooden or stone-tipped plows. Harvesting became quicker with stronger sickles that retained a sharp edge longer. These improvements increased food production, which in turn supported larger populations and freed more people to focus on trades, crafts, or other specialized jobs.

In regions like Mesopotamia, where irrigation was key, bronze tools helped maintain canals and dikes. Workers could dig more effectively or repair breaches faster. This further tied metal to the fate of these early civilizations. Societies that harnessed bronze tools for farming, water management, and infrastructure had a better chance to thrive, giving them an edge over their neighbors who were still working mostly with stone or wooden tools.

12. Ritual Significance of Metal

In the early Bronze Age, metal objects also held symbolic or religious importance. People sometimes placed precious metal items—like ornate weapons, jewelry, or small figurines—in graves. These items might have been offerings to the gods or signs of the dead person's status. Metal could represent wealth, power, or divine favor. A finely made bronze dagger or axe might be adorned with designs that held cultural or spiritual meaning.

Such rituals remind us that the dawn of the Bronze Age was about more than just practical improvements. People did not only see bronze as a stronger tool; they also saw it as something special and even magical. The process of turning raw ore into gleaming metal connected them to mysterious forces. In many cultures, metalworkers had a special place in society, sometimes acting as ritual specialists who understood the secrets of fire and transformation.

13. Challenges and Conflicts

While the Bronze Age brought many benefits, it also introduced new challenges. Conflicts could arise when different groups competed for control of metal sources or trade routes. Raids became more likely once warriors had access to bronze weapons. This pushed some communities to develop defensive structures or form alliances with powerful neighbors. Other groups might be forced to migrate to avoid conflicts, taking their culture and knowledge of metals with them to new lands.

Natural disasters like droughts, floods, or epidemics also posed threats. If a particular region suffered a severe crop failure, its population might decline or be forced to move, altering local balances of power. The story of the Bronze Age is not just about progress and expansion, but also about how societies responded to the many obstacles they faced. At the dawn of this era, people still lacked the advanced political structures or widespread trade networks that would come later. They often relied on local leaders or ad-hoc alliances to solve big problems.

14. Artistic and Cultural Beginnings

In these early Bronze Age communities, art began to flourish in new ways. Some of the earliest metal objects, such as pins, brooches, or decorative plaques, displayed simple designs. Over time, craftspeople experimented with more complex shapes and patterns, sometimes inlaid with precious stones or other metals. Ceramics also evolved during this period, as potters used new techniques or decorative styles, influenced in part by contact with other regions.

Mythologies and storytelling traditions likely grew too, though much of that oral tradition is lost to us now. People might gather around fires, in communal halls, or in temple courtyards to tell tales of gods, heroes, and mythical events. These stories served as a cultural glue, binding communities together with shared beliefs and histories. While we do not have direct written records of all these tales from the earliest Bronze Age phases, later myths and epics (like the Sumerian or Egyptian stories) suggest a rich oral tradition that was already forming.

15. Health and Diet in Early Bronze Age Societies

Though the Bronze Age brought many advancements, people's daily life could still be tough. Diets often revolved around grains like barley or wheat, along with vegetables, fruits, and occasionally meat from domesticated animals such as goats, sheep, and cattle. The surplus of grain was crucial for feeding growing populations, but malnutrition could still happen if crops failed or if people did not have access to a varied diet.

Diseases were a constant challenge. Large settlements led to issues with waste management, clean water, and the spread of illnesses. People did not understand germs the way we do today, but they developed communal practices to maintain some level of cleanliness. In some places, drainage systems and public wells were created, hinting that leaders recognized the importance of sanitation. However, life expectancy was still lower compared to modern times, and infant mortality rates were high. Even so, the dawn of the Bronze Age marked a period of overall population growth, suggesting that the benefits of agriculture and metal tools outweighed the risks.

16. Early Seafaring and Coastal Communities

In some regions, such as the Aegean Sea, coastal communities began to develop rudimentary seafaring skills. Wooden boats were used to travel between islands, and eventually, people learned to cross larger stretches of open water. Maritime trade introduced a new dimension to the Bronze Age economy. Goods could move more quickly by sea than over difficult land routes. Islands that had metal resources or valuable goods could flourish as trade hubs.

This maritime activity also spurred cultural exchange. It was easier for ideas, beliefs, and even art styles to travel from one island to another. Over time, entire civilizations—like the Minoans on Crete—would become known for their seafaring abilities. But at the dawn of the Bronze Age, these developments were just beginning. People were still experimenting with boat designs, navigation methods, and ways to handle cargo on rough seas.

---

17. Transition from Subsistence to Surplus

One of the biggest social changes at the dawn of the Bronze Age was the shift from a subsistence-level economy to one that could generate and store surplus. Subsistence farming means growing just enough food to feed one's own family or community. Surplus means producing extra that can be traded or stored for future use. Metal tools played a big role here by increasing agricultural efficiency. As more surplus was generated, not everyone needed to work the fields. Craftspeople, traders, priests, and other specialists became increasingly common.

This shift also led to more complexity in social hierarchy. As some individuals or families accumulated wealth in the form of metal tools, jewelry, or stored grain, they gained more influence. They could hire laborers or sponsor building projects. The dawn of the Bronze Age was, in many ways, the dawn of more pronounced social stratification. Wealthy elites emerged, and they often used that wealth to commission larger houses or tombs and display luxury items made of metal.

18. Learning Through Trial and Error

It is important to remember that there was no single "instruction manual" for how to transition into the Bronze Age. Early societies learned through experimentation. Some might have noticed that adding a certain kind of ore to copper made it stronger. Others discovered new smelting techniques by accidentally overheating ore or changing the type of furnace they used. News of such discoveries spread slowly, through traders, travelers, or migrating groups.

In many ways, the dawn of the Bronze Age was a period of great curiosity. Each new method of metal production could lead to unexpected advances. Craftspeople realized they could create new shapes or designs by pouring molten metal into molds. This was different from older methods that relied mostly on hammering and shaping. As people refined their metalworking skills, the potential uses of bronze grew, setting the stage for even more dramatic social changes.

---

19. The Wider World

Though we often focus on the "cradles of civilization" in the Near East, the dawn of the Bronze Age also influenced Europe, parts of Asia, and North Africa. In Europe, the transition was slower in some regions, but eventually, local groups began to acquire or produce bronze tools. Over time, megalithic cultures that built large stone monuments (like Stonehenge) came into contact with bronze-working societies. Across Asia, each region's path varied, but China, as we will see in later chapters, developed an elaborate bronze culture with advanced casting techniques.

This interconnectedness was still in its early stages. Not every corner of the Old World felt the impact of bronze right away. Still, the trend was clear: metalworking was a game-changer. Wherever it spread, it brought the chance for societies to grow, trade, and defend themselves more effectively. The dawn of the Bronze Age was thus a story unfolding across vast distances, linking communities that once might have seemed isolated.

20. Conclusion: Setting the Stage for Further Developments

The dawn of the Bronze Age was an exciting time in human history. It was marked by slow but important transformations in technology, social structure, and daily life. People learned to mine copper and occasionally tin, leading to early experiments with metal alloys. Settlements grew larger as agriculture became more productive, and trade routes began to span longer distances. Religion and leadership also evolved, as people who controlled resources—especially metals—rose to new levels of power.

CHAPTER 2: THE EMERGENCE OF BRONZE TECHNOLOGY

Introduction

Bronze did not appear out of nowhere. It was the result of countless experiments with copper and other ores—mainly tin—that led to an alloy stronger and more durable than copper alone. In this chapter, we will focus on how bronze technology emerged, spread, and changed the course of history. We will look at the process of smelting copper and how adding tin or other metals enhanced its properties. We will also explore why bronze was so valued, how it shaped crafts and warfare, and how it stimulated trade across vast regions.

The switch from using mostly stone or pure copper to using bronze might seem like a technical detail. But in fact, it set off a ripple effect that touched every aspect of society. Bronze tools and weapons lasted longer, cut deeper, and had a range of uses. This allowed more advanced farming, helped carve large structures, and made armies more formidable. The quest for tin and other resources opened new trade routes. In short, the emergence of bronze technology was a turning point that pushed societies into a new era of complexity and power.

---

1. The Metallurgical Breakthrough: Mixing Copper and Tin

Bronze is typically made by mixing about 90% copper with 10% tin, although exact ratios varied. Sometimes other metals like arsenic, lead, or zinc were present in small amounts, either by accident or on purpose. The key was discovering that copper became harder, more durable, and easier to cast when combined with tin. This was a huge breakthrough in metallurgy, but it did not happen overnight. Early metalworkers might have stumbled upon copper-tin ores in the same location, discovering that the resulting metal had better qualities than pure copper. Over time, they refined the process, learning the best ratios of copper to tin to produce different grades of bronze.

Smelting involved heating the metal ore to a high temperature in a furnace. The metals would melt and separate from the rock, allowing the molten metal to be collected. This process required a strong heat source, often charcoal, and a controlled airflow to reach the temperatures needed to melt copper (which melts at around 1085°C). Tin has a lower melting point (around 232°C), so it was often added later or found naturally in the ore. Managing these temperatures required skill and the right furnaces or pits. Early furnaces were typically made of clay or stone, with openings that allowed bellows or blowpipes to feed air into the fire.

2. Early Evidence of Bronze Production

The earliest signs of bronze production can be traced back to regions in the Near East and Southeast Europe, dating to the late 4th and early 3rd millennium BCE. In places like Sumer (in Mesopotamia) and ancient Anatolia, archaeologists have found tools, weapons, and casting molds that point to intentional bronze-making. These artifacts show that by this stage, craftspeople were not just accidentally discovering bronze but deliberately creating it.

In China, bronze technology developed later, but once it did, it took on a distinct character. Chinese bronzes were often made using advanced casting techniques in piece-mold systems, which we will explore in later chapters. Meanwhile, the Indus Valley Civilization created bronze tools and ornaments, and in Egypt, bronze gradually replaced copper for many purposes. Each region had its own style and methods, shaped by local resources, cultural traditions, and the needs of the people.

3. Casting and Shaping Bronze

One of the advantages of bronze over stone was that it could be melted and poured into molds. Craftspeople created molds from clay or stone, carving out the shape they wanted for tools, weapons, or decorative items. The molten bronze would fill the mold, and once it cooled, the mold was broken or opened to reveal the newly shaped object. This method allowed for more standardized production, meaning items could be made more consistently in larger quantities.

Hammering and shaping the cooled bronze was also possible. While casting made it easier to mass-produce certain objects, hammering refined the edges or added details. The flexibility of bronze to be cast or hammered made it a preferred material for all sorts of tools—axes, daggers, chisels, saws, and more. This versatility contributed to its popularity and helped drive the economies of Bronze Age civilizations.

4. Why Bronze? Advantages over Copper and Stone

Pure copper tools were an improvement over stone in some ways, but copper was relatively soft. It would bend or dull after repeated use. Adding tin made the metal harder and more resistant to wear. A bronze axe would hold its edge longer, a bronze sword would be stronger in battle, and a bronze chisel could cut into wood or stone more effectively. These qualities had a profound impact on daily life and warfare.

Stone tools could still be useful for certain tasks, and in many areas, stone remained in use alongside bronze for quite some time. But as more regions discovered or imported tin, bronze eventually overtook stone in most important tasks. Bronze tools meant carpenters could fashion more sophisticated wooden items—furniture, planks for building boats, and even detailed carvings. Farmers could plow deeper into the soil and harvest more efficiently. Scribes and artists could produce intricate seals, figurines, and ceremonial items that showcased a level of detail stone could not match.

5. The Tin Problem: A Rare and Crucial Resource

Tin is not as widely found as copper. This fact created a constant demand for tin and spurred long-distance trade networks. Some of the known ancient tin sources included regions in modern-day Afghanistan, the Iberian Peninsula, parts of Central Europe, and Cornwall in Britain (though Cornwall's tin may have been exploited more in the later Bronze Age). Because tin was harder to come by, controlling access to tin could make a society rich and powerful.

Merchants who specialized in tin became valuable links between mining regions and the growing city-states that needed bronze. Tin may have traveled by land via caravan routes or by sea in small ships or boats. The result was increased interaction between cultures, along with competition and sometimes conflict over mining sites. The "tin problem" was that without tin, you could not easily make high-quality bronze. This pushed many early states to venture beyond their borders to secure a steady supply.

6. Bronze as a Status Symbol

Because it was so valuable, bronze items also served as status symbols. In many Bronze Age societies, owning a bronze sword or a beautifully crafted bronze vessel signaled wealth and power. Royal tombs often contained lavish bronze artifacts, indicating that the elite had the means to acquire and commission these items. Temples, too, might display or store bronze objects as offerings to the gods.

This status aspect encouraged artisans to develop more artistic and decorative styles. Handles of daggers might be ornamented with intricate patterns, or large ceremonial axes might feature images of mythical creatures. This union of art and metallurgy would shape the cultural identity of numerous Bronze Age civilizations, adding a layer of glamour and mystery around bronze artifacts.

7. Effects on Warfare

The emergence of bronze technology changed warfare significantly. Although stone-tipped spears and arrows could still kill, bronze weapons offered more durability and sharper points. Warriors armed with bronze swords, spears, and helmets had an advantage. Over time, entire armies began to equip themselves with bronze gear, which included not just weapons but also shields and protective armor (though early armor was often made from leather or layered materials reinforced with bronze scales).

Chariots also became important in some regions, such as the Near East and Egypt. The wheels and fittings of chariots often included bronze components that made them lighter and sturdier than older wooden designs. These chariots could carry archers swiftly across battlefields, adding a new dynamic to warfare. As we will see in later chapters, the need for bronze weaponry and the development of professional armies played a role in the rise of larger kingdoms and empires.

8. Agricultural Advancements

Beyond warfare, bronze tools were crucial in agriculture. A bronze plowshare could break tougher soil than a simple wooden blade, allowing farmers to cultivate land more efficiently. Sickles and scythes made from bronze retained their sharpness longer, speeding up the harvest and minimizing crop loss. This meant that larger fields could be tended by fewer laborers, increasing the potential for surplus.

Irrigation works also benefited from bronze. Shovels, picks, and other implements helped dig canals and water channels. Societies like those in Mesopotamia, which heavily relied on irrigation, gained a lot from improved metal tools. By making the land more productive, these tools helped support larger populations, which in turn supported more specialized workers—priests, scribes, traders, and metalworkers themselves.

9. Specialized Craftsmen and Workshops

As bronze gained popularity, specialized workshops emerged. Skilled metalworkers might pass their craft down through families or train apprentices. In larger city-states, these workshops might be sponsored by the palace or temple, ensuring a steady supply of bronze tools and weapons. Artisans experimented with different alloys, casting techniques, and decorative methods. Over time, each region developed its own "school" of bronze craftsmanship. Some areas became known for weapon smithing, while others specialized in making ritual vessels or jewelry.

These craft specialists often lived in or near urban centers. Their work was in high demand, not just locally but sometimes abroad through trade connections.

This gave them a measure of importance, though they were not always part of the elite. Still, the presence of skilled metalworkers enhanced a city's reputation and power. After all, a city that could produce large numbers of bronze weapons had a better chance of defending itself or projecting force onto others.

10. Cultural Exchange and Influence

The widespread desire for bronze tools and weapons also accelerated cultural exchange. Traders moving metals and finished products across regions did more than just pass along materials—they brought stories, religious ideas, styles of art, and even new technologies. For example, a decorative motif or casting technique developed in one workshop could inspire artisans in distant lands. This blending of ideas contributed to a cosmopolitan atmosphere in some of the major trade hubs.

In certain cases, we see the blending of artistic styles that could not have existed if not for the movement of craftspeople and goods across long distances. Symbols or deities from one culture might appear in the artwork or religious ceremonies of another. While each region maintained its unique identity, these interactions helped push innovation. This cross-pollination of ideas was one of the most important side effects of bronze technology and the trade networks that sprang up around it.

11. Emerging Economic Systems

As bronze objects became more central to everyday life, economic systems began to adapt. In some places, bronze became a form of wealth that could be stored or exchanged. Ingots of standardized shapes and weights were used as a form of currency in trade dealings. Temples and palaces might collect and redistribute bronze, controlling the flow of valuable metal through society. This control could make or break economies, especially if external trade routes were disrupted.

The concept of debt, wages, and taxation took shape in part because of the need to manage resources like grain and metal. Record-keeping became more sophisticated, and scribes documented transactions, inventories, and agreements. Over time, these economic systems would become even more complex, laying the groundwork for advanced financial practices in later centuries. But it was the introduction and spread of bronze technology that helped spark these changes, forcing societies to figure out how to manage a resource that was in high demand and not always easy to acquire.

12. Religious and Ceremonial Objects

Bronze was not limited to practical and military uses. It also found a prominent place in religion and ceremony. Large bronze bells, gongs, or other musical instruments were used in temples for rituals. Statues of gods, animals, or mythical creatures were cast to adorn temple complexes or palatial courtyards. Bronze mirrors, plates, and other ritual items took on sacred importance, reflecting the belief that metal carried a special, almost divine quality.

In some cultures, it was common to bury bronze objects as offerings to gods or ancestors, or to place them in tombs with the deceased. These acts could signify respect, devotion, or the hope that the item would accompany the deceased into the afterlife. The craftsmanship on these ceremonial objects was often exquisite. Artisans used fine engraving, inlays of precious stones, and designs featuring mythological scenes. Such treasures reveal how deeply bronze influenced not just the material culture but also the spiritual life of Bronze Age societies.

13. Environmental Impact

While Bronze Age societies did not have the large-scale pollution issues of modern industries, the emergence of bronze technology did have environmental effects. Mining copper and tin was labor-intensive and required clearing forests for both mine shafts and the charcoal needed to fuel furnaces. Trees were cut down to produce the charcoal that kept the smelters running at high temperatures. This could lead to deforestation in areas around major mining sites.

Overgrazing by larger herds of animals, made possible by more efficient farming, also placed stress on local ecosystems. Irrigation projects could alter rivers and wetlands. While these changes were relatively small compared to modern times, they did mark a shift in human interaction with nature. Societies that managed resources well could maintain a stable environment, but those that overexploited resources risked decline.

14. Spread of Bronze in Europe and Asia

Bronze technology reached Europe from the Near East and Anatolia through trade routes crossing the Balkans and the Mediterranean. Groups in Central and Northern Europe started to adopt bronze for tools and weapons as they gained access to tin and learned smelting techniques. Over centuries, local cultures emerged that blended older Neolithic traditions—such as megalithic tombs—with new metalworking skills. Europe's Bronze Age is often linked with the building of impressive structures and the creation of distinctive metal artifacts like swords, axes, and jewelry.

In Asia, apart from the well-known developments in Mesopotamia and the Indus Valley, regions further east also began to use bronze. China's Bronze Age developed a sophisticated set of rituals and vessels that left behind a rich archaeological record. Meanwhile, Central Asian cultures, through contact with either Mesopotamia or other centers, incorporated bronze into their own traditions. Overland routes like the steppe corridors helped spread metalworking knowledge, even if at a slower pace than sea routes.

15. Artistic Styles and Techniques

As bronze artisans refined their skills, different artistic styles appeared. Engraving, embossing, and inlay work became popular. Some items showcased geometric patterns, while others depicted animals, gods, or scenes of daily life. Symbolism played a key role—an animal might represent fertility, strength, or a particular deity. Because bronze objects could last a long time if cared for, they were often passed down through generations or placed in the graves of honored individuals.

Techniques like lost-wax casting might have been developed or refined during this period in certain regions. This method involved creating a wax model of the item, then covering it with clay or plaster. Once heated, the wax melted away, leaving a mold that could be filled with molten metal. This allowed for incredibly detailed work and contributed to the intricate bronze statues found in some Bronze Age cultures.

16. Political Implications of Bronze

The emergence of bronze technology had major political implications. Rulers who controlled metal resources or trade routes gained leverage over their neighbors. The ability to equip an army with bronze weapons could tip the balance of power. Alliances might be formed or broken based on access to tin or copper. In some cases, city-states built strong walls and defensive structures, demonstrating the link between metal-fueled warfare and the need for fortifications.

Diplomacy, too, might involve the exchange of bronze gifts. A visiting ruler might offer fine bronze weapons or decorative items to a neighboring king as a sign of good faith or an attempt to form a marriage alliance. These gestures underscored how valuable bronze was, not just for practical use but also for symbolic and political purposes. Over time, as states expanded, control over metal trade routes or mining regions became a common reason for conflict.

17. Bronze and Social Hierarchy

Social classes became more pronounced in many Bronze Age societies, partly due to the concentration of wealth and power among those who owned or controlled bronze production. Craftsmen, while not typically at the top of the social ladder, gained a special status for their expertise. Merchants dealing in metals also found opportunities for profit. At the top were rulers, nobles, or priests who claimed authority over the distribution of bronze and other resources.

Meanwhile, farmers, laborers, and slaves bore the brunt of the hard work—mining for ores, tending fields, or constructing city walls. The emergence of bronze technology did not eliminate social inequalities; in fact, it often magnified them. The gap between those who had access to metals and those who did not grew wider, shaping the social and economic structures of Bronze Age civilizations.

18. Everyday Objects and Domestic Life

Bronze was not only reserved for warriors, elites, or priests. In many cultures, everyday domestic objects were made of bronze. Needles, pins, small knives, cooking pots, and fishhooks became more common in households. These items made daily tasks easier and sometimes safer. A bronze knife stayed sharper than a stone one, and a bronze pot conducted heat more evenly over a fire.

Still, bronze was expensive. Many poorer families might only own a few small bronze items and rely on wood, bone, or stone for other needs. Over time, as production increased, bronze did become more accessible. This shift allowed modest households to experience some benefits of metal technology, though the finest bronze goods remained in the hands of the wealthy or powerful.

19. The Growth of Metallurgical Centers

Some regions became famous for their metallurgical skill. These places, often near copper or tin mines, turned into bustling centers of production. Skilled artisans might produce items not only for local use but also for export. Traveling merchants would come to these centers to buy finished bronze objects or raw ingots, then sell them elsewhere. This boosted the local economy, attracting more laborers, craftsmen, and traders, creating a cycle of growth.

Cities that specialized in metallurgy sometimes left behind heaps of slag (the waste product of smelting) and broken molds. These archaeological traces show the scale of production. As the Bronze Age progressed, certain city-states grew wealthy from the trade of bronze items, investing in monumental architecture, temples, or palaces. Over time, these centers played a key role in shaping regional politics, art, and culture.

CHAPTER 3: MESOPOTAMIAN BRONZE CIVILIZATIONS

Introduction

Mesopotamia is often called the "Cradle of Civilization" because some of the earliest complex societies emerged there. Located between the Tigris and Euphrates Rivers in what is now roughly the region of modern-day Iraq, Mesopotamia had fertile soil that supported large-scale agriculture. During the Bronze Age, the people of Mesopotamia developed city-states, introduced advanced irrigation systems, and used bronze technology to transform warfare, crafts, and daily life.

In this chapter, we will look at how bronze fit into the larger story of Mesopotamian history. We will explore key groups like the Sumerians, Akkadians, Babylonians, and Assyrians. We will also examine social structures, religion, trade, and the political scene that linked these city-states and kingdoms together. By the end of this chapter, you will see how bronze played a vital role in Mesopotamian accomplishments, from their military tactics to their building projects and cultural development.

---

1. The Land Between Two Rivers

Mesopotamia literally means "the land between rivers." The region's geography included rich alluvial plains, which flooded periodically. These floods deposited nutrients that made the soil very fertile, ideal for growing grain such as barley and wheat. However, the timing of floods could be unpredictable. To manage water resources, the people built canals, dikes, and reservoirs. These irrigation systems required organized labor, skilled planning, and leadership.

As agricultural output rose, populations increased. Villages grew into towns, then into the famous city-states of Mesopotamia. With surpluses of grain, people could pursue specialized tasks. Some became scribes, priests, merchants, or metalworkers. Over time, these specializations led to greater complexity in social hierarchies and government. Mesopotamia's environment was thus both a blessing and a challenge. Without regular rains, they depended on rivers. To adapt, they built sophisticated irrigation networks, which set the stage for the region's Bronze Age developments.

2. Early Sumerians and the Rise of City-States

The earliest known urban civilizations in Mesopotamia are collectively referred to as Sumerian. These city-states, including Uruk, Ur, Lagash, and Eridu, emerged in the southern part of Mesopotamia. Each city-state was built around a central temple dedicated to a patron god or goddess. Priests held powerful roles in these theocratic societies, overseeing rituals, managing surplus grain, and organizing labor.

During the Bronze Age, Sumerian artisans began to use bronze for tools, weapons, and various items for temple use. The city-state of Ur, for example, became a major center of cultural and economic activity, in part due to its location near the Persian Gulf, which facilitated trade in metals and other goods. Sumerians developed cuneiform writing, pressing wedge-shaped signs into clay tablets. Although writing itself is not a direct product of bronze technology, the need to manage resources such as metals, grain, and labor encouraged better record-keeping methods.

3. The Importance of Bronze in Sumerian Society

As Sumerian populations grew, competition over land, water sources, and trade routes intensified. Bronze weapons—like spears, swords, and axes—provided an edge in conflicts. Those city-states that could equip their warriors with bronze weapons often overcame those relying on stone or simple copper. Bronze tools also helped dig irrigation canals faster and maintain city walls more effectively.

Temple complexes benefited from bronze by commissioning artistic items like statues and ritual vessels. Priests and rulers displayed these bronze objects as symbols of power and divine favor. Skilled metallurgists learned to cast bronze using clay molds, sometimes decorating the finished pieces with simple patterns or inscriptions. Such items became markers of status and religious devotion. In short, the introduction of bronze had a wide impact: it boosted military strength, improved infrastructure projects, and enriched cultural and religious practices.

4. Political Organization and Leadership

In the earliest phases of Mesopotamian civilization, priest-kings known as "en" or "ensi" often ruled the city-states. They combined religious authority with administrative power. Over time, secular kings (lugal) also rose to prominence. Rivalries between city-states were common. Alliances shifted as each city aimed to control more farmland, trade opportunities, and precious resources, including metals.

As societies became more complex, rulers constructed palaces that rivaled the temples. These palaces served administrative functions and showcased the political might of the king. Bronze played a part here: not only were the palace gates sometimes fitted with bronze fixtures, but the king's guards often carried bronze-tipped spears to protect the royal courts. These symbols of authority and power demonstrated how important bronze had become in shaping both the image and the reality of Mesopotamian rule.

---

5. The Akkadian Empire: Sargon's Conquests

Around the mid-3rd millennium BCE, a powerful figure named Sargon rose to prominence in Mesopotamia. He established the Akkadian Empire, uniting many Sumerian city-states under one rule. Sargon's conquests depended on organized armies equipped with bronze weapons. Soldiers carried bronze-headed spears, axes, and daggers. Bronze-capped chariot wheels and fittings also became more common, enabling swift movement on the battlefield.

The Akkadian Empire fostered trade with distant lands. They imported raw materials like metals and stone, which Mesopotamia lacked. This network stretched toward Anatolia, the Levant, and possibly even farther, bringing in tin for bronze. The empire's administrative structure grew more sophisticated as well. Officials recorded taxes, labor rosters, and tribute from conquered regions on clay tablets. Bronze tools helped them build roads and fortifications, further strengthening the empire's grip on the territory.

6. Naram-Sin and the Height of Akkadian Power

One of Sargon's successors was Naram-Sin, who declared himself a "God of Akkad." He continued campaigns throughout Mesopotamia and beyond, using the empire's robust military to dominate neighboring regions. Bronze technology made it easier to produce weapons on a large scale, and the spoils of war often included prisoners, livestock, and precious goods such as metals.

Under Naram-Sin, monumental art flourished. One famous piece from this period, though often studied by later generations, depicts him as a larger-than-life figure leading his troops to victory. While stone steles were common, bronze figurines and plaques also commemorated the empire's glory. Some were placed in temples to honor the gods and showcase the ruler's devotion. The Akkadian Empire at its height was a shining example of how bronze-equipped militaries could forge vast realms under a single authority.

---

7. The Fall of Akkad and Shifting Power

Over time, the Akkadian Empire faced internal rebellions and external pressures from groups like the Gutians, who invaded from the Zagros Mountains. Environmental factors, such as drought, may have further weakened the empire. Cities fell into chaos, trade routes became unsafe, and metal supplies were disrupted. Without stable leadership or secure resources, Akkad's dominance crumbled.

Yet the idea of unifying Mesopotamia under one rule did not vanish. Other powers would eventually arise, taking advantage of the bronze-based technologies that had become widespread. After Akkad's decline, a Sumerian renaissance took place, most notably during the Third Dynasty of Ur (Ur III), which worked to rebuild cities, reaffirm temple traditions, and restore farmland. Bronze continued to be crucial for these efforts, enabling both defense and construction projects.

8. The Third Dynasty of Ur (Ur III)

The Ur III period, often dated to around the late 3rd millennium BCE, saw a resurgence of Sumerian culture under kings like Ur-Nammu and Shulgi. Ur-Nammu is famous for building ziggurats—massive temple towers—in many cities. Bronze tools and chisels helped shape the mudbrick or baked brick used in these structures, while bronze decorative pieces adorned ceremonial areas.

Ur III rulers standardized weights and measures, facilitating trade and the collection of taxes in grain or livestock. Detailed administrative records show how the state managed irrigation, distributed rations, and organized labor. Bronze weapons continued to protect the realm from incursions, and bronze was a key export to nearby regions that could not produce it themselves. Although the Ur III state was strong, it eventually faced external threats and internal divisions, leading to its downfall. This pattern—rise and fall of city-states—would repeat throughout Mesopotamia's history.

---

9. Babylon: Hammurabi and the Old Babylonian Period

After the decline of Ur III, various city-states and small kingdoms jockeyed for power. Babylon rose from this environment, guided by rulers who extended their influence over neighboring territories. The most famous of these kings was Hammurabi (18th century BCE). His conquests brought many regions under Babylon's rule, and bronze weapons were crucial to his armies' success. Additionally, Babylon's growing control of trade routes allowed it to secure tin for making bronze.

Hammurabi is best known for his law code, which outlined rules and punishments for various crimes. Although the code itself was inscribed on a stone stele, bronze writing tools and other metal objects played a supporting role in Babylon's bureaucracy. Scribes managed data on clay tablets, recording harvests, trade deals, and legal cases. The Old Babylonian period was thus marked by a blend of administrative sophistication and military might, both of which benefited from bronze technology.

10. Mesopotamian Trade Networks in the Bronze Age

Throughout the Bronze Age, Mesopotamian city-states engaged in widespread trade. Caravans and riverboats carried surplus grain, wool, leather goods, and especially textiles to distant markets. In exchange, Mesopotamians received metals such as copper and tin, as well as luxury items like precious stones or exotic woods. Maritime routes extended along the Persian Gulf, reaching lands that could supply vital resources.

This flow of goods helped Mesopotamian cities flourish. Craftsmen in metal workshops turned imported raw copper and tin into bronze weapons, tools, and ceremonial objects. Temples also commissioned lavish bronze statues. Rulers might receive tribute in metal ingots, further boosting their political power. While local copper mines existed in places like the Iranian highlands, the constant demand for tin in particular encouraged long-distance connections, which tied Mesopotamia to other major Bronze Age centers.

---

11. Bronze in Daily Life

Not everyone in Mesopotamia lived in a palace or served in an army. Ordinary people still felt the influence of bronze in their day-to-day activities. Farmers used bronze sickles for harvesting crops. Carpenters employed bronze saws and chisels to shape wood for furniture, carts, or boat parts. Fishermen used bronze hooks, making their work more efficient. Even small household items like pins, needles, and mirrors could be crafted from bronze.

However, bronze remained relatively expensive compared to simpler materials like clay, wood, or stone. Poorer families might own only a few metal tools or might borrow or rent them. Still, as the Bronze Age progressed, metal items became more common, giving ordinary people more ways to improve their work and daily tasks. This gradual shift improved agricultural yield and craftsmanship, contributing to the region's overall prosperity.

12. Religion and Bronze Artifacts

Religion deeply influenced Mesopotamian society. Each city had a patron deity, and people built towering ziggurats to honor these gods. Bronze played an important role in religious rituals. Temples might display bronze statues of deities, often adorned with precious stones or intricate designs. Priests could carry ceremonial bronze implements during festivals, sacrifices, or purification rites. Musical instruments made of bronze, such as bells or clappers, might accompany processions or temple ceremonies.

Worshipers offered bronze figurines, weapons, or utensils to gain divine favor or to thank the gods for blessings. These were placed in temple treasuries, hidden from public view, or sometimes buried as dedicatory objects. The presence of so many bronze items in religious contexts shows how the material was associated not just with practical or martial power, but also with spiritual and cultural life.

---

13. Warfare Tactics and Technology

Bronze weaponry in Mesopotamia included spears, daggers, swords, and socketed axes. Bows with bronze arrowheads were also common. Armies typically consisted of foot soldiers supported by light chariots. Bronze fittings in chariot wheels and harnesses made these vehicles lighter and more reliable than older, all-wood designs. Chariot crews could quickly strike an enemy's flank or pursue fleeing forces.

Cities in Mesopotamia fortified themselves with walls made of mudbrick, sometimes reinforced or adorned with bronze gates. Defenders atop the walls hurled spears and shot arrows at attackers. Sieges were grueling affairs, as invaders tried to breach walls or starve the city into surrender. Control of water sources was a vital aspect of warfare—armies might divert canals or dam rivers to deprive a rival city of irrigation or drinking water. Bronze tools and weapons played a central role in both offensive and defensive strategies.

14. Social Structure and Class Divisions

Mesopotamian society during the Bronze Age was stratified. At the top were rulers—kings or priest-kings—followed by high officials, priests, and scribes. Wealthy merchants and landowners also held significant influence. Skilled craftsmen, including metalworkers, ranked lower than nobles but were still respected for their expertise. Peasants, who made up the majority of the population, worked the land or served in large building projects. Slaves, often prisoners of war or debt slaves, occupied the lowest rung.

Bronze items often signified status. Elites wore bronze jewelry or owned elaborately decorated bronze weapons. A lavish bronze dagger could identify someone as part of the upper class. Meanwhile, farmers or common soldiers might share communal bronze tools, with personal items limited to a few basic pieces. Despite these inequalities, the widespread availability of bronze tools did gradually improve living standards and create some mobility for skilled artisans or traders.

15. Literature, Myth, and Epic Traditions

Mesopotamia is famous for its myths and epics, such as the Epic of Gilgamesh. Although the content of these stories is not strictly tied to bronze, they do feature heroic warriors wielding mighty weapons and embarking on grand quests. These tales were written in cuneiform on clay tablets and recited by storytellers in royal courts or temples. Bronze instruments, like small cymbals or harps fitted with metal parts, might have accompanied these performances.

Such epics reinforced the idea of the heroic king or warrior, a figure who could protect the land and earn the favor of the gods. In daily life, real rulers tried to match these heroic ideals by commissioning grand building projects, expanding their territories, and ensuring the prosperity of their people. Bronze technology gave them a practical edge in warfare and construction, bridging the gap between mythic heroism and real-world accomplishments.

16. Art and Sculpture

Mesopotamian art was diverse, ranging from cylinder seals with tiny engravings to large relief carvings and statues. Bronze sculpture appeared frequently in temples and palaces, depicting gods, animals, and sometimes worshipers in humble poses. Artisans used the lost-wax casting method or clay molds to achieve fine details. Figures might show clothing folds, facial expressions, or even inscriptions praising a deity or ruler.

Metal relief panels could decorate wooden doors or furniture, telling stories of the king's victories or religious offerings. Wall paintings also existed, though fewer survive. Many artworks emphasized religious or royal themes, suggesting a close relationship between political power and divine favor. In this environment, bronze served not only as a functional material but also as a medium of artistic expression, reflecting the beliefs and ambitions of Mesopotamian society.

---

17. The Assyrian Emergence in the North

While cities like Ur, Uruk, and Babylon dominated southern Mesopotamia, the northern region—centered around the city of Assur—also rose to power in the Bronze Age. Early Assyria began as a city-state and expanded over time. Like their southern neighbors, the Assyrians relied on bronze for weapons, chariots, and tools. They established trade connections that stretched into Anatolia, where they exchanged textiles and tin.

Assyrian merchants set up trading colonies in distant lands, creating networks that brought in metals and other valuable resources. Over time, Assyrian rulers developed formidable armies. Their success in warfare rested on disciplined troops armed with bronze-tipped spears and arrows, supported by chariots. Although the greatest expansion of the Assyrian Empire would come in later periods (often called the Iron Age), the foundations were laid in this earlier Bronze Age context.

18. Interactions with Neighboring Regions

Mesopotamia's position between multiple geographical areas—Anatolia to the northwest, the Iranian plateau to the east, and the Levant to the west—placed it at a crossroads of cultural exchange. Bronze Age Mesopotamians influenced, and were influenced by, civilizations such as the Hittites in Anatolia and the Elamites to the east. Sometimes these relationships were peaceful, marked by trade and diplomacy; at other times, they involved warfare or tribute.

Imported goods could include timber from the Levant, copper from Cyprus, tin from the Zagros region or beyond, and precious metals from further afield. Mesopotamian merchants introduced their cuneiform script to neighboring lands, and foreign scribes adapted it for their own languages. Bronze was thus part of a broader tapestry of exchanges that shaped religion, language, and art across the ancient Near East.

---

19. Decline, Shifts, and the Late Bronze Age

The Bronze Age in Mesopotamia was not a single, uninterrupted era of growth. City-states and empires rose and fell. Climate fluctuations sometimes caused drought or floods that weakened the region's agricultural base. Rival powers jostled for supremacy, leading to destructive wars that could devastate crops and disrupt trade. In some periods, large populations migrated, bringing new ideas or stirring conflict.

Nevertheless, by the Late Bronze Age (roughly the mid-2nd millennium to around 1200 BCE), Mesopotamia had firmly established itself as a major center of urban life, governance, and metalworking. Empires like Babylon and Assyria continued to compete for dominance. Bronze remained a critical material, though advances in ironworking were on the horizon. The complex heritage of Mesopotamia—law codes, literature, irrigation methods, and city planning—would influence future civilizations even after the Bronze Age ended.

CHAPTER 4: BRONZE AGE EGYPT

Introduction

Egypt's history spans thousands of years, but the Bronze Age period stands out as a time of remarkable change and growth. Situated along the Nile River, Egypt benefited from annual floods that provided fertile silt for agriculture. As populations expanded, communities grew into organized states under strong rulers, eventually giving rise to the powerful pharaohs of the Old, Middle, and New Kingdoms. Though Egypt's most iconic monuments—such as the Great Pyramids—were constructed mostly in the Old Kingdom (which some scholars consider to be on the early edge of the Bronze Age)—the wider Bronze Age (especially the Middle and New Kingdoms) witnessed even greater strides in trade, warfare, and governance.

In this chapter, we will explore how bronze technology influenced Egypt's military, economy, religion, and daily life. We will also look at the role of the Nile in shaping the Egyptian worldview and social order. From mighty temples to elaborate tombs, from complex hieroglyphic records to stunning artwork, Bronze Age Egypt offers countless mind-blowing achievements that stemmed in part from the careful use of metal resources.

---

1. The Nile River and Agricultural Surplus

Ancient Egypt's prosperity started with the Nile. Each year, the river flooded, depositing nutrient-rich silt on farmland. When the waters receded, farmers planted crops like wheat, barley, and flax. The predictable nature of these floods allowed Egyptians to plan agricultural cycles with remarkable accuracy. This annual rhythm led to consistent harvests, which in turn supported population growth and state development.

Bronze tools gradually improved farming efficiency. Metal plowshares cut deeper into the soil, and bronze sickles sped up the harvesting process. Although the earliest phases of Egyptian civilization relied on stone or copper tools, the spread of bronze by the Middle Kingdom made large-scale agriculture more manageable. With stable food supplies, Egypt could free more laborers for construction projects, craft workshops, and military service, fueling the growth of the kingdom.

2. Early Dynastic Foundations and the Old Kingdom

Before we delve into the full swing of Bronze Age Egypt, it is important to recognize the Old Kingdom as the era that built the foundational structures of Egyptian society. Pharaohs became central figures of power, considered divine or semi-divine. Massive building projects like the pyramids of Giza demonstrated the state's ability to mobilize labor and resources. Though these pyramids are often associated with stone, copper and early bronze tools also played a role in shaping blocks, cutting canals, and managing equipment.

During the Old Kingdom, local administration was organized into nomes (districts), each overseen by a governor (nomarch). Pharaohs, assisted by viziers and scribes, collected taxes in the form of grain and labor. This system provided the workforce for building monuments and maintaining irrigation. While bronze was not yet as widespread as it would be later, the stage was set for further developments in metal usage, especially once the Middle Kingdom arrived.

---

3. The Middle Kingdom and Bronze Expansion

The Middle Kingdom (roughly 2050–1650 BCE) is often viewed as a "golden age" of Egyptian culture and governance. Pharaohs like Mentuhotep II and Senusret III worked to stabilize the country after periods of disunity. Under their rule, trade networks expanded south into Nubia and possibly eastward toward the Red Sea and Levant. With these trade routes, Egypt gained increased access to raw materials, including metals.

Bronze became more common during the Middle Kingdom. Craftsmen produced bronze tools for farming, carpentry, and stonecutting. In warfare, Egyptian soldiers began to carry bronze-tipped spears, daggers, and eventually swords. Bronze chisels and drills made it easier to carve intricate hieroglyphs into stone temple walls. Although Egypt is not rich in tin, it imported this metal to alloy with copper, ensuring a steady supply of bronze. The Middle Kingdom's relative peace and prosperity allowed artisans and scribes to refine their skills, leading to an outpouring of art, literature, and monumental architecture.

---

4. Trade Routes and Connections

Egypt's search for metals pushed it to establish trade relations with neighboring lands. Copper could be sourced from the Sinai Peninsula, while gold was mined in the Eastern Desert and Nubia (though gold is not an alloy component for bronze, it was highly valued). Tin, essential for making bronze, had to come from more distant regions—possibly parts of the Near East or the Mediterranean world. Egyptian merchants bartered grain, linen, papyrus, and crafts in exchange for metals, precious stones, incense, and exotic woods.

Coastal trade via the Mediterranean and Red Sea also emerged, though the Nile remained the primary highway for internal commerce. By transporting goods along the river, the state efficiently moved large quantities of grain, stone blocks, and metal ingots. Bronze fittings and metal implements were crucial for constructing sturdy boats, some of which sailed as far as the land of Punt (likely located near the Horn of Africa). These trade expeditions expanded Egypt's wealth and cultural horizons.

---

5. Fortifications and Military Campaigns

As bronze weapons improved, Egypt became more capable of projecting power beyond its borders. During the Middle Kingdom, several fortresses were built along the southern frontier with Nubia. These strongholds served to guard trade routes and secure valuable resources, such as gold mines. The fortresses were often equipped with bronze-tipped arrows, spears, and garrison forces trained in organized formations.

The Hyksos intrusion into Egypt during the Second Intermediate Period (roughly 1650–1550 BCE) tested Egyptian military strength. The Hyksos brought new warfare techniques, including more advanced bows and horse-drawn chariots. Initially, the Hyksos gained control over parts of Lower Egypt. However, Theban rulers in Upper Egypt adapted to these challenges, adopting chariot warfare and improving their bronze weaponry. Eventually, the Theban prince Ahmose expelled the Hyksos, ushering in the New Kingdom—a period often seen as the pinnacle of Bronze Age Egypt.

6. The New Kingdom: Imperial Ambitions

The New Kingdom (circa 1550–1070 BCE) is frequently called Egypt's imperial age. Pharaohs like Thutmose III, Hatshepsut, Amenhotep III, and Ramesses II expanded Egyptian influence to its greatest extent, controlling territories in Nubia to the south and reaching into the Levant and Syria. This expansion was fueled by a professional army equipped with bronze swords (the khepesh was one famous curved sword), spears, and improved chariots. Charioteers wore armor reinforced with bronze scales or plates, giving them an edge in close combat.

Victories in battle brought plunder, tribute, and captives back to Egypt. The pharaoh's prestige soared, and temples were enriched with new wealth. Skilled metalworkers, including foreign craftsmen, arrived or were captured to serve the state. The demand for bronze soared as more weapons were needed, and large building projects required metal tools. Egypt's imperial reach thus depended significantly on its mastery of bronze technology and its ability to secure tin through trade or tribute.

---

7. Temples, Tombs, and Monumental Architecture

Religion in Egypt revolved around a complex pantheon of gods. Pharaohs built monumental temples to honor these deities and to display their own power. The construction of temples at Karnak and Luxor, as well as mortuary complexes in the Valley of the Kings, required vast resources. Bronze chisels, drills, and adzes allowed laborers to shape large stone blocks with more precision and speed than with stone or copper tools alone.

The tombs of pharaohs and nobles often included bronze grave goods—mirrors, razors, small statues, or ceremonial weapons. These items were believed to help the deceased in the afterlife. Tomb paintings and inscriptions depict craftspeople forging metal objects or carrying them as precious offerings. In some cases, entire sets of bronze tools or chariots were buried with important individuals. The lavish use of bronze in such burials underscores its significance as a symbol of wealth, power, and divine favor.

8. Religious Rituals and Bronze Implements

Egyptian religion placed great importance on ritual purity and ceremonial acts. Priests performed daily offerings in temple sanctuaries, washed statues of the gods, and lit incense. Bronze vessels, censers, and other implements were commonly used in these rituals because they could be finely crafted and maintained. Bronze could be polished to a bright shine, reflecting sunlight or torchlight, giving it a sacred aura.

Outside the temple, processions would carry statues of the gods on wooden barques fitted with bronze decorations. Musicians might accompany these events with bronze sistrums—rattles used in worship—creating a stirring, rhythmic sound. These ceremonies reinforced the idea that the pharaoh and priesthood were keepers of cosmic order. Bronze objects, being both durable and gleaming, represented the eternal nature of the gods and the ongoing life of the land.

9. Daily Life: Tools, Crafts, and Household Items

Bronze's influence spread beyond the grand temples and palaces. Carpenters relied on bronze saws, chisels, and adzes for furniture-making and boat-building. Stonecutters used bronze tools to shape limestone and granite blocks for construction. Farmers wielded bronze sickles during harvest, improving efficiency. Cooks and butchers used bronze knives in kitchens and markets. Even fishermen might have bronze hooks for catching fish in the Nile.

Women of higher status possessed bronze mirrors, hairpins, and tweezers for personal grooming. Bronze needles and awls helped in textile production. Though these items were more expensive than their wooden, bone, or stone counterparts, they offered advantages in durability and precision. Over time, as bronze became more widely available, middle-class families could afford certain metal items, improving comfort and efficiency in everyday tasks.

10. The Evolution of Egyptian Warfare

Egyptian warfare evolved dramatically in the Bronze Age. Initially, armies were raised from peasant conscripts. Over time, professional soldiering developed, especially under New Kingdom pharaohs who needed permanent forces for campaigns in distant lands. Bronze arrowheads, spear tips, and swords were standard, while improved bow designs increased range and accuracy.

Chariots became the elite strike force on the battlefield, manned by a driver and an archer. Bronze components, such as rivets and reinforcements, reduced the vehicle's weight and increased its durability. The best archers could fire arrows rapidly while the chariot maneuvered. Egyptian records, such as inscriptions on temple walls, frequently boast of pharaohs charging into battle on chariots, with the gods granting them victory. While glorified in art and texts, these achievements were grounded in practical bronze technologies that gave Egyptians a strategic and tactical edge.

---

11. Administration and Record-Keeping

A sophisticated bureaucracy underpinned Egypt's stability. Scribes, trained in the art of hieroglyphs and hieratic script, documented harvests, distribution of grain, temple offerings, and troop movements. Though the writing was done on papyrus with reed brushes and inks, bronze played a role in broader administrative tasks. Bronze seals or signet rings stamped official documents or clay sealings, authenticating deliveries and storage.

The government had to organize massive labor forces for canal maintenance, pyramid building, and temple expansions. Bronze tools helped dig channels and shape stone blocks. Surplus food from efficient agriculture supported these large work gangs, who toiled for the state at certain times of the year. This close relationship between well-managed resources, bureaucratic skill, and available metal tools kept Egypt's economy humming, even through changes in dynasties.

---

12. Nubia and the Flow of Gold and Bronze

Nubia, located south of Egypt, was rich in gold and other resources. Egyptians built fortresses in Nubia, not just for military control but also to secure trade routes. The region provided ivory, ebony, and sometimes copper or other metals. Bronze production in Egypt thus relied on a steady flow of copper from Sinai and Nubia, as well as tin from more distant lands. This made Nubia crucial to Egypt's economic health.

Egyptian culture influenced Nubia, and Nubian cultures in turn left their mark on Egypt. Intermarriage, exchange of goods, and shared deities fostered connections. Bronze items found in Nubia sometimes bear Egyptian-style decorations, reflecting this cultural blending. Over time, local Nubian states also mastered metalworking, creating their own variations of bronze tools and weapons. However, during the height of the New Kingdom, Egypt maintained the upper hand in this relationship, thanks to its powerful bronze-armed military forces.

13. Art and Iconography in the Bronze Age

Egyptian art is famous for its consistency and symbolic depth. Paintings, reliefs, and statues often show gods, pharaohs, and scenes of daily life in a stylized form. Bronze contributed to this visual culture in several ways. Sculptors created small bronze statues of deities, animals (like the Apis bull), or symbolic figures (like the scarab). Some large statues, though less common, were cast in bronze to stand in temple courtyards or near palace entrances.

Jewelry made with bronze, gold, and semi-precious stones was also significant. Pectorals, bracelets, and collars might include bronze elements for structure and decoration. The bright sheen of polished bronze contrasted well with colored stones like carnelian, lapis lazuli, and turquoise. These pieces served not only as personal adornments but also as amulets invoking protection or blessing. Artisans refined the lost-wax casting and hammering techniques, achieving high levels of artistry that remain awe-inspiring.

14. Religious Transformations and the Amarna Period

One notable event in the New Kingdom was the religious revolution under Pharaoh Akhenaten (14th century BCE). He elevated the worship of the Aten—a form of the sun god—to unprecedented importance, reducing the influence of other gods. During this time, artistic styles changed, showing more naturalistic and relaxed portrayals of the royal family. Although the Amarna period was relatively short, it left a distinctive mark on Egyptian art and religion.

Bronze objects continued to be produced, though some changes in style are evident. The shift in religious focus did not undo the technical achievements made so far. Craftsmen still made weapons, tools, and ritual items in bronze. After Akhenaten's death, Egypt largely returned to its traditional deities under rulers like Tutankhamun. The wealth of bronze artifacts found in Tutankhamun's tomb—daggers, chariot fittings, and small statues—reflects the ongoing significance of bronze in royal and funerary contexts.

15. Tombs of Nobles and Craftsmen

Not only pharaohs, but also high officials and skilled craftsmen could afford tombs equipped with bronze items. In places like Deir el-Medina, a village of workers who built the royal tombs in the Valley of the Kings, excavations reveal how craftsmen lived. They had access to better tools and sometimes owned small bronze statues or personal objects. Tomb paintings from these individuals' graves show scenes of daily life, including metalworking, carpentry, and fishing with bronze hooks.

Though these individuals were not part of the royal family, they enjoyed a status above the average peasant. Their specialized knowledge of tomb construction and decoration made them valuable to the state. The presence of bronze in their homes and burial items indicates how deeply metal technology had penetrated everyday Egyptian culture by the Late Bronze Age.

16. Economic Shifts and External Pressures

By the late New Kingdom, Egypt faced economic challenges and political strife. Long military campaigns drained resources, and the cost of maintaining distant territories grew burdensome. Trade routes were disrupted by conflicts in the Near East, making it harder to secure tin and other raw materials necessary for bronze production. At home, priests of Amun in Thebes gained significant power, challenging the authority of the pharaoh in some periods.

Foreign incursions also tested Egypt's military. Sea Peoples and Libyan tribes pushed into the Nile Delta, weakening the central administration. Even with formidable bronze weapons, the overstretched Egyptian forces struggled to fend off every threat. Over time, the government lost its firm grip on conquered lands, reducing its ability to collect tribute and secure metals. These pressures contributed to a gradual decline, part of the broader wave of turmoil known as the Late Bronze Age collapse across much of the Eastern Mediterranean.

17. Cultural Achievements Despite Challenges

Despite the mounting problems, Late Bronze Age Egypt continued to produce notable cultural achievements. Temples in Karnak, Luxor, and other cities underwent expansions. Artistic styles saw refinements in sculpture, painting, and architecture. Bronze tools played a role in shaping relief carvings on temple walls and statues that depicted the gods and the pharaohs who worshipped them.

Literature, such as the story of the "Tale of Wenamun," reflects the changing political landscape, with Egyptian officials facing difficulties abroad in acquiring cedar wood and other resources. These texts provide insights into the final stages of the Bronze Age in Egypt, a period of both cultural richness and growing instability. They depict a realm trying to maintain its traditions and influence while grappling with new realities of diplomacy and resource scarcity.

18. The Onset of the Iron Age and Shifting Technologies

The Bronze Age in Egypt gradually yielded to the Iron Age, beginning around the late second millennium BCE into the first millennium BCE. Iron tools and weapons, though initially rare and costly, eventually became more common. They were stronger than bronze and, after mastering the smelting and forging processes, easier to produce once local sources of iron ore were developed or acquired. This shift did not happen overnight—bronze remained in use for a considerable time, especially in ceremonial contexts. However, the advantage that bronze once gave in warfare and construction faded in comparison to iron's potential.

Egypt's political fortunes also shifted. Nubians, Assyrians, Persians, and others would later rule parts of Egypt. But the legacies of the Bronze Age did not disappear; the monumental buildings, religious practices, and cultural memory continued to shape future dynasties. Pharaohs still built on the foundations laid by their Bronze Age predecessors, even as the world around them evolved in new directions.

19. Legacy of Bronze Age Egypt

Bronze Age Egypt left an indelible mark on history. Its colossal temples, royal tombs, and intricate art fascinated neighboring lands. The pharaohs of the Middle and New Kingdoms demonstrated how a well-managed state, with access to metal resources, could maintain power for centuries. Their armies, armed with bronze-tipped spears and swords, projected authority deep into Nubia and the Levant. Its scribes recorded achievements, religious texts, and administrative details on papyrus, preserving knowledge for future generations.

The religious beliefs of the Egyptians also shaped perceptions of kingship and the afterlife. The idea of a ruler as a divine or semi-divine being influenced later cultures. Their solar worship, temple architecture, and funerary customs inspired awe and sometimes imitation. Even as the Bronze Age ended, Egypt remained a symbol of longevity and splendor, in large part due to the accomplishments it had achieved during its centuries of economic and political strength.

CHAPTER 5: THE MINOANS AND THE BRONZE AGE AEGEAN

Introduction

Far out in the eastern Mediterranean Sea lies the island of Crete, home to one of the most intriguing Bronze Age civilizations: the Minoans. For many centuries, these island dwellers built impressive palace complexes, ran busy ports, and traded far and wide. Their influence reached other islands in the Aegean and beyond. They created a unique culture, a writing system that still puzzles us, and artwork filled with lively colors and bold motifs. Much about Minoan civilization seems peaceful on the surface, yet they had to adapt to natural disasters, competition from mainland groups, and the challenges of island life.

In this chapter, we will explore how the Minoans came to prominence during the Bronze Age, how they developed their society around palace centers, and how their religious and cultural practices set them apart. We will also look into their extensive trade networks, connections with neighboring regions, and the mysterious reasons behind their eventual decline. By the end, you will see why many still find the Minoans remarkable—an island society that harnessed bronze, achieved great prosperity, and left behind a legacy both colorful and puzzling.

---

1. Crete's Geographic Advantages

The island of Crete sits at a crossroads in the eastern Mediterranean. To the north lie mainland Greece and the Aegean islands, to the east the coast of the Levant, and to the south and west lie the pathways toward Egypt and Libya. This location made Crete a natural meeting point for traders, sailors, and travelers from different lands. Crete also has a varied landscape, with fertile plains, mountainous areas, and natural harbors. Farmers could grow olives, grapes, and grains; shepherds raised goats and sheep in the rugged highlands; fishermen harvested the surrounding waters.

With these resources, Crete was never short on food. This stability allowed the population to grow and experiment with more complex social structures. The mild climate helped too, meaning sea travel was feasible for much of the year.

The sea was both a protective barrier against large-scale invasion and a gateway for trade. Over time, Cretans learned to build strong ships, navigate the waves, and forge connections with distant lands. These benefits laid the groundwork for the Minoans' rise in the Bronze Age.

2. Early Settlements and the Dawn of Minoan Culture

Archaeological findings (which we will simply describe as ancient remains, to keep our focus on the Bronze Age) suggest that Crete had small farming and fishing communities well before 3000 BCE. As time passed, these early inhabitants learned about metals—first copper, then bronze. By the third millennium BCE, people on Crete had begun forging bronze tools and weapons, following the same gradual path of metallurgical discovery seen in other parts of the world.

The rise of the first palace complexes around 2000 BCE (a timeframe often linked to the start of what researchers call the Protopalatial or Old Palace period) signaled a new era. Populations were growing, and leadership structures must have become more centralized. The word "palace" might be misleading if one thinks only of a royal building. Minoan palaces served as administrative, economic, and religious centers, distributing goods, conducting ceremonies, and housing storage facilities for surplus. Over time, these complexes grew in size and complexity, hinting at a refined society with specialized crafts and clear social hierarchies.

3. Palace Centers: Knossos, Phaistos, Malia, and Zakros

The four most famous palace sites on Crete are **Knossos**, **Phaistos**, **Malia**, and **Zakros**. Each developed unique architectural layouts but shared certain features. They typically had large central courtyards, numerous storage magazines (long, narrow rooms) for goods like grain, oil, and wine, and sophisticated drainage and plumbing systems. Corridors branched out in ways that sometimes seemed maze-like, leading to smaller chambers, workshops, and living areas.

- **Knossos**: This is the largest and most well-known Minoan palace center. It boasted multiple stories, grand staircases, and vibrant wall paintings

(frescos) featuring themes like bull-leaping, processions, and nature scenes. The layout was so complex that later Greek myths associated it with the Labyrinth and the legendary Minotaur.
- **Phaistos**: Located in south-central Crete, Phaistos had a commanding view of the Mesara Plain. This palace complex likewise featured storerooms, a grand courtyard, and fine potteries known for their elegant shapes and decorations.
- **Malia**: In north-central Crete, Malia's palace site revealed massive storage facilities where pithoi (large clay jars) were kept. It also had open courts and workshops that showed a bustling economic life, with metals, textiles, and ceramics likely produced and traded here.
- **Zakros**: On the eastern edge of Crete, Zakros controlled maritime routes toward Cyprus and the Near East. Its palace had direct access to the sea, facilitating trade in metals—especially copper and tin—for bronze-making, as well as luxury goods from eastern lands.

The shared features of these palaces point to a common Minoan cultural framework, but each center likely had its own local elite managing the flow of resources. The fact that multiple palaces thrived at once suggests that power may have been divided among different regions of Crete, or perhaps loosely united under a central authority based in Knossos in some eras.

---

4. Minoan Craftsmanship and Bronze Working

The Minoans became skilled metalworkers, crafting bronze tools, weapons, and artistic objects. They needed copper and tin for bronze, neither of which were abundant on Crete itself. This scarcity of raw materials pushed them to trade with other regions—likely Cyprus for copper and possibly parts of Anatolia or far-away lands for tin. Once acquired, the metals would be smelted in workshops near the palaces or port towns. Craftsmen developed techniques like hammering, casting with stone or clay molds, and, on some occasions, more advanced methods such as lost-wax casting.

Bronze made farm tools stronger and more durable. Axes, sickles, and chisels helped farmers clear fields, harvest grain, and maintain irrigation ditches. Builders and carpenters used bronze saws to cut timbers for ships, furniture, and palace structures. In warfare, bronze-tipped spears and daggers could be found, though archaeological evidence suggests the Minoans were not as militaristic as some contemporary groups. Still, they definitely recognized the value of having reliable metal weapons for defense against pirates or rival powers.

Minoan artists also experimented with metal for decorative items: bronze pins, jewelry, and small figurines. These items sometimes displayed swirling, naturalistic motifs—octopuses, dolphins, flowers—reflecting the Minoans' close ties to the sea and nature. Metals like gold or silver might be combined with bronze for added ornamentation, underscoring the wealth that passed through their trade networks.

5. The Minoan Writing Systems: Linear A and More

One of the enduring mysteries of Minoan culture is their undeciphered script known as **Linear A**. Surviving examples appear on clay tablets, seals, and various administrative objects found in Minoan palaces. Since scholars have not fully translated Linear A, our knowledge of Minoan governance, religion, and social organization relies heavily on archaeology rather than written texts. Before Linear A, there was an earlier script called Cretan hieroglyphic, which is also not fully understood. Later, the Mycenaeans adapted a version of Minoan writing to create **Linear B**, which has been deciphered—but that pertains mainly to Mycenaean Greek, not the original Minoan language.

What we can glean from the records is that Minoans had a structured method of accounting. The clay tablets often record goods—oil, wine, grain—and possibly workforce details. Seals found on storage jars or boxes suggest a system of labeling, indicating who owned or managed the goods. These administrative practices highlight the organizational complexity within Minoan palatial centers. The fact that so much remains unknown about the Minoan language adds to their mystique, leaving a large part of their beliefs and history hidden behind undeciphered script.

6. Minoan Religion and Ritual

Artwork and artifacts reveal much about Minoan religious practices. The bull appears frequently in Minoan art, leading many to believe that it held a special place in their mythology and rituals. Frescos depict a practice called **bull-leaping**, showing young men or women vaulting over the back of a charging bull. The exact meaning is unclear—whether it was a religious ceremony, a rite of passage, or a form of entertainment. Bulls' heads, crafted in stone or ceramic, appear in palaces, some designed as libation vessels for pouring liquids during rituals.

Minoans also worshiped goddesses or female figures, often represented in statues with raised arms. These "Snake Goddesses" or "Priestesses" wear open-fronted dresses and hold snakes, symbols that might represent fertility, renewal, or the chthonic (earth-based) aspects of religion. Small shrines and peak sanctuaries on mountaintops further suggest that Minoan worship extended into the landscape, not just confined to palace temples. Offerings of pottery, figurines, and even bronze daggers have been found in these shrines. The blending of nature worship, animal symbolism, and possible goddess-centered devotion sets Minoan religion apart from many other Bronze Age traditions.

---

7. The Art of Fresco Painting

Minoan palaces were famous for their vibrant frescos—wall paintings made by applying pigment onto wet plaster, allowing the colors to bond with the surface. Scenes often depicted daily life, marine themes, or religious events. Popular motifs included dolphins, fish, octopuses, and plants, reflecting the island's environment. Human figures appear in stylized but dynamic poses, with slender waists, broad shoulders, and flowing hair.

Some frescos portray processions of men or women carrying offerings, possibly for a religious festival. Others show athletic feats like bull-leaping or boxing. The bright colors—blues, reds, yellows, whites—lend a sense of energy and movement. This art form was not merely decorative; it likely had cultural and spiritual meaning. Depicting nature alongside human activities might have symbolized the Minoans' harmonious relationship with the land and sea, as well as their devotion to deities linked to fertility and growth.

8. Maritime Trade and Influence

From an early stage, the Minoans proved themselves capable sailors. They built long, sleek ships for trading, fishing, and perhaps a form of naval patrol. Crete's location allowed them to establish connections with mainland Greece, the Cycladic islands, Anatolia (modern-day Turkey), Cyprus, the Levant, and Egypt. Such expansive maritime reach brought in metals, timber, luxury items, and ideas from abroad. In return, Minoan crafts—especially pottery—circulated widely.

One type of Minoan pottery, known as **Kamares ware**, features intricate designs in white and orange on a dark background. Another style, sometimes called **Marine Style**, depicts sea creatures swirling around the vessel's surface. These styles show up in distant ports, suggesting that Minoan goods were highly valued. The trade routes also allowed the Minoans to import the tin necessary for making bronze, a crucial resource for tools and weapons. Over centuries, these seafaring ventures helped Minoan culture spread throughout the Aegean, influencing art styles, religious symbols, and perhaps administrative practices in neighboring regions.

---

9. Social Structure and Palatial Administration

Although we lack detailed written records, we can infer certain aspects of Minoan social organization from palace layouts, art, and artifacts. The presence of grand palaces suggests a hierarchy: elites or rulers of some sort managed resources, stored surplus goods, and sponsored building projects. Below them might have been priests, scribes, merchants, craftsmen, and farmers. Some depictions show individuals dressed in elaborate clothing or jewelry, likely signifying wealth or status.

Many scholars believe Minoan society allowed some level of female authority, given the prominence of female figures in art and religious contexts. However, the exact roles of women remain unclear without decipherable texts. Rulers might have claimed divine sanction, bridging political power with religious duties, though we do not have direct evidence of a single "king" like in other Bronze Age states. Instead, Minoan governance might have been more collective or regionally distributed, with various palace centers operating in cooperation or competition.

10. Daily Life in Minoan Crete

For most Minoans, life revolved around farming, crafts, or trade. In coastal towns, fishermen and sailors found work on the ships that traversed the Aegean. Inland, villagers tended fields of barley, wheat, olives, and grapes. Herds of sheep provided wool for textiles, while goats supplied milk. Surpluses of oil, wine, and grains were brought to palaces, which functioned like redistribution centers. Craftspeople used bronze tools in carpentry, pottery-making, and stone-carving workshops.

Homes in smaller settlements were often built from stone and mudbrick, sometimes two stories high if resources permitted. They had simple layouts and basic furniture. Cooking was done on hearths using clay pots, and families stored food in large vessels. The mild climate allowed for an outdoor lifestyle, with courtyards or terraces for family gatherings. Entertainment might include music, dancing, athletic competitions, or local festivals honoring various deities. Though life could be demanding, especially during harvest times, Minoan art suggests a society that valued festivity, nature, and communal activities.

---

11. The Role of Women in Minoan Culture

As mentioned, women appear prominently in Minoan art. They are shown participating in processions, engaging in religious ceremonies, and sometimes depicted at the center of ritual activities. This portrayal could hint at a society where women held significant status, at least in spiritual or ceremonial roles. Some frescos even show what might be female figures handling large jars or leading processions, though it is uncertain whether these scenes reflect ordinary social dynamics or highly ritualized events.

Snake Goddess figurines, with their elaborate dresses and exposed breasts, have often been interpreted as symbols of fertility or representations of powerful female deities. While we should not jump to the conclusion that Minoan Crete was a complete matriarchy, the evidence suggests that women had a notable presence in the religious and possibly administrative spheres. This is somewhat different from many other Bronze Age societies, where male kings and warriors typically dominated public life.

12. Defensive Measures and Possible Military Activity

Although Minoan art rarely depicts large-scale battles, that does not mean the Minoans were a purely peaceful people. Living on an island offered some natural protection, but pirates or rival traders could still pose threats. Coastal towns may have had watchtowers, and Minoan fleets might have patrolled important shipping lanes. Small bronzes of swords and daggers, along with armor fragments, point to at least some martial readiness.

Some scholars think that the lack of massive city walls (compared to, say, the Mycenaeans' fortified palaces on mainland Greece) means the Minoans were less militarized. Others argue they relied on a strong navy for defense rather than on land-based fortifications. The emphasis on bulls, dancing, and vibrant nature in their artwork might reflect a cultural preference for ritual and trade over warfare. Still, the presence of high-quality bronze weapons indicates that Minoan leaders understood the importance of armed security—especially if they wished to protect their wealth and maintain trade dominance.

---

13. The Eruption of Thera (Santorini)

A major volcanic eruption on the nearby island of Thera (modern-day Santorini) took place sometime in the mid-second millennium BCE. This catastrophic event is often linked to the decline of the Minoans. The eruption was colossal, possibly creating tsunamis that hit Crete's northern coastline, damaging harbors, ships, and coastal settlements. Thick layers of volcanic ash may have affected agriculture or forced people to relocate. While the exact timeline of the eruption and its impact on Crete is still debated, there is little doubt it disrupted trade routes and daily life.

The psychological impact might have been significant, too. If the Minoans saw this disaster as an omen or a punishment from the gods, it could have shaken their religious convictions or social order. Over time, weakened infrastructure and reduced economic power may have left Crete vulnerable to outside forces, including the rising power of the Mycenaeans from mainland Greece.

14. Competition and Interaction with Mainland Greece

The Mycenaeans, centered on the Greek mainland, were influenced by the Minoans but also followed their own path. They built heavily fortified palaces, developed Linear B (adapted from Minoan Linear A), and pursued military expansions. By the mid-late Bronze Age, Mycenaeans were establishing footholds in the Aegean, including some Cretan sites. In some cases, they might have arrived as peaceful traders or settlers, adopting aspects of Minoan art and culture. In other scenarios, they might have come as conquerors, exploiting Crete's weakened state after the Thera eruption or internal strife.

Evidence from Knossos suggests a Mycenaean takeover around 1450 BCE. Some palaces were destroyed around this time, and the ruling elites may have been replaced by Greek-speaking newcomers who introduced different burial practices, art styles, and administrative methods. The once-thriving Minoan civilization did not disappear instantly, but its character changed under new influences. Over time, Mycenaean control deepened, folding Crete into a broader Aegean world that was increasingly dominated by mainland powers.

15. Art and Culture Under Foreign Influence

Even after possible Mycenaean domination, Minoan art and culture continued in a hybrid form. Potters and fresco artists still created vibrant pieces, but new styles emerged, reflecting Mycenaean tastes. The use of Linear B scripts in palace administration replaced or overshadowed Linear A. Burial customs shifted from Minoan communal tombs to Mycenaean-style shaft graves or tholos tombs in some areas.

Many small towns and rural communities carried on traditional crafts, but palace-based production may have changed hands or priorities. Trade networks also shifted, with more routes leading to and from Mycenaean-controlled ports on the mainland. Some local elites might have adapted to new rulers, using Greek titles or forging alliances with Mycenaean overlords. Others may have resisted, but we have little direct evidence. The combination of natural disaster, foreign pressure, and internal factors led to what we call the "final" phases of Minoan society.

16. Late Minoan Period and Collapse

The period following 1450 BCE is often called the Late Minoan period. Some palace sites were rebuilt or modified under Mycenaean influence, while others remained in ruins. The great palaces at Knossos and Phaistos still saw activity, but the distinctly Minoan character was diluted. By around 1200 BCE—close to the broader Bronze Age collapse in the eastern Mediterranean—these centers also fell into decline or were abandoned.

This collapse was not unique to Crete; it affected many major powers across the region. Disruptions in trade, possible migrations or invasions, and the breakdown of palace economies led to a "dark" period from which it took centuries to recover. For Crete, this meant the end of the classical Minoan tradition and the rise of smaller communities that would later evolve into different forms of Greek culture. Though much knowledge of Minoan religious practices, language, and government was lost, their cultural imprint remained strong. The memory of a splendid island civilization lingered in later Greek myths about King Minos, the Labyrinth, and the Minotaur.

---

17. Minoan Achievements in Shipbuilding

Since the Minoans relied heavily on maritime trade, shipbuilding was an essential craft. They built swift vessels with high prows, likely powered by both oars and sails. These ships carried goods like olive oil, wine, pottery, and metal ingots across the Aegean. Some may even have ventured as far as Egypt or the Levant. Bronze tools for carpentry—saws, chisels, adzes—made it easier to shape sturdy timber hulls.

Harbors at places like Amnissos, near Knossos, or Kommos in southern Crete, served as key embarkation points. Goods would be loaded onto ships for export, while arriving vessels brought in copper, tin, luxury items, and possibly exotic animals or plants. Successful voyages required knowledge of winds, currents, and navigation by the stars. The expertise the Minoans gained in seafaring contributed greatly to their prosperity and helped them exert soft power across the Aegean region, influencing art, religion, and commerce in distant communities.

18. Crafts: Pottery, Textiles, and Stone Vessels

Minoan craftsmanship was not limited to bronze tools and weapons. Pottery production boomed, with specialized workshops creating pieces for everyday use and high-quality exports. **Kamares ware**, known for bold, curving designs in contrasting colors, became a symbol of Minoan creativity in the Protopalatial period. Later pottery styles incorporated marine life, floral motifs, and more geometric patterns.

Textile production was another vital craft. Spinning and weaving were likely done by women, using wool from local sheep or linen from flax. Bronze needles, pins, and weaving tools made the work easier. Minoan fabrics, though not surviving in great quantity, appear in art, showing colorful patterns and intricate designs.

Stone vessels also stand out in Minoan art. Craftsmen carved local stone into vases, bowls, and ritual vessels. Some were purely functional; others were highly decorative, with carved relief scenes of animals, plants, or religious symbols. Bronze chisels and abrasives likely aided these stone-carving processes. Such vessels could be important trade items, gifts to foreign dignitaries, or precious temple donations.

19. Minoan Legacy and Cultural Influence

Although the Minoan civilization eventually declined, its impact lived on. Many elements of later Greek culture bear traces of Minoan origins. For example, the Mycenaeans incorporated Minoan religious symbols, script, and artistic motifs into their own palatial world. Myths about Crete—like the Minotaur legend—found their way into Greek storytelling, reflecting the memory of a powerful island culture that once inspired awe.

In the broader Bronze Age context, the Minoans exemplify how a seafaring, trade-focused society could thrive and shape the culture of an entire region. Their advanced building techniques, complex palaces, and sophisticated art proved that an island civilization could stand shoulder to shoulder with mainland powers like Egypt or Mesopotamia. While the Minoans did not conquer vast territories, they built a network of economic and cultural ties that gave them stability and prosperity for centuries.

CHAPTER 6: THE MYCENAEANS

Introduction

When people think of ancient Greece, they often envision temples, philosophers, and later city-states like Athens and Sparta. But centuries before the "Classical" age, the mainland was home to the Mycenaeans—fierce warrior-kings who built fortified palaces, commanded naval forces, and engaged in widespread trade. They lived in the late Bronze Age, partially overlapping with the Minoans of Crete. Over time, the Mycenaeans rose to dominance in the Aegean region, forging a realm that extended across mainland Greece, the Cycladic islands, and even parts of Crete. They left behind massive fortress-palaces, gold-laden tombs, and the earliest known written form of Greek, inscribed in Linear B.

In this chapter, we will discover how the Mycenaean civilization grew from modest beginnings into a significant Bronze Age power. We will examine their imposing citadels, burial practices, religious beliefs, warfare, and far-reaching trade networks. We will also see how they adapted and absorbed elements of Minoan culture, only to surpass Crete in regional influence. As we approach the end, we will explore the mysterious collapse that eventually brought Mycenaean dominance to a close, setting the stage for a later era of Greek history.

---

1. The Mainland Setting and Early Societies

Mainland Greece is marked by rugged mountains, fertile plains, and a coastline dotted with natural harbors. In the early Bronze Age, small agrarian communities grew in valleys where they could farm wheat, barley, and olives. The coastline encouraged fishing and seafaring, though these early groups were not as focused on maritime trade as the Minoans were. Over time, as bronze technology spread, local elites began to compete for resources. Settlements in central and southern Greece started to expand, giving rise to more complex societies.

Connections with Crete introduced new ideas in architecture, metalworking, and possibly administration. By the Middle Bronze Age, some mainland settlements—like Mycenae, Tiryns, and Thebes—showed evidence of rising wealth and social hierarchy. Fortifications appeared, though smaller than the later colossal walls. Increasing contact with Minoan traders exposed mainland communities to advanced shipbuilding and the concept of a palatial economy. A transition was underway, paving the path toward what would be recognized as "Mycenaean" culture.

2. The Palaces of Mycenae, Tiryns, and Pylos

By around 1600–1500 BCE, the Mycenaeans were building powerful palaces that served as administrative, economic, and military hubs. **Mycenae** in the northeastern Peloponnese became the most famous of these centers, lending its name to the entire civilization. The fortress at Mycenae sat atop a hill, protected by massive "Cyclopean" walls made of enormous stones. Through a grand entrance known as the **Lion Gate**, visitors entered a citadel containing a palace complex, storerooms, and royal grave circles.

Tiryns, another formidable site, had similarly impressive walls and a well-planned palace with a central megaron—an architectural feature consisting of a large hall with a central hearth. **Pylos**, located in Messenia, showcased a sprawling palace known for its elaborate frescoes and numerous Linear B tablets. Unlike Mycenae and Tiryns, Pylos did not have equally massive walls, but it was still strategically situated, controlling coastal routes and fertile lands nearby. Each palace center included workshops, storerooms, living quarters for elites, and shrines for worship. Together, they formed the backbone of Mycenaean power.

3. Linear B: The Oldest Known Greek Writing

One of the most significant Mycenaean legacies is **Linear B**, a script adapted from Minoan Linear A. Unlike Linear A, Linear B has been deciphered and is recognized as an early form of the Greek language. Scribes incised symbols onto clay tablets for record-keeping. These tablets, often stored in palace archives, detailed lists of goods, personnel, and religious offerings.

Examples from Pylos provide a glimpse into Mycenaean administration. Tablets mention specialized workers—smiths, leatherworkers, chariot-makers—along with rations allocated to them. Records also note offerings to gods and the production or distribution of bronze, reflecting the significance of metal in their economy. The written documents confirm that Mycenaean palaces were carefully managed societies, with scribes keeping track of everything from grain harvests to bronze ingots. Though the Linear B texts are largely administrative, they help us understand the organizational complexity behind Mycenaean power.

4. Mycenaean Religion and Pantheon

The Mycenaean religion was an early form of the Greek pantheon. Some Linear B tablets list offerings to deities who appear in later Greek mythology, such as Zeus, Hera, Poseidon, and possibly Athena. However, we do not have extensive myths preserved from Mycenaean tablets; most references are short and tied to palace accounts of sacrifices or gifts. Still, the existence of these names hints that Mycenaeans worshiped gods who would later be central to Greek culture.

Mycenaean shrines likely existed within palatial complexes or in nearby areas. Certain figurines discovered in palace storerooms or grave goods might depict deities or worshipers. Ritual vessels and bull iconography, borrowed from the Minoans, appear in Mycenaean contexts, indicating that they absorbed aspects of Minoan religious practices. Over time, the Mycenaeans blended local beliefs with imported ideas, forging a religious tradition that laid foundations for classical Greek theology and myth.

5. Warrior Culture and Military Organization

In contrast to the relatively open and less-fortified Minoan palaces, Mycenaean citadels bristled with defensive walls. Their society placed a high value on warfare and the display of martial prowess. **Grave Circle A** at Mycenae, dating to around 1600–1500 BCE, contained weapons, gold masks (including the famous "Mask of Agamemnon"), and other treasures, showing that elite burial was often accompanied by symbols of power and warrior identity.

Chariots played a role in Mycenaean warfare, as indicated by numerous references on Linear B tablets and artistic depictions. Bronze was indispensable: swords, spears, arrowheads, and protective gear were fashioned from it. The

Mycenaeans also appear to have used advanced composite bows, another technology possibly influenced by eastern contacts. Ships carried warriors on raids or expeditions across the Aegean, showing that the Mycenaeans, like the Minoans, recognized the importance of naval strength.

An elite warrior class likely surrounded the king (often called the *wanax* in Linear B texts). Another figure, called the *lawagetas*, might have served as a military leader under the king. Together, they coordinated the palace's resources—bronze ingots, horses, chariots, and manpower—to maintain control and expand influence. Warfare provided spoils, glory, and captives, some of whom may have been taken as slaves or laborers in the palace.

---

6. Burial Customs: Shaft Graves and Tholos Tombs

The Mycenaeans are famous for their grand burial practices. Early on, elite families were interred in **shaft graves**, deep rectangular pits lined with stone. The Grave Circles at Mycenae contained multiple shaft graves filled with lavish goods—gold diadems, weapons, jewelry, and intricately decorated masks. These items emphasized the importance of status in the afterlife, suggesting that the Mycenaeans believed in preserving one's rank beyond death.

Later, the Mycenaeans built **tholos tombs**, also known as beehive tombs. These large, corbel-vaulted structures were cut into hillsides, featuring a long passageway (dromos) leading to a circular burial chamber with a high, domed roof. The best-known examples are the so-called **Treasury of Atreus** at Mycenae and the **Tomb of Clytemnestra**. Though named by later observers after legendary figures, their original occupants remain uncertain. Many of these tombs were robbed in antiquity, but enough artifacts remained to show they once housed rich grave goods. Tholos tombs served the ruling families, reinforcing their dominance and connecting them with ancestral prestige.

---

7. Palace Economies and Redistribution

Mycenaean palaces functioned as central points for collecting and redistributing resources. Farmers and craft workers owed a portion of their produce to the palace. In return, the palace provided protection, infrastructure, and possibly rations during difficult times. Linear B tablets record large stocks of grain, oil, and wine, as well as wool used for textiles. Metallurgical workshops within or near the palaces processed copper and tin into bronze. Smiths turned this bronze into tools, weapons, and fittings.

This palace-based economy allowed for specialized labor. Some scribes oversaw flocks of sheep or herds of cattle, ensuring a steady supply of wool or hides. Others tracked the output of metal workshops. The scale of production was significant, enabling Mycenaean states to field well-armed troops and engage in long-distance trade. This intricate system required strong leadership, administration, and a consistent supply of raw materials—particularly the tin needed for bronze, which had to be imported.

8. Mycenaean Seafaring and Trade Networks

Though not as renowned as the Minoans for maritime trade, the Mycenaeans were still skilled seafarers. They expanded their influence across the Cyclades, Crete, and even reached into the eastern Mediterranean. Shipbuilding advanced as they adopted or adapted Minoan techniques, and ports on the Greek mainland served as gateways for trade. Mycenaean pottery, easily recognized by its shapes and decoration, has been found across the Aegean and along the coasts of the Levant, Cyprus, and Italy.

This trade brought them metals (copper from Cyprus, tin from more distant lands), luxury items like ivory and glass, and possibly new warfare or building technologies. In exchange, they likely exported oil, wine, textiles, and finely crafted bronze weapons. As the Mycenaeans established political control over Crete, some Minoan ports and workshops came under their administration, further expanding their reach. Maritime routes were not always peaceful; raids and piracy could disrupt shipping, prompting the Mycenaeans to maintain armed vessels and to build alliances with strategic coastal towns.

9. Cultural Borrowing from the Minoans

When the Mycenaeans first encountered the Minoans, they found a sophisticated, palace-based civilization with advanced craft techniques and extensive trade connections. Impressed, the Mycenaeans began to adopt Minoan features. Artistic motifs such as spirals, marine themes, and floral patterns migrated into Mycenaean pottery and frescoes. The Mycenaeans also learned to write from the Minoans, modifying Linear A into Linear B for their own language.

Religious symbols like the bull, double axe, and certain goddess figures likewise appeared in Mycenaean art, though often placed in a more militaristic or regal context. Over time, the Mycenaeans moved from imitation to dominance, particularly after they took control of Crete around 1450 BCE. Still, they never lost the flair for color and decoration inherited from Minoan models. A blending of these styles created a unique Mycenaean aesthetic that can be seen in palace frescoes featuring hunting scenes, processions, or mythic creatures like griffins.

10. Society and Social Hierarchy

Mycenaean society was stratified, centered on the palace. At the top was the king (*wanax*), who held ultimate authority over land, resources, and military decisions. Below him were high-ranking officials like the *lawagetas* (possibly a war leader) and local governors (*ko-re-te*), who managed specific regions or tasks. Scribes formed an educated class responsible for administration. Skilled craftsmen—metalworkers, potters, builders—occupied a respected position since their labor was crucial to the palace's success.

Farmers and herders formed the bulk of the population, living in smaller settlements around the palace centers. They owed tribute or taxes in the form of produce or labor. In return, they received some protection from raids or invasions. Slaves or captured peoples from foreign campaigns provided additional labor, often working in palace workshops or large construction projects. The royal family and nobility flaunted wealth through elaborate burials, lavish feasts, and displays of gold or bronze objects, further solidifying social divisions.

11. The Mycenaean Heartland: Argolid and Beyond

The region known as the Argolid, in the northeastern Peloponnese, was home to both **Mycenae** and **Tiryns**, making it a crucial hub of power. The fertile plains, proximity to the sea, and trade routes linking the Gulf of Argos to the Aegean gave local rulers a strategic advantage. They could control the movement of goods and troops, shaping alliances with smaller nearby settlements. This concentration of resources and leadership helped Mycenae, in particular, to become a legendary seat of power in later Greek myths (such as the stories of King Agamemnon).

Elsewhere on the mainland, places like **Thebes** in Boeotia and **Orchomenos** rose as regional players, each with its own palace. **Sparta** in Laconia and **Athens** in Attica may also have had smaller Mycenaean palatial centers or significant structures, though not all have left as clear a record. The unifying theme across these sites is the presence of fortifications, palatial administration, and a shared material culture that we call "Mycenaean." Still, they were not a single unified empire in the modern sense, but rather a network of loosely affiliated or competing states that recognized common cultural traits.

---

12. Warfare and Weaponry: A Closer Look

Mycenaean warriors carried a variety of bronze weapons:

- **Swords**: Several types have been uncovered, including long, slim blades suitable for thrusting and shorter, sturdier blades used for slashing. Many were ornate, with inlaid decoration or gold hilts, signifying the status of their owners.
- **Spears**: Bronze spearheads came in different shapes, from leaf-shaped to triangular. Spears were common among foot soldiers, providing reach and thrusting power in battle.
- **Daggers**: Often decorated with precious metals and scenes of hunts or battles, these were both functional and ceremonial.
- **Shields**: Early Mycenaean shields could be large and rectangular ("tower shields") or figure-of-eight-shaped, possibly influenced by Minoan designs. Later forms were smaller and more maneuverable.
- **Armor**: Some references exist to bronze scale armor or plate armor, though it was likely limited to elite warriors. There is also the notable **Dendra panoply**, a full-body bronze armor found near Argos, showcasing advanced protective gear.

Chariots were crucial for rapid movement, possibly used in shock tactics or for archers. Representations in art and on seals depict chariots with two horses and a driver plus a warrior. The cost to maintain chariots, horses, and specialized personnel implies that they were symbols of high status, used primarily by aristocrats or royal retinues.

13. Hunting as a Noble Pastime

Hunting scenes appear frequently in Mycenaean art, including images on daggers or frescoes. The boar hunt in particular had strong cultural significance, as wild boars were dangerous animals that tested a warrior's courage and skill. Hunts provided an opportunity for elites to demonstrate bravery and bond with fellow nobles or warriors. They also supplied meat for feasting, an important social event that reinforced alliances and hierarchical structures.

Much like warfare, hunting required high-quality bronze weapons. Spears and arrows with sharp bronze tips gave hunters a lethal advantage. Dogs might assist, as indicated by scenes in Mycenaean art or references in later Greek epics. The spoils of a successful hunt—boar tusks, deer antlers—could decorate helmets, belts, or palace walls. For the Mycenaeans, hunting was an arena where aristocratic masculinity and prestige shone, second only to the battlefield.

14. Feasting and Displays of Wealth

Feasts were a central feature of Mycenaean palace life. Elite gatherings in the megaron (the palace's main hall) involved abundant food, wine, and entertainment. Bronze vessels and utensils were used to serve and consume food. Large cauldrons, spits, and mixing bowls found in palace storerooms reflect the scale of these events. Singing, dancing, and possibly the recitation of heroic tales could enliven the atmosphere.

Such feasts served both political and social purposes. Rulers could display generosity, distributing portions of meat and wine to favored guests, cementing loyalty. Foreign dignitaries or allied leaders might be invited, fostering diplomatic ties. Feasts also reinforced the social hierarchy, as only the upper classes would partake in these lavish events. Meanwhile, common laborers and farmers remained outside the palace, carrying on their tasks but occasionally benefiting from redistributed goods or smaller communal celebrations.

---

15. Interaction with the Wider Bronze Age World

Mycenaean connections went beyond the Aegean. Texts from Hittite records occasionally mention a land called "Ahhiyawa," which some scholars interpret as a reference to Mycenaean Greeks. Trade with the Hittites, Egyptians, and other Near Eastern powers included exchanges of metals, textiles, and finished goods. Mycenaean pottery has been found in the Levant, on Cyprus, and in coastal Anatolia, indicating robust commerce by sea.

In some stories, Mycenaean warriors or raiders might have ventured into foreign lands in search of plunder or mercenary service. The later Greek epics (though composed centuries afterward) preserve a memory of Mycenaean-era heroes journeying across the seas to fight in far-off places. Whether or not these epics reflect specific historical events, they echo the fact that Mycenaean influence extended well beyond the Greek mainland, shaping and being shaped by international interactions.

---

16. The Question of the Trojan War

According to later Greek tradition, the Trojan War took place near the end of the Mycenaean period, supposedly around the 12th or 13th century BCE. The epics *Iliad* and *Odyssey*, attributed to Homer, describe a grand coalition of "Achaeans" (Mycenaean Greeks) laying siege to the city of Troy in northwestern Anatolia. Archaeological excavations at the site often identified as Troy (or Ilion) show evidence of destruction layers that may align with a conflict during the Late Bronze Age.

However, the exact historical reality of the Trojan War remains uncertain. If a conflict did occur, it might have involved trading disputes or alliances gone sour, typical of the complex politics of the time. For the Mycenaeans, controlling or influencing the straits leading to the Black Sea could have been strategically valuable for trade. While we cannot confirm every heroic tale, the existence of a city called Troy, combined with widespread turmoil in the region during the late 2nd millennium BCE, suggests that elements of the epic stories could derive from real events tied to Mycenaean expansion or rivalry.

17. Signs of Decline and the Late Helladic Period

By around 1200 BCE, signs of trouble appeared in Mycenaean society. Many palaces show evidence of fire and destruction, possibly from invasions, internal strife, or natural disasters. The once-thriving trade networks began to falter, making it difficult to obtain tin for bronze. Disruptions across the eastern Mediterranean—often associated with the so-called "Sea Peoples" or widespread migrations—contributed to instability. In some places, local uprisings or rivalries might have led to palace burnings.

As central authority weakened, the palatial system collapsed. People fled fortified sites, and population centers shifted. Writing in Linear B disappeared, indicating a breakdown in administrative systems. Over time, iron began to replace bronze, but the knowledge and organization once held by palace scribes and craftsmen were lost or diminished. The result was a centuries-long period of reduced literacy, simpler material culture, and smaller political units—a time often called the "Greek Dark Age."

18. Possible Causes of the Collapse

The Mycenaean collapse was probably not caused by a single event but a combination of factors:

1. **External Invasions or Raids**: Groups from outside the Aegean might have seized the opportunity to attack weakened palaces.
2. **Internal Conflicts**: Succession disputes or power struggles could have led to civil unrest and the burning of palaces.
3. **Economic Strain**: Trade disruptions limited the flow of tin, making bronze production harder. Rising costs for maintaining armies and building projects might have overstretched resources.

4. **Natural Disasters**: Earthquakes and droughts could have compounded the crisis, straining agriculture and infrastructure.

Regardless of the exact mix of causes, the result was a dramatic shift in the region's political and economic landscape. Large palaces and the elaborate bureaucracy they represented vanished, replaced by smaller, simpler communities. Many once-glorious sites lay abandoned, leaving behind ashes and ruins.

---

19. Legacy of the Mycenaeans

Though the Mycenaean civilization collapsed, its memory and influence did not vanish. The oral traditions that would later become the Greek epics likely preserved some notion of Mycenaean heroes, grand palaces, and far-reaching voyages. Mycenaean tombs, citadels, and leftover artifacts shaped the myths and legends of classical Greece. Even the Greek language carried forward words and religious concepts that may have originated in the Mycenaean period.

Centuries later, Greek city-states emerged with new forms of government, art, and warfare. Yet they continued to reference the heroic age of Mycenae as a time of legendary kings and mighty deeds. The enduring fascination with this age can be seen in stories of Agamemnon, Menelaus, Achilles, and Odysseus—characters who, if not historically identical to real figures, reflect cultural memories of the Mycenaean era. For historians and enthusiasts alike, the Mycenaeans represent a formative stage in Greek civilization, bridging the gap between the Minoan world and the classical heights to come.

CHAPTER 7: BRONZE AGE ANATOLIA AND THE HITTITES

Introduction

Anatolia, often called Asia Minor, is a vast peninsula that connects the Near East with southeastern Europe. During the Bronze Age, this region became home to a remarkable array of peoples and cultures. Among them, the Hittites rose to great prominence, establishing one of the most powerful empires of the time. They built strongholds on the rugged plateau, formed alliances and rivalries with neighboring states, and became known for their chariots and skill in forging political and military power.

In this chapter, we will explore the geography of Anatolia, the many Bronze Age communities that thrived there, and the complex developments that gave rise to the Hittite Empire. We will examine how bronze technology fueled agricultural expansion, trade, and warfare. We will also look at the Hittite capital of Hattusa, the nature of Hittite kingship, and their conflicts and treaties with neighboring powers such as Egypt. By the end, you will see how the Hittites became a major force in the Bronze Age and left an enduring mark on the region's history.

---

1. Geography and Early Settlements in Anatolia

Anatolia is surrounded by the Black Sea in the north, the Aegean Sea in the west, and the Mediterranean Sea in the south. The interior consists of a high plateau intersected by mountain ranges and broad valleys. This varied landscape supported different forms of economic activity: farming in the fertile river basins, herding in the uplands, and trade along coastal routes or caravan paths that crossed the region.

Well before the Bronze Age, small communities populated Anatolia, practicing agriculture and animal husbandry. As time passed, they discovered copper deposits in the mountainous areas. This opened the path to metalworking and eventually to the creation of bronze. By the Early Bronze Age (roughly the third millennium BCE), several city-states began to form. Archaeologists (focusing only on ancient remains for our purposes) have identified numerous fortified settlements indicating that warfare, trade, and organized leadership were already features of these early societies.

Local resources included copper, silver, and gold. Tin was typically imported—possibly from distant regions such as Central Asia or the Zagros area—to produce bronze, the prized alloy of the era. Because Anatolia was located between Mesopotamia, the Levant, and the Aegean, its communities served as intermediaries in the exchange of metals, textiles, and other goods. Over time, this strategic position would lay the foundation for more complex states to emerge.

2. The Assyrian Trade Colonies and Influence

One important milestone in Anatolia's Bronze Age history was the arrival of Assyrian traders from Mesopotamia. They established "trade colonies" (called *karum* in some ancient texts) in the early second millennium BCE, setting up enclaves near key Anatolian cities. The most famous was at Kanesh (also spelled Kültepe in modern naming, but we will avoid modern references and just note it as an ancient site).

These traders brought textiles, tin, and other goods from Mesopotamia in exchange for Anatolian metals, especially silver. They introduced cuneiform writing to the region, using clay tablets to record commercial contracts and correspondence. This influx of ideas and materials helped shape the local Anatolian polities, some of which grew wealthier and more organized. Leadership figures formed alliances, minted standardized weights for trade, and possibly learned advanced methods of administration and record-keeping from the Assyrians.

Eventually, native powers began to consolidate control over these trade routes. Among them, a group in central Anatolia, later identified as the Hittites, rose in prominence. They recognized the advantages of controlling trade and securing resources such as metals. By absorbing or defeating rival city-states, they gradually laid the groundwork for an empire that would dominate the region for centuries.

3. The Rise of the Hittite Kingdom

The Hittites spoke an Indo-European language, which sets them apart from many neighboring populations who spoke Semitic or other language families.

They established themselves in central Anatolia, around the region of the Halys River (often referred to in ancient texts). Over time, they began to build a political entity sometimes called the Old Hittite Kingdom, centered at Hattusa.

Traditional accounts attribute the unification to leaders like Labarna and Hattusili I (though the exact details can be murky). What is clear is that these early kings waged wars against rival kingdoms in Anatolia and perhaps even campaigned in northern Mesopotamia or the Levant. By doing so, they gained control of trade routes and extracted tribute from conquered cities. Bronze tools and weapons played a key role in these military ventures, allowing the Hittites to equip their chariots, infantry, and siege operations effectively.

The central plateau of Anatolia, with its rugged terrain and resource-rich hills, provided both a natural defense and the potential for wealth through mining. The Hittites capitalized on these advantages, forging alliances with local chiefs or subduing them outright. Over several generations, this kingdom became a formidable force, capable of challenging even the long-standing powers of Mesopotamia and the Levant.

---

4. Hattusa: The Hittite Capital

At the heart of the Hittite world lay **Hattusa**, perched on a strategic rocky outcrop, surrounded by fortifications. Massive stone walls encircled the city, with gates adorned by stone reliefs depicting lions or sphinxes. Within the walls stood administrative buildings, temples, granaries, and residences for the king's court. There was also a royal citadel—built on higher ground—where the palace and major religious structures existed side by side.

The city included elaborate water management systems: canals, cisterns, and underground passages. This ensured a steady water supply during sieges or droughts. As the empire grew, so did Hattusa. Texts from the site mention records of tribute, royal decrees, treaties with foreign powers, and religious ceremonies, all written in cuneiform script adapted for the Hittite language. Scribes employed clay tablets and cylinder seals, reflecting a blend of Mesopotamian writing influence and local administrative needs.

Temple complexes in Hattusa dedicated worship to a range of gods—some from the original Hittite pantheon, others adopted from conquered lands. The result was a cosmopolitan religious scene that paralleled the empire's political tapestry. Bronze offerings or ritual implements might have been presented to these deities, symbolizing the metal's significance in both worldly and divine affairs.

5. Religion and Mythology

Hittite religion was a rich mixture of indigenous Anatolian beliefs and deities absorbed from neighboring regions. The king often served as the high priest, performing ceremonies to ensure the favor of the pantheon. Deities like the Storm God or the Sun Goddess were central figures, often connected to agriculture and warfare. The Storm God, in particular, symbolized the power of weather—crucial for farming and for victory in battle.

The Hittites produced mythological texts that refer to divine struggles and heroic deeds, though many details remain fragmentary. Some references describe the Storm God fighting a dragon-like creature, echoing parallels in Mesopotamian or wider Near Eastern myth. In daily life, people visited local shrines, offered food, drink, or metal objects, and sought blessings for crops, livestock, and family well-being. The concept of sacred oaths was extremely important—violations of treaties or promises might be feared as offenses against the gods, risking divine wrath.

Large festivals gathered people from across the empire to Hattusa or other major cult centers. These events involved processions, feasts, and sacrifices, creating a shared sense of identity and loyalty to the crown. Bronze altars, incense burners, or ceremonial weapons often played a role, affirming that metal was not just a tool of warfare but also a medium connecting mortals and the divine realm.

6. Administration, Law, and Society

Hittite society included the king at the top—sometimes called the "Great King"—followed by royal family members, noble families, and local governors. Officials managed provinces and city-states, collecting taxes and overseeing the distribution of goods. Slaves, prisoners of war, and lower-class farmers composed the bulk of the labor force, working in agriculture or crafting. Skilled artisans and scribes held higher status due to their importance in metalworking, record-keeping, and temple service.

Law codes, some preserved on tablets, covered topics like theft, injury compensation, and property disputes. They also addressed religious offenses. Punishments could be harsh, but certain reforms appear to have mitigated extreme penalties over time. The Hittites took treaties and oaths very seriously, binding vassals or conquered rulers to their authority under threat of curses invoked before the gods. This diplomatic approach, combined with military might, helped the Hittites govern a culturally diverse empire.

Within local communities, everyday life likely revolved around tending fields of wheat and barley, raising livestock, and participating in communal religious rites. Bronze tools improved farming, enabling deeper plowing and more efficient harvesting. Merchants traveled between cities, bringing tin, textiles, and finished bronze objects. Households utilized pottery, cloth, and simple furniture, with metal items—knives, pins, small tools—being valued possessions. While the nobility enjoyed lavish banquets, simpler folk survived on cereals, dairy, and occasional meat or fish.

7. Military Strength and Chariot Warfare

One of the hallmarks of Hittite power was their skill in warfare, particularly the use of **chariots**. These light, horse-drawn vehicles offered speed and mobility on the battlefield. Bronze fittings for the chariot's wheels and axles reduced weight and enhanced durability. The Hittite chariot often carried three men—one to drive, one to fight with spear or bow, and another to shield them. This design contrasted with some rivals who employed only two-man chariots.

Infantry armed with bronze swords, spears, and shields supported the chariot corps. Some references mention heavier fortifications or siege tactics used against walled cities. The Hittites also practiced diplomacy by forging alliances or signing treaties with city-states that could supply troops or resources. Through a combination of efficient administration, well-trained charioteers, and a reliable supply of bronze weapons, the Hittites created a formidable military force capable of challenging major powers like Mitanni, Babylonia, and even New Kingdom Egypt.

A strong military not only protected the empire's trade routes and borders but also allowed the Hittite kings to assert influence over distant regions. They could demand tribute, secure access to metals, or intervene in local politics. The prestige of victory in battle enhanced the king's reputation, reinforcing his position as both ruler and high priest.

8. Conflicts and Alliances with Neighboring Powers

The Hittites found themselves in a dynamic geopolitical environment. To the south lay the region of Syria and the kingdom of Mitanni, while further east were the Assyrians and Babylonians. To the west lay Arzawa and other smaller states, and beyond that the Aegean world. Each of these zones had its own ambitions and resources, making diplomacy and warfare constants in Hittite history.

A major rivalry developed between the Hittites and Mitanni over control of northern Syria. The region was vital for trade routes leading to Mesopotamia and the Levant. At times, the Hittites campaigned extensively in Syria, capturing cities and imposing Hittite-style administration. In other periods, they faced setbacks as Mitanni or local rulers rebelled. Meanwhile, Babylonia, under different dynasties, intervened diplomatically or militarily to protect its interests or expand. The Assyrians also emerged as a rising threat, pressuring the Hittites from the southeast in later periods.

One of the most notable rivalries was with New Kingdom Egypt under pharaohs like Seti I and Ramesses II. Both the Hittites and Egyptians vied for control over the strategic lands of Canaan and Syria. This competition culminated in several battles, most famously the Battle of Kadesh (around the 13th century BCE). While this battle is often portrayed in Egyptian records as a great pharaonic victory, the Hittites likely fought to a stalemate, preserving their hold on much of Syria. Ultimately, the two powers signed one of the earliest known peace treaties, dividing spheres of influence in the region. This treaty was sealed by royal marriages and oaths made before the gods, reflecting the Hittites' emphasis on sworn pacts.

---

9. The Battle of Kadesh and Its Aftermath

The Battle of Kadesh stands out as a defining moment in the Late Bronze Age. Ramesses II led Egyptian forces north, hoping to wrest control of strategic Syrian towns from Hittite authority. Muwatalli II, the Hittite king at the time, gathered a large coalition, including charioteers from different parts of his empire. The two sides clashed near the Orontes River. Hittite chariots initially ambushed the Egyptian vanguard. Ramesses II claimed he fought back heroically and forced the Hittites to retreat.

Despite Egyptian temple reliefs celebrating victory, the reality was more complex. The Hittites managed to hold most of Syria even after the battle, indicating at least a drawn outcome. Both sides suffered casualties and realized that perpetual warfare was exhausting their resources. Not long after, Ramesses II and Hattusili III (brother and successor to Muwatalli II) negotiated a peace treaty. This accord recognized zones of control, promoted diplomatic ties, and ended major hostilities between the two empires.

The treaty stands as an example of Bronze Age diplomacy—both pragmatic and sacred. Each side swore oaths under the watch of their gods. Royal women married into each other's courts, signifying a bond that was not to be broken lightly. This arrangement stabilized the region for some time, allowing the Hittites to focus on internal affairs and dealings with other neighbors.

10. Cultural Exchanges and Trade

Hittite territory spanned multiple cultural zones, including populations that spoke Luwian, Hurrian, Hattian, and other languages. As they conquered or allied with these groups, the Hittites absorbed cultural practices, deities, and artistic elements. In turn, they spread their own administrative structures, religious rites, and material culture. This mix led to a vibrant cultural tapestry within the empire.

Trade was essential to the Hittite economy, with metal resources like silver, copper, and iron ore found in Anatolia. Though the widespread use of iron would come more into focus after the Bronze Age, the Hittites had some early experience with it, using it for ceremonial or precious objects. Bronze, however, remained the everyday backbone of tools and weapons. Tin, a key component, had to be imported through complex routes that connected to distant lands.

Exports from Hittite territories could include wool, textiles, and finished metal goods. In turn, they imported luxury items like ivory, fine pottery, glass from the Levant, and specialized resources such as cedar wood from the mountains of Lebanon. The Hittite presence in Syria gave them access to ports on the Mediterranean coast, facilitating both trade and communication with distant regions.

11. Daily Life Under Hittite Rule

For ordinary people, life in the Hittite realm revolved around farming, herding, and village affairs. The central government demanded taxes and labor, especially during building projects or wartime. Villagers produced grain, wine, and oil; herders raised sheep, goats, and cattle. Bronze plowshares and sickles made agriculture more productive. Carpenters and masons used bronze tools for construction, crafting everything from simple homes to monumental structures in the capital.

In local shrines, villagers offered small gifts—perhaps figurines or bits of metal—to regional gods who oversaw their fields and flocks. Seasonal festivals likely punctuated the year, coinciding with sowing or harvest times. Craftspeople in towns and cities specialized in pottery, weaving, woodworking, or metalworking, selling their goods in markets or supplying the palace. Travel could be hazardous, given the mountainous terrain and the risk of bandits, but caravans under palace protection traversed major routes to connect different provinces.

Social hierarchies were clear: the nobility and priestly class commanded respect, controlling wealth and religious authority. Scribes, intimately familiar with cuneiform, served in administrative offices. Warriors enjoyed status and land grants in return for their service. Commoners worked the land or served local lords, while slaves—often war captives—performed menial tasks. Despite these disparities, a shared sense of identity gradually formed under Hittite governance, reinforced by religion, trade, and the benefits of a stable empire (when not embroiled in war).

12. Hittite Legal and Diplomatic Traditions

The Hittites established a formal legal system, some of which survives on clay tablets. Their laws covered issues such as theft, murder, and even aspects of personal conduct. Interestingly, certain reforms appear to have reduced the severity of punishments—some earlier death penalties changed to fines or restitution. The aim may have been to maintain social harmony in a large empire with diverse populations.

Diplomacy was another defining trait. The Hittites crafted treaties that bound vassal states with loyalty oaths. These treaties often invoked a pantheon of gods as witnesses, threatening dire curses on anyone who broke the agreement. This religious and legal framing provided a powerful deterrent against rebellion. To enforce treaties, the Hittites placed garrisons in strategic cities or married princesses into local royal families, ensuring a measure of loyalty or at least a stable alliance.

In times of transition, such as the death of a king or a significant military setback, internal power struggles sometimes erupted. Royal succession could be contested by princes or by influential nobles. Such disputes might lead to intrigue or civil strife, undermining the empire's cohesion. Nonetheless, the overall tradition of law and oath-based diplomacy helped the Hittites maintain unity through many challenges.

13. The Height of Hittite Power

Under kings like Suppiluliuma I, Mursili II, and later Hattusili III, the Hittites reached the peak of their power in the 14th and 13th centuries BCE. They held sway over large parts of Anatolia, northern Syria, and occasionally beyond. They kept the Assyrians in check for a time, defeated Mitanni, and rivaled Egypt for control of the Levant. Hattusa became a bustling imperial capital, with a complex bureaucracy managing tribute, trade, and military campaigns.

Massive building projects took place in Hattusa, expanding temples and constructing new fortifications. The empire's scribes produced archives that touched upon religious rituals, diplomatic correspondence, land grants, and legal disputes. The official language of court was Hittite, but Luwian, Hurrian, and other tongues were heard in the streets and outlying regions. Royal propaganda portrayed the king as chosen by the gods to maintain order and peace—though in practice, these were still turbulent times with frequent warfare.

Despite the militaristic emphasis, there were periods of relative stability that allowed cultural flourishing. The Hittite elite sponsored art—stone reliefs, wall paintings, gold and bronze adornments—showcasing both local styles and foreign influences. Craftsmen refined chariot designs, improved metal casting, and developed new agricultural tools. This synergy of artistry, technology, and power made the Hittite Empire a leading force in the Bronze Age world.

14. Internal Strife and Economic Pressures

Maintaining a large empire was costly. Armies had to be paid or at least provisioned, building projects demanded labor and materials, and trade routes required protection from raiders. Over time, the Hittites faced growing challenges from new powers like Assyria, which gained strength and encroached on once-Hittite territories. In the west, various local kingdoms also tested Hittite control, sometimes forming coalitions against them.

Economic disruptions could arise if tin supplies were cut off or if foreign conquests failed to yield expected tributes. Crop failures due to drought, or natural disasters such as earthquakes, could strain the empire's food reserves. Meanwhile, internal factionalism within the royal family sometimes led to power struggles. A rebellious prince or general might gather support from disaffected nobles, hoping to seize the throne. These internal upheavals weakened central authority, making it harder to respond to external threats.

As the 13th century BCE drew on, the Bronze Age world grew more unstable. Raiders, migrations, and shifting alliances disrupted trade and toppled once-mighty states. Although the Hittites tried to adapt, forging new alliances or reorganizing their military, they could not fully withstand the wave of changes that swept the region. Eventually, the empire began to lose its grip on outlying territories, retreating closer to its core lands in central Anatolia.

---

15. The Fall of Hattusa and the Empire's End

Around the start of the 12th century BCE, Hattusa was destroyed. The exact circumstances remain uncertain—whether it was an attack by invading forces, an uprising within the empire, or a result of widespread chaos known to have hit many Bronze Age civilizations. Some historians connect the destruction to the movements of unidentified "Sea Peoples" or to the expanding power of Assyria, but the evidence is not conclusive.

In any case, the royal dynasty collapsed. Hattusa was abandoned as a political center, and the various provinces either fell to local rulers or were taken over by neighboring states. Without a unifying kingship, the Hittite Empire splintered. Some populations fled or migrated, possibly establishing smaller Neo-Hittite states in southeastern Anatolia and northern Syria. These successor states continued certain Hittite traditions for a time, but they did not recreate the grand empire.

The decline of Hattusa mirrored a broader pattern in the eastern Mediterranean. Great city-states and kingdoms from Greece to the Levant faced turmoil, leading to what many call the Late Bronze Age collapse. Trade networks broke down, administrative centers burned, and writing systems vanished in some regions. The once-powerful Hittites receded into history, leaving behind only ruins and tablets that later generations would unearth, revealing a lost empire's achievements and struggles.

---

16. Cultural Legacy and Influence

Despite its abrupt fall, the Hittite civilization left a lasting legacy in Anatolia and beyond. Their legal and diplomatic traditions influenced successor kingdoms, demonstrating the importance of formal treaties and oath-making. Their cuneiform texts in Hittite, Luwian hieroglyphic inscriptions, and other documents preserved mythologies, historical accounts, and religious rituals that enrich our understanding of Bronze Age thought.

Many of the smaller states that emerged after the empire's collapse were culturally linked to the Hittites, sometimes referred to as "Neo-Hittite" or "Syro-Hittite" states. They continued certain architectural forms, religious iconography, and linguistic practices. These regional powers played a role in bridging the Bronze Age and Iron Age worlds, at least until larger empires like Assyria absorbed them.

In the broader Bronze Age narrative, the Hittites stand alongside Egypt, Babylon, Assyria, and other major players. Their treaties with Egypt are among the earliest surviving diplomatic agreements, underscoring their place in the story of international relations. Their skill in chariot warfare influenced neighbors, and their approach to governance—balancing conquest with alliances—became a model for how to hold a diverse empire together.

17. Hittite Metallurgy and Technological Contributions

Bronze lay at the heart of Hittite military and economic power. They established workshops in major cities, producing not only weapons and tools but also decorative objects for the palace and temples. The empire's control over metal-rich areas ensured a steady supply of copper and silver. Tin remained a strategic import that required steady trade ties or successful military campaigns to secure.

Some evidence suggests the Hittites began experimenting with iron smelting and forging earlier than many of their neighbors, though iron would not fully replace bronze until well after the Bronze Age ended. Still, the reputation of "Hittite iron" in later tradition might reflect their early knowledge. During the Bronze Age proper, however, it was the skillful production and use of bronze that made their chariots deadly and their tools efficient. Carpenters, stonemasons, and farmers all benefited from the improved metal edges on saws, chisels, and plowshares.

These technological advances circulated through Anatolia and neighboring lands via trade, warfare, and diplomacy. Thus, Hittite metallurgy contributed to a broader regional development, reinforcing the idea that the Bronze Age was a time of interconnected progress rather than isolated civilizations.

---

18. Everyday Art and Architecture

While Hattusa's monumental walls and grand temples are the most visible reminders of Hittite architecture, smaller settlements also featured distinctive building styles. Houses often had mudbrick walls on stone foundations, arranged around courtyards. Pottery included both utilitarian wares for cooking and storage as well as finer vessels for serving at elite banquets.

Stone reliefs carved into rock faces or city gates depicted gods, animals, and mythological scenes. These public artworks served both religious and political purposes, showing the king's role as a mediator between the people and the divine. Some sites outside the capital, like Yazılıkaya, contained rock-cut reliefs in a natural sanctuary setting, illustrating a pantheon of deities in procession. Bronze figurines or ritual implements might accompany these depictions, emphasizing the union of art, religion, and politics.

In the realm of craft production, textiles played a significant role. Women in household workshops likely did much of the spinning and weaving, while palace-run workshops produced high-quality textiles for trade or for the king's use. Leatherworking, woodworking, and stone-carving also flourished, often aided by bronze tools that made detailed craftsmanship possible. The combined effect was a society where artistry existed at many levels, from the practical to the ceremonial.

19. Legacy of Hittite Diplomacy and Myth

The Hittites' approach to diplomacy, marked by carefully negotiated treaties, royal marriages, and religiously sanctioned oaths, influenced how later states viewed interstate relations. Though the empire collapsed, its memory lingered in the region. Some references to the "land of Hatti" or "people of Hatti" appear in writings of other Near Eastern civilizations that rose to prominence afterward, indicating that the Hittite name had a lasting resonance.

Myths and religious practices did not vanish, either. Certain stories, gods, and rituals made their way into the cultural mix of subsequent eras. Neo-Hittite states carried forward aspects of Hittite tradition, blending them with local customs. While much of the specific Hittite literature has only partially survived on clay tablets, what remains reveals a complex worldview that saw the cosmos as an interplay of divine forces, with kings and priests acting as mediators.

In the larger timeline of the Bronze Age, the Hittites stand out as an example of how a relatively small group can rise to imperial status through strategic use of resources, effective military organization, and skilled diplomacy. Their success—followed by their sudden disappearance—mirrors the fate of many Bronze Age empires, reminding us of the fragility that even powerful states faced in a world dependent on volatile trade routes and vulnerable to natural or human-made catastrophes.

CHAPTER 8: THE INDUS VALLEY CIVILIZATION

Introduction

Across a vast region in what is now the northwestern part of the Indian subcontinent, a remarkable urban culture blossomed during the Bronze Age. Known today as the **Indus Valley Civilization** (often also referred to as the Harappan Civilization in some contexts), it extended over hundreds of settlements, large and small, from river plains to coastal areas. This civilization flourished around the same time as Mesopotamia and Egypt, engaging in trade, practicing sophisticated town planning, and demonstrating advanced engineering skills.

In this chapter, we will examine how the Indus Valley Civilization utilized bronze technology to support agriculture, crafts, and trade. We will explore their well-planned cities, such as Mohenjo-daro and Harappa, which featured impressive drainage systems and grid-like layouts. We will also consider their still-undeciphered script, the nature of their society, possible religious beliefs, and the factors that may have contributed to their decline. Through these details, we will see how the Indus culture stands out as an innovative and influential Bronze Age civilization, even though many of its secrets remain hidden in inscriptions we cannot yet read.

---

1. Geography and Environment

The Indus Valley Civilization took shape in the floodplains of the Indus River and its tributaries, spanning parts of what is now western South Asia. Seasonal floods brought fertile silt that supported abundant agriculture, including wheat, barley, peas, and cotton (one of the first areas where cotton was grown and woven into cloth). The climate during the Bronze Age might have been somewhat wetter than in later centuries, making agriculture more reliable.

In addition to the Indus River system, some settlements grew along the now-dry Ghaggar-Hakra River (sometimes associated with the mythical Saraswati River of later texts). Ports on the Arabian Sea coast connected Indus merchants to long-distance trade routes. This environment allowed for large populations to develop, supported by irrigation and careful flood management. In such a setting, bronze tools and weapons began to play a role in building and defending these urban centers.

Unlike civilizations that built large-scale monuments like pyramids or ziggurats, the Indus people put their energies into urban infrastructure—streets laid out in grids, well-constructed houses of baked bricks, and drainage systems that rank among the most advanced of the ancient world. Their approach to city planning suggests a society that valued practicality, public health, and a certain uniformity across widely scattered sites.

2. The Emergence of Urban Centers

By around 2600 BCE, settlements in the Indus region began to evolve into true cities. **Mohenjo-daro** and **Harappa** are the most famous, each covering hundreds of hectares and housing tens of thousands of residents at their peak. Other major sites include Dholavira, Ganweriwala, and Rakhigarhi. These urban centers shared common features: a "citadel" area on raised ground, which may have contained public buildings or storage facilities, and a "lower town" where most people lived and worked.

The streets of these cities were laid out in a grid pattern, intersecting at right angles. Houses varied in size but were generally built from standard-sized baked bricks. Many had multiple rooms, and some even had private wells and bathing areas. Drains from houses connected to covered brick sewers running along the streets, carrying wastewater away from the settlement—a level of municipal infrastructure not seen in many other Bronze Age cultures.

This uniformity suggests strong central planning or at least a commonly accepted set of standards for construction. The lack of massive royal palaces or distinctly grand temples raises questions about how Indus society was organized. It is possible that political power was distributed among local elites or councils rather than a single, towering monarchy. Bronze tools, including chisels and saws, helped shape the fired bricks and stone used in these carefully engineered cities.

3. Trade, Economy, and Use of Bronze

Trade was a cornerstone of the Indus economy. Archaeological evidence reveals goods such as semi-precious stones (carnelian, lapis lazuli), shell, and metals being exchanged among the Indus cities and with distant lands. Indus seals bearing distinctive animal motifs—like the unicorn, bull, or elephant—have been found in Mesopotamia, suggesting direct or indirect contact via maritime or overland routes. The Indus region likely exported cotton textiles, beads, and possibly foodstuffs like grain. In return, they imported raw materials for bronze production, especially tin, which was scarce in the local environment.

Bronze in the Indus Valley was used for tools (axes, knives, chisels) and small objects such as mirrors or decorative items. Weapons like bronze spears or arrowheads have been found, though the Indus people do not appear to have placed as much emphasis on militarism or warfare as some other Bronze Age societies. Their fortifications seem geared more toward flood control and storage security rather than purely defensive walls, though limited warfare or conflict may still have occurred.

The uniform weight and measure systems across the Indus cities suggest a regulated economy. Cubical weights made of stone have been discovered in standardized increments, probably used in trade for measuring precious materials or goods. This system implies a form of bureaucracy or at least a shared cultural practice ensuring fairness and uniformity. Bronze scales or measuring tools might also have been used, though most surviving examples are stone or terracotta, indicating that bronze was relatively precious.

---

4. Seals and the Indus Script

One of the most intriguing aspects of the Indus Valley Civilization is their script, found on small seals and pottery fragments. The seals often depict animals—bulls, rhinoceroses, elephants, or the mythical unicorn—accompanied by short sequences of symbols. These symbols remain **undeciphered** to this day, although many attempts have been made to unravel their meaning.

We do not know if the script represents a language related to later South Asian tongues or if it is completely different. The brevity of most inscriptions (often just a few characters) and the lack of a bilingual text have hampered decoding efforts. If deciphered, these seals might reveal details about ownership, trade transactions, or religious ideas. Some may represent the names of merchants or denote the origin of goods.

What we do see is the high quality of craftsmanship in seal production. They were carved with bronze or stone tools, showing fine detail in both the script and the animal images. Seals could be pressed into clay to mark goods or shipments, a common practice in many Bronze Age economies. The existence of a script points to a literate or semi-literate society with organized commerce and administration, even if we cannot fully glimpse their records.

5. Social Structure and Daily Life

The uniformity of Indus cities has led some to propose that the civilization was more egalitarian than Mesopotamia or Egypt—at least at first glance. There are no towering pyramids, no obvious palaces, and no large-scale tombs loaded with grave goods to mark a ruling dynasty. Still, differences in house sizes indicate social stratification: larger homes with courtyards and wells may have belonged to wealthier families, while smaller or simpler dwellings housed common people.

Daily life for most inhabitants likely involved farming, livestock management, or craft production. Farmers sowed wheat, barley, peas, and cotton. Craftspeople spun cotton into textiles, made pottery on fast wheels, and carved ornaments from stone or shell. Metalworkers forged bronze implements, which were traded or used locally. The presence of standardized brick sizes throughout settlements suggests centralized or widely shared guidelines, maybe enforced by local councils or a merchant class.

Bathing and cleanliness appear to have been cultural priorities. Many homes had bathing areas, and the drains were meticulously maintained. Public bath structures, like the famous "Great Bath" at Mohenjo-daro, might have served ritual or communal purposes. This emphasis on hygiene is unique among many Bronze Age societies, reflecting a societal focus on water management and personal cleanliness.

6. Religious Beliefs and Rituals

Although the lack of decipherable texts leaves much unknown about Indus religion, artifacts and city layouts offer clues. Seals depict animals and possibly deities or mythic figures. One famous motif, sometimes called the "Pashupati seal," shows a horned figure seated in a posture that some suggest resembles a later Hindu god associated with animals or a proto-Shiva concept. Such interpretations remain speculative, but they indicate that the Indus people likely had a complex religious system involving animal symbolism and possibly fertility cults.

Small terracotta figurines, often of female forms, might represent mother goddesses or fertility symbols. Others show male figures, children, or animals in daily life scenes. Large communal structures, like the Great Bath, might have been used for religious purification or social gatherings. The citadel areas could have housed temples or administrative sites with religious significance.

We do not see large idols or monumental temple complexes akin to Mesopotamian ziggurats or Egyptian pyramids. This might suggest a different approach to worship—perhaps more domestic or localized to neighborhoods. Rituals may have centered on water, hearth, or smaller shrines. Bronze items, such as ritual vessels or small figurines, could have played a part in ceremonies, but direct evidence is limited.

---

7. Craft Specialization and Artistry

The Indus Valley Civilization displayed advanced craft specialization. Bead-making workshops produced delicate carnelian beads, often heat-treated to achieve vibrant colors. Potters turned out fine, standardized wares featuring red or black slips, sometimes decorated with simple geometric or plant motifs. Metalworkers made bronze tools, mirrors, and ornaments with considerable skill. Stone carvers produced seals, statuary, and architectural elements.

One famous artifact is the so-called "Dancing Girl" figurine from Mohenjo-daro, cast in bronze. It depicts a young female figure in a confident pose, wearing bangles on her arms. The artistry suggests not just technical skill in metal casting but also a refined aesthetic sense. Other statuettes, though rare, indicate an interest in human form and expression.

The scale of craft production suggests an economy with organized labor, possibly supervised by guilds or local authorities. Large kilns, bead-polishing tools, and leftover materials found at sites imply that these crafts were produced in significant quantities—likely for both local use and export. Traders carried these goods along river routes or by sea, linking the Indus region to a broader Bronze Age network.

8. Urban Planning and Public Works

The urban layout of Indus cities stands out as a testament to meticulous planning. In Mohenjo-daro, wide streets dividing the city into rectangular blocks reflect a sense of order. Many buildings were oriented to catch prevailing winds, aiding ventilation in a hot climate. The "Great Bath" measures about 12 meters by 7 meters and is lined with watertight bricks, fed by a well or infiltration from a higher water source. Stairs on each end allowed bathers to descend into the water.

Drainage systems remain one of the most impressive aspects. Each house had a connection to a covered drain in the street, which led waste and water outside the settlement. Manholes and inspection points suggest regular maintenance. This level of public hygiene stands in contrast to many ancient cities where waste often accumulated on streets. The presence of such advanced infrastructure implies authorities who could mobilize labor, enforce building codes, and maintain civic amenities for large populations.

Fortified areas in some cities served as administrative or protective enclaves. Thick walls and elevated platforms guarded against flooding and perhaps marauders, although evidence of large-scale warfare is minimal. The consistent design across settlements hundreds of kilometers apart indicates either a unified political entity or strongly shared cultural norms for city-building.

9. Connection to Other Bronze Age Civilizations

The Indus people did not exist in isolation. Artifacts bearing Indus seals have been found in Mesopotamia, indicating trade or direct contact. Mesopotamian texts mention a land called "Meluhha," which might correspond to the Indus region. Goods from Indus ports, possibly including textiles, timber, and grain, would have made their way westward, while returning caravans or ships brought tin, silver, and other commodities needed for bronze-making.

To the east, the Indus civilization likely influenced cultures in the Gangetic plains, though major urban development in that region came later. The coastline along the Arabian Sea might have facilitated voyages southward or westward, linking them to maritime trade routes. Lothal, a site near the coast, had a structure interpreted by some as a dockyard, supporting the idea of an active shipping trade.

Despite these connections, the Indus Valley Civilization maintained distinct cultural traits: their script, their standardized brick sizes, their urban sanitation systems, and a relatively modest approach to monumental art or architecture. Bronze usage was practical and commercial rather than focused on forging massive armies, suggesting they relied more on economic and cultural ties than on military conquest.

---

10. Peaceful Society or Hidden Conflicts?

A noticeable aspect of the Indus civilization is the apparent lack of clear evidence for large-scale warfare. Unlike the fortified palaces of Mycenae or the warlike steles of Mesopotamia, Indus art does not glorify battles or show kings smiting enemies. While we do find weapons—arrowheads, spears, and occasional hints of conflict—there is little sign of mass destruction or frequent city-burning that might indicate long wars.

This has led to interpretations that the Indus culture was more peaceful or diplomatically inclined. Some argue that strong trade ties and shared urban ideals helped avoid large-scale conflicts. Others caution that absence of evidence is not evidence of absence—wooden fortifications, ephemeral conflicts, or unrecognized forms of warfare could have existed. The truth may lie somewhere in between, with the Indus people engaging in smaller-scale skirmishes or local defense without developing a strong culture of conquest.

Regardless, the emphasis on civic planning rather than monumental fortresses does stand out. The Indus social structure might have prioritized collaboration and commerce, making them distinctive among Bronze Age powers that often thrived on conquest. Bronze arms likely played a role in policing trade routes or defending city gates, but full-time armies or elaborate chariot tactics seem less prominent here than in places like Mesopotamia or Anatolia.

11. Environmental Changes and Decline

By around 1900 BCE, many Indus cities began to show signs of decline. Public works like drainage and wells fell into disrepair, and the uniformity of building standards eroded. Populations at major sites decreased, with some cities gradually abandoned. Smaller settlements continued, but the cohesive urban culture dissipated. Scholars have proposed several possible causes:

1. **Shift in Rivers**: Geological changes might have altered the course of the Indus or the Ghaggar-Hakra system, depriving cities of water or flooding them uncontrollably.
2. **Climate Change**: A change in monsoon patterns or prolonged droughts could have reduced agricultural yields, forcing migrations or social upheaval.
3. **Trade Disruption**: Shifts in trade routes, possibly due to changing political conditions in Mesopotamia or elsewhere, might have undermined the Indus economy.
4. **Sociopolitical Factors**: Internal social changes, class conflicts, or the breakdown of central coordination might have led to fragmentation.

No single theory conclusively explains everything. More likely, a combination of environmental stress, declining trade opportunities, and local power shifts caused the Indus urban centers to wane. The once-sophisticated cities no longer maintained their complex infrastructure, and their script vanished from historical view, leaving only archaeological remains for later ages to uncover.

---

12. Continuity and Cultural Transformation

Although the great Indus cities collapsed, many aspects of their culture probably lived on among rural populations. Settlements continued along rivers, people farmed the land, and crafts like pottery-making evolved. Over centuries, new cultural and linguistic groups emerged in the region, blending old traditions with incoming influences. The memory of Indus achievements faded in oral histories, overshadowed by later civilizations that rose in northern and western parts of the subcontinent.

Nonetheless, certain hallmark practices—like well-planned settlements or advanced craft techniques—may have persisted in localized forms. The Indus region remained a crossroads for trade and migrations, linking Central Asia with the subcontinent's interior. Communities adapted to new river courses or changing political dynamics, forming smaller, more localized cultures that formed the transition into subsequent eras.

In the larger story of the Bronze Age, the Indus Valley Civilization stands out for its extensive urban networks, emphasis on public infrastructure, and far-reaching trade relations. Their approach to bronze usage was pragmatic—focusing on tools and moderate levels of weaponry rather than forging large standing armies. Their script and imagery still puzzle modern researchers, hinting at untold stories of governance, religion, and daily life in one of the ancient world's most remarkable but mysterious civilizations.

---

13. Material Culture: Pottery and Ornaments

Indus pottery often features bright red surfaces with black designs, sometimes geometric or floral. The potters' skill in firing large batches to uniform quality indicates specialized workshops. Small terracotta figurines depict animals or human forms, possibly toys or votive objects. Many of these figurines show careful craftsmanship, though produced in large numbers for common use.

Beads were another significant craft, with extensive bead-working industries found at sites like Chanhu-daro. Craftsmen shaped stones—especially carnelian—into beads that were polished to a gleaming finish. Shell bangles and ornaments were also popular, indicating a taste for decorative personal adornment. Gold and silver appear in limited quantities, mainly in beads or small ornaments for the elite, showcasing some level of wealth concentration.

Metal objects (mostly copper-bronze) include tools like razors, saws, fishhooks, and chisels. Figurines cast in bronze—rare but notable—display advanced techniques akin to lost-wax casting. These artifacts reveal a well-developed craft tradition that supported everyday needs and also catered to a desire for aesthetic refinement. The wide distribution of such items across the Indus sphere underscores the integrated nature of their market systems.

14. Water Management and Agriculture

The Indus people were highly adept at managing water resources. Besides the impressive urban drainage systems, they built wells throughout their cities, often lined with bricks. These wells provided a reliable water supply for domestic use and likely helped mitigate the impact of droughts or unpredictable river flooding.

Farmers benefited from the seasonal flooding of the Indus and its tributaries, which fertilized fields with fresh silt. They grew a range of crops—wheat, barley, pulses, sesame, and cotton. The presence of cotton is especially noteworthy, as it gave them an advantage in producing textiles that could be traded or used locally. Surpluses of grain supported the growth of cities, enabling specialists to focus on crafts, trade, or administration instead of subsistence farming.

Bronze sickles and plowshares may have improved yields, though wooden implements still played a major role. The typical plow might have been a simple scratch-plow, but with a metal edge it could break through heavier soils. Storage facilities within the city—likely large granaries—helped regulate food supplies. This capacity for managing resources contributed to the Indus civilization's ability to support large urban populations over several centuries.

---

15. Artistic Themes and Iconography

While we cannot read their script, the Indus seals provide a window into their artistic and symbolic world. Animals—such as bulls, buffaloes, elephants, rhinoceroses, and the unique "unicorn" motif—often appear alone or in combination. The repeated depiction of the so-called "unicorn," which may be a stylized bull with a single horn, has led to much speculation about its significance. It could represent a clan totem, a deity, or a trade guild emblem.

Some seals feature ritual scenes, including figures standing before altars or trees, possibly signifying worship. The presence of repeated motifs suggests a shared set of religious or cultural images across the Indus region. Figurines portraying pregnant women or mother figures may point to a focus on fertility and the continuity of life, common in many ancient societies.

Sculptures like the "Priest-King" from Mohenjo-daro—a bearded male figure wearing a robe with trefoil designs—highlight a possible elite or revered individual. The calm expression and carefully carved details suggest a sophisticated artistic tradition. Although the Indus people did not leave behind massive statues or rock-cut reliefs like other Bronze Age cultures, their smaller-scale art reveals a consistent aesthetic linking religion, commerce, and social identity.

16. Sociopolitical Organization: Cities Without Palaces?

One of the enduring mysteries of the Indus civilization is how they governed themselves. The typical Bronze Age pattern—powerful kings in palaces, grand temples for state-sponsored religion—does not appear evident in Indus cities. Instead, we see uniform city planning, standardized bricks, and communal facilities such as bathhouses and granaries, but no distinct royal buildings or monumental tombs.

It is possible that power was vested in councils of merchants or elders, or that local elites ruled in a more collective manner. The prosperity of trade might have encouraged cooperation rather than conquest. Cities may have been administratively linked, sharing standards for weights, measures, and urban layouts.

Alternatively, some scholars suggest that we simply have not recognized the "palaces" because they were not built in a style we can easily distinguish. The largest buildings on the citadel mounds could have been multipurpose: storing grains, hosting ceremonies, or accommodating officials. Whatever the case, the Indus approach to governance seems less centered on overt displays of individual rulership and more on efficient civic management.

17. The Role of Bronze in Indus Warfare and Defense

While Indus cities do not exhibit the same evidence of militarism seen in other Bronze Age cultures, they nonetheless crafted bronze weapons. Arrowheads, spears, and axes have been found, albeit not in large caches. City walls or platforms might have helped deter raiders or manage floods, or both. Some settlements show gateways and bastions that could serve defensive functions if needed.

In times of conflict, Indus defenders may have mustered armed militias rather than professional standing armies. Bronze weapons likely supplemented wooden clubs, bows with stone or bronze-tipped arrows, and possibly slings. Without extensive written records describing wars or conquests, it is difficult to assess how often these weapons saw actual use. The overall impression is that while the Indus people recognized the need for defense, their primary focus lay in trade, agriculture, and urban life rather than territorial expansion or frequent warfare.

This relative emphasis (or lack thereof) on warfare allowed the Indus civilization to flourish for centuries without being overshadowed by a single militaristic ruler. Their cohesion, based on shared culture and economic interdependence, likely contributed to the stability of large urban centers spread across the region.

18. Possibilities of Cultural or Population Movements

As the Indus civilization declined, populations might have migrated eastward toward the more fertile lands of the Ganges Valley, where later historical developments took shape. Some communities adapted to changing river courses, shifting to areas with better water access. Others may have dispersed into smaller villages, preserving certain Indus practices while adopting new cultural influences from steppe migrations or local tribal groups.

This transformation was not necessarily a single cataclysmic event; it could have been a gradual process of changing priorities. Cities like Mohenjo-daro shrank, their once-great drainage systems clogged by silt and debris. Crafts became more localized, and the unifying style of Indus pottery gave way to regional variants. Over generations, the distinct Indus identity faded, though elements of its heritage likely endured in the agricultural methods, craft techniques, and social customs of successor communities.

19. Comparison with Other Bronze Age Civilizations

When we place the Indus Valley Civilization alongside Mesopotamia, Egypt, the Minoans, Mycenaeans, and the Hittites, we see both shared and unique features:

- **Urbanization**: The Indus cities were meticulously planned, with advanced drainage rivaling or surpassing anything in Mesopotamia or the Aegean.
- **Absence of Monumental Kingship**: Unlike the pharaohs of Egypt or the warrior-kings of Mycenae, Indus rulers (if they existed in that form) did not build grand tombs or palaces.
- **Script**: The undeciphered Indus script is shorter and more elusive than cuneiform or hieroglyphics. Its secrets remain locked.
- **Trade Emphasis**: Like Mesopotamia, the Indus region thrived on commerce, connecting resource-rich highlands and coastal ports.
- **Bronze Use**: Tools and weapons were made of bronze, but Indus society appears less militaristic than the Hittites or Mycenaeans.

These comparisons highlight how the Bronze Age was diverse, with each region finding its own path to complexity. The Indus Valley stands out for its communal infrastructure, standardized systems, and emphasis on civic cleanliness. The lack of decipherable texts limits our knowledge, yet it also maintains the Indus allure: a civilization advanced in urban planning, commerce, and craft, yet mysterious in its governance and beliefs.

CHAPTER 9: ANCIENT CHINA IN THE BRONZE AGE

Introduction

In many people's minds, ancient China is connected with dynasties that built long-lasting traditions in governance, philosophy, and art. The Bronze Age in China set the foundation for much of what would come later. Though the timeline may differ from the Bronze Age developments in Mesopotamia, Egypt, or the Indus Valley, China's path was equally remarkable. Early cultures discovered how to cast bronze for ritual vessels, weapons, and tools. Over time, powerful rulers arose, claiming the divine right to govern, and used bronze to display wealth and authority.

In this chapter, we will explore how bronze technology emerged in ancient China, focusing on the **Xia**, **Shang**, and **Zhou** periods, which many scholars associate with China's Bronze Age. We will examine the importance of bronze in warfare, ritual practices, and state-building. We will also look at urban centers, social structures, religion, and how China's unique casting techniques allowed artisans to create some of the most elaborate bronze pieces of the ancient world.

---

1. The Geographic Setting

China's heartland during the Bronze Age was centered around the Yellow River (Huang He) and its tributaries. The region's fertile loess soil supported farming of millet in the north, while the Yangtze Basin further south favored rice cultivation. Rivers served as transportation routes, connecting emerging states with distant settlements. The varied terrain—plains, hills, and river valleys—enabled communities to specialize in different crops and resources, leading to trade within and beyond their home regions.

The annual floods of the Yellow River could be unpredictable, sometimes causing destructive events that harmed settlements. In response, populations built dikes and irrigation channels, requiring organized labor and governance. This necessity for coordination may have contributed to the rise of centralized authority, a step that paved the way for the Bronze Age dynasties.

2. Early Metallurgy and the Dawn of Bronze

Before bronze became widespread, many Chinese communities used stone and bone tools. Gradually, people discovered native copper, which they hammered and heated to create rudimentary implements. The earliest traces of copper objects in northern China date to periods before 2000 BCE. Over time, these groups learned that mixing copper with tin or lead created a stronger and more versatile alloy—bronze.

In certain areas, local deposits of copper, tin, and lead were found, though not all resources existed in one place. This drove trade and sometimes warfare, as different chiefdoms or states competed to control essential mines. Smelting and casting methods continued to improve, allowing craftsmen to produce higher-quality bronze goods. By the time we reach what many consider the start of the Bronze Age in China—often associated with the **Xia Dynasty**—bronze-casting techniques were already becoming sophisticated.

---

3. The Question of the Xia Dynasty

Traditionally, Chinese history speaks of the **Xia Dynasty** (often dated roughly 2100–1600 BCE) as the first ruling house. Whether the Xia truly existed as a formal dynasty or represented a cluster of early Bronze Age chiefdoms remains a topic of debate. Excavations at places like Erlitou (an important archaeological site) have revealed large buildings, workshops, and evidence of bronze production. These discoveries suggest that a centralized authority may have controlled the region, managing labor, storing grain, and producing bronze vessels.

If the Xia did exist, it would mark a key transition from scattered Neolithic cultures to a more unified Bronze Age society. Bronze ritual objects, such as simple tripod vessels, appear at sites linked to the Xia period, hinting at the early use of bronze in ceremonial contexts. This focus on bronze rituals foreshadows what would happen under the later Shang Dynasty, when bronze vessels became central to royal and ancestral worship.

---

4. The Rise of the Shang Dynasty

Following the Xia, historical accounts place the **Shang Dynasty** (ca. 1600–1046 BCE) as the next major power. The Shang era is better documented, with clear archaeological sites like Zhengzhou and Anyang (also known as Yin). The Shang kings ruled over a broad territory and conducted warfare against rival states, capturing laborers, farmland, and important resources—especially those needed for bronze.

Shang society revolved around a ruling elite who claimed a direct relationship with ancestors and deities. In large cities, they built palatial areas, ritual temples, and workshops for making bronze vessels and weapons. The scale of bronze production was enormous. Workers mined ore, transported it, and smelted it in large furnaces. Skilled artisans then poured molten bronze into clay or stone molds. One of the Shang's greatest achievements was their **piece-mold casting** technique, which allowed for intricate designs and inscriptions on bronze items.

5. Piece-Mold Casting: A Chinese Specialty

Unlike the lost-wax process used in some other parts of the world, ancient Chinese bronze casters developed a **piece-mold** method. First, they fashioned a clay model of the final vessel. Then, they formed a negative clay mold around it, which they could cut into multiple segments. After removing the original model, the mold pieces were reassembled, leaving a hollow space that matched the shape of the vessel. Molten bronze was poured into this cavity. Once cooled, the mold was broken or removed to reveal the newly formed object.

This technique enabled artisans to produce bronzes with high-relief decorations, swirling patterns, and zoomorphic motifs—like the famous **taotie** mask (a stylized monster face). These designs were not just decorative; they also held symbolic or religious meaning, possibly linked to ancestral or spirit worship. The ability to cast large and complex bronzes set Shang China apart from many other Bronze Age cultures.

6. Ritual Bronzes and Ancestral Worship

Bronze vessels—like **ding** (cauldrons), **gui** (food containers), and **zun** (wine vessels)—played a pivotal role in Shang (and later Zhou) religious life. The Shang kings and nobles conducted ceremonies that involved offerings of food, wine, and possibly animal sacrifices to their ancestors. These rituals were meant to maintain a harmonious relationship between the living and the spirit world. Bronze vessels were central to these ceremonies, reflecting both piety and prestige.

Carved or cast inscriptions on some vessels recorded events, lineage references, or dedications to ancestors. The artistry displayed in these objects underscored the wealth and power of the elites who commissioned them. Over time, the quantity and size of ritual bronzes grew, indicating that controlling the production of bronze was a way for rulers to express their authority. The bronzes thus symbolized a cosmic link between Heaven, Earth, and the royal clan.

7. The Oracle Bones and Early Writing

One of the most important legacies of the Shang Dynasty is the **oracle bone** inscriptions. These were typically cattle scapulae or turtle plastrons, which priests or diviners used for communicating with ancestors and deities. A hot poker or rod was applied to the bone, causing cracks to form. The diviner interpreted these cracks to answer questions about warfare, harvests, the weather, or royal affairs.

Written inscriptions on the bones recorded the questions, and sometimes the answers or outcomes. This script is recognized as an early form of Chinese writing and shows direct continuity with later Chinese characters. Oracle bone texts often mention the use of bronze weapons in warfare, tributes paid by conquered regions, and offerings made in bronze vessels. These inscriptions provide an invaluable glimpse into the concerns, beliefs, and administrative practices of the Shang court.

8. Social Structure and Labor Organization

Shang society was stratified. At the top stood the king, supported by a network of nobles and military chiefs. Priests and diviners played crucial roles, managing religious ceremonies and communicating with the ancestors. Skilled artisans—particularly bronze-casters—occupied a privileged position due to their specialized knowledge. Commoners farmed the land, tended livestock, and provided labor for large building projects.

Bronze production demanded a complex supply chain: miners to extract copper and tin ore, transporters to move raw materials, smelters to refine the metal, and foundry workers to cast finished items. This degree of organization indicates a strong central authority. The king or nobles might conscript labor or levy taxes in the form of grain or manpower. In return, they offered protection and the promise of spiritual intercession with the ancestors, who were believed to bestow blessings on the realm.

9. Warfare, Chariots, and Weapons

The Shang Dynasty engaged in frequent warfare, aiming to expand territory, control trade routes, and gather captives for labor. Bronze was vital for crafting spears, axes, and daggers. An important development was the introduction of the **horse-drawn chariot**—though it is uncertain if the chariot was invented locally or introduced from steppe cultures further north. The earliest chariots in China date to the late Shang period, appearing in elite burials alongside valuable bronzes.

These chariots served as mobile command platforms for warfare or perhaps as status symbols for Shang elites. Warriors armed with bronze ge (a type of dagger-axe) and spears could overwhelm less advanced foes. Control of bronze weaponry gave the Shang aristocracy a decisive edge over rival chiefs. The spoils of war—land, captives, livestock—reinforced their power and wealth, forming the basis of a cycle in which successful warfare led to greater resource control, which in turn fueled more campaigns.

10. The Late Shang Period and Royal Burials

Archaeological discoveries at **Anyang** (also called Yin, the last Shang capital) provide vivid evidence of the dynasty's grandeur and brutality. Royal tombs yielded vast arrays of bronze vessels, jade ornaments, and weapons. Some tombs also contained chariots and horses, sacrificed to accompany their masters in the afterlife. The scale of human sacrifices, found in certain royal burials and ritual pits, shocked later observers but underscored the depth of Shang spiritual beliefs regarding the afterlife and ancestral needs.

These grand burials highlight the wealth accumulated by the Shang rulers. Precious goods arrived through tribute or trade with distant regions. Jade, turquoise, and seashells adorned many objects, while elaborate gold or bronze fittings complemented wooden chariots and coffins. Such luxury was not available to ordinary people. Their graves were simpler, reflecting lower social standing. Yet this disparity fueled the grandeur of the court and reinforced the notion that the king stood at the pinnacle of a divinely sanctioned hierarchy.

11. The Fall of the Shang and the Rise of the Zhou

The Shang Dynasty's power waned over time, possibly due to internal strife, overextension, and rebellion among vassal states. By the mid-11th century BCE, a growing power called the **Zhou** began challenging Shang dominance. The Zhou people lived to the west of the Shang heartland and adopted many of the same cultural practices, including bronze casting and ancestral rites.

According to traditional accounts, King Wu of Zhou launched a decisive campaign against the last Shang king, who was described as a tyrant ruling without virtue. The Zhou forces defeated Shang armies, seized the capital, and took control of the region. This transition did not end the Bronze Age. Instead, the Zhou continued and even expanded the use of bronze for both ritual and military purposes. However, it did mark a shift in political ideology, as the Zhou promoted the concept of the **Mandate of Heaven** to legitimize their rule.

12. The Early Zhou Dynasty and the Mandate of Heaven

Under the **Zhou Dynasty** (1046–256 BCE), bronze remained central to governance. The Zhou kings claimed they had received the Mandate of Heaven—an authority granted by a supreme deity or cosmic force—because they were more virtuous than the Shang. If a ruler became corrupt or neglected his people, Heaven would withdraw its mandate and grant it to a more worthy house. This idea shaped Chinese political thought for centuries, linking moral conduct to rightful rule.

Bronze vessels continued to play a role in state rituals and ancestral offerings. The Zhou kings established a feudal-like system, granting territories to relatives or trusted nobles. In return, these lords provided military support and tribute. Each local court possessed its own bronze foundries, replicating the central rituals on a smaller scale. Over time, the quantity and variety of bronze objects increased, and inscriptions grew longer, recording genealogies, conquests, and moral lessons.

13. Advances in Bronze Casting and Decoration

During the Zhou, new decorative styles emerged. Motifs became more stylized, with geometric patterns and inscriptions sometimes surpassing the large taotie masks of the Shang. Craftsmen experimented with inlaid designs, inserting gold, silver, or semi-precious stones into the bronze surface. The piece-mold method evolved, allowing for multi-layered decoration.

Some Zhou bronzes carried lengthy inscriptions, commemorating great deeds of nobles or recording land grants. These texts illustrate how bronzes had become not only ritual implements but also documents of political and familial identity. They were treasured heirlooms, passed down across generations, linking the living community with ancestors and with Heaven's mandate. The level of artistry reached new heights, and the influence of these casting techniques would persist in Chinese metalwork for centuries.

14. Social Changes and the Well-Field System

Under the early Zhou, there were attempts to organize farmland through a system sometimes known as the "well-field" arrangement. The land was divided into nine equal squares. Each square belonged to a peasant family, while the central square was worked communally for the local lord. Although it is unclear how extensively this system was implemented, it reflects the Zhou concern with regulating agriculture, labor, and tribute.

Bronze tools—plowshares, knives, and sickles—helped to some degree. However, much of farming still relied on wooden or stone implements. Bronze was relatively precious, and weapon production often took priority. Nevertheless, higher-ranking nobles might own bronze-tipped plows or adorn their farming gear with bronze to signify status. This interplay between agriculture and aristocracy underlined the Zhou's power structure, which depended on a well-fed populace and loyal landholders.

---

15. Warfare in the Zhou Era

The Zhou period saw ongoing conflicts. Rival nobles fought each other for territory and influence, especially as the central royal power weakened over generations. Bronze weapons—spears, dagger-axes (ge), and swords—were essential in these battles. Armies expanded, with chariots still functioning as elite vehicles. However, infantry forces grew larger, and archery gained greater importance.

Over time, fortifications improved, with earthen walls and watchtowers. Some local lords developed specialized foundries to equip their troops, forging strong alliances or clashing with each other in a struggle for dominance. The concept of the Mandate of Heaven implied that a ruler who won battles and stabilized the realm might be favored by Heaven. This added an ideological layer to warfare, making victory not just a matter of territory but also a sign of divine approval.

---

16. The Transition to Iron and Its Impact

Even though we focus on the Bronze Age, it is important to note that by the later Zhou era, knowledge of ironworking began to spread. Iron tools and weapons offered advantages—harder edges and potentially cheaper production once the process was refined. Over time, this shifted the balance away from bronze, though bronze remained valuable for ceremonial objects, musical instruments, and status items.

As iron gained ground, large-scale armies armed with iron swords and crossbows emerged, changing the nature of warfare. The older aristocratic chariot-based combat gave way to massed infantry formations. This transformation contributed to the eventual fragmentation of the Zhou realm, leading to the **Spring and Autumn** and **Warring States** periods, in which many smaller states vied for supremacy. While that era lies beyond the core Bronze Age, the seeds of these changes were planted during the later Zhou.

17. Urban Centers and Daily Life

During both the Shang and Zhou periods, many people lived in walled towns or small cities, though the largest urban centers were the royal capitals. Inside these walls, elites occupied grand compounds, while commoners lived in simpler dwellings made of wood and rammed earth. Markets sold goods like grains, vegetables, fish, cloth, and pottery. Bronze items, being more expensive, were typically reserved for nobility—either as functional weapons/tools or as ritual and decorative pieces.

Farming communities outside the walls paid tribute in grain or livestock. Seasonal festivals involved feasting, drinking, and ancestral rites. Musicians used bronze bells and chimes in court ceremonies. Such instruments required precise casting to produce the correct tones. In daily life, most laborers wore hemp or linen garments. Those of higher rank might afford silk, a luxury that symbolized status. Meanwhile, the presence of bronze in a household item or personal ornament was a mark of privilege.

---

18. Religious and Philosophical Currents

Although major philosophical traditions like Confucianism or Daoism would become prominent in later periods, the Bronze Age set the stage for them. Ancestral worship, reverence for Heaven, and the belief in moral governance shaped the Zhou ideology. Rulers were seen as responsible for maintaining harmony between humans and the spirit world. They performed sacrifices and consulted oracles to ensure that the ancestors and deities were appeased.

Some of these ideas—like the Mandate of Heaven—later influenced Confucius and other thinkers, who stressed virtue, proper rites, and moral leadership. The roots of these philosophies lie in the Bronze Age worldview that placed spiritual forces at the core of political authority. In this sense, the elaborate bronze vessels and the ceremonies they supported were not mere decorations but tangible expressions of a deep spiritual and moral order.

19. Cultural Exchange and Peripheral Regions

The early Chinese states did not exist in isolation. They interacted with neighboring peoples in the northeast, northwest, and south. Trade or tribute might bring horses, jade, or other goods into the Shang and Zhou domains. Some peripheral groups adopted bronze technology for their own purposes, occasionally leading to alliances or conflicts with the central states.

Chariots, for instance, might have originated through contact with steppe nomads who had experience with horses. Western regions contributed tin or other metals. Maritime trade along the eastern coast may have been limited compared to land routes, but local communities still exchanged shells, salt, or fish for bronze tools or ornaments. These interactions extended the influence of Chinese bronze culture beyond the Yellow River basin. Over centuries, that cultural sphere grew, eventually forming the background for a more unified empire in later times.

CHAPTER 10: BRONZE AGE EUROPE

Introduction

Europe's Bronze Age is a vast tapestry of regional cultures. Stretching from the Atlantic coasts of Iberia and the British Isles to the plains of Central Europe and beyond, many different groups adopted and adapted bronze technology in their own ways. Unlike the centralized states of Mesopotamia, Egypt, or China, Europe's Bronze Age societies often formed smaller tribal groups or regional confederations, though some areas saw the emergence of more complex chiefdoms or proto-kingdoms.

In this chapter, we will journey through Europe's Bronze Age, looking at how bronze arrived, spread, and transformed local societies. We will discuss famous cultural horizons such as the **Bell Beaker**, **Unetice**, **Tumulus**, **Urnfield**, and the **Nordic Bronze Age**. We will examine their burial practices, art styles, trade routes, and the role of bronze in everything from farming to warfare. By the end, you will see how Europe's Bronze Age was both varied and interconnected, setting the stage for future developments in the Iron Age.

---

1. Early Bronze Age Foundations

Bronze technology reached Europe gradually, traveling from regions where metallurgy was already established—such as the Near East and Anatolia—through the Balkans into Central Europe. Some of the earliest evidence of copper use in Europe dates back to the later Neolithic or Chalcolithic, but true bronze (copper alloyed with tin) became more common in the third millennium BCE.

In certain areas, local sources of copper and tin were exploited. For example, the ores in the eastern Alps and parts of the British Isles became crucial for bronze production. Overland trade routes developed to move raw metals or finished objects. Maritime connections along the Mediterranean coast also spread knowledge of casting techniques. As small communities discovered bronze's superiority over stone tools and weapons, they adopted these new methods, spurring social changes that sometimes led to greater hierarchies and inter-regional contacts.

2. The Bell Beaker Culture

One of the best-known phenomena of the Early Bronze Age in Europe is the **Bell Beaker culture** (roughly 2800–1800 BCE), named after the distinctive pottery vessels shaped like inverted bells. These beakers were often found in graves, sometimes with archery equipment, copper daggers, or ornaments of gold. The Bell Beaker phenomenon spanned wide areas of western and central Europe, suggesting a vast network of shared practices.

While not a single ethnic group or empire, Bell Beaker communities seem to have shared ritual and stylistic elements, facilitating the spread of metalworking knowledge. The presence of copper daggers and other metal items in Bell Beaker burials demonstrates the growing importance of bronze technology. Trade routes likely moved metals from the resource-rich regions (like the Iberian Peninsula or the western Alps) to areas where copper and tin were less abundant. This culture set the stage for further developments, as local traditions blended with these widespread Beaker influences.

---

3. Unetice and the Growth of Bronze Networks

Following the Bell Beaker phase, various regional cultures emerged, each refining bronze metallurgy. One of these was the **Unetice culture** (roughly 2300–1600 BCE), centered in parts of Central Europe (modern regions around eastern Germany, Czech lands, and Poland). Unetice is notable for its well-crafted metal items—daggers, axes, halberds—often placed in hoards or burials. These finds suggest a growing social stratification, as certain individuals were buried with lavish assemblages of metal artifacts.

Unetice communities engaged in long-distance exchange. Amber from the Baltic coast, tin from the Erzgebirge or even further afield, and possibly gold from the Carpathian region circulated in these networks. The presence of standardized metal types across wide distances points to specialized workshops and skilled artisans. Over time, Unetice gave rise to other regional groups, each building upon the expanding knowledge of bronze casting. Elite individuals may have controlled trade in metals, reaping social prestige and power in the process.

4. Metallurgical Advances in Europe

As bronze use intensified, European smiths developed new casting methods. Initially, simple open molds or bivalve molds were used for small daggers and axes. Over time, more sophisticated techniques arose, allowing for socketed axes, longer swords, and decorated spearheads. Tools like sickles, chisels, and awls made farming and carpentry more efficient.

The presence of tin remained a limiting factor. Much of Europe had copper, but tin was rarer, primarily available in places such as Cornwall in Britain, parts of Brittany, the Iberian Peninsula, or beyond Europe's frontiers. This scarcity elevated tin to a highly traded commodity. Control of tin sources or trade routes conferred wealth and influence. Coastal communities or those near navigable rivers often prospered by becoming intermediaries in this exchange.

---

5. Burial Practices: Barrows and Megaliths

As elites emerged, they often displayed status in death. In many regions, individuals of high rank were buried under **barrows** (also called tumuli), large earthen or stone mounds covering a grave chamber. The Tumulus culture (around 1600–1200 BCE in Central Europe) takes its name from these grand barrow burials. Grave goods frequently included bronze weapons, jewelry, and sometimes exotic items like amber or gold, reflecting the deceased's power or social connections.

In parts of Atlantic Europe—like Britain, Ireland, and Brittany—earlier megalithic traditions continued, though the large communal tombs of the Neolithic gave way to smaller barrows for select individuals. Some barrows show extended inhumations with richly furnished grave sets. These burials, combined with the distribution of prestige goods, suggest a ruling class whose authority may have rested on controlling resources like metals, farmland, and trade routes.

---

6. The Nordic Bronze Age

While Central Europe saw the rise of Tumulus and Urnfield cultures, the far north developed its own Bronze Age traditions—often referred to as the **Nordic**

Bronze Age (around 1700–500 BCE) in regions including southern Scandinavia (modern Denmark and southern Sweden). Though tin was scarce there, local people imported it through trade, forging distinctive swords, axes, and personal ornaments.

The Nordic Bronze Age is famous for its rock carvings, which depict ships, sun symbols, and scenes of agriculture or warfare. These carvings hint at a maritime worldview, with seafaring likely important for both fishing and long-distance contacts. Large lurs (bronze musical horns) and other ritual objects found in Denmark display high craftsmanship. Burials varied: some individuals rested in oak coffins under barrows, their bodies placed with well-preserved textiles and bronze goods. This environment reveals a hierarchical society with an elite that could afford exotic bronze items and ceremonial displays.

7. Artwork and Symbolism

Bronze Age Europe produced a wide variety of artistic expressions, often linked to religious beliefs or status. Geometric designs on swords, daggers, and shields might signal the owner's identity or regional style. Spiral and sun motifs were widespread, possibly reflecting solar cults or seasonal cycles crucial to agrarian societies.

Gold was used for delicate torcs, diadems, and other ornaments, especially in Atlantic regions (e.g., Ireland, Britain, northern France). These items suggest skilled metalworkers who knew how to hammer and shape precious metals. The lavish golden lunulae from Ireland or gold hats in Central Europe (conical headgear decorated with solar symbols) exemplify the wealth and ritual significance attached to these items. Bronze figurines also appear occasionally, though less commonly than in the Chinese or Near Eastern contexts. When they do surface, they might represent deities, ancestors, or mythic heroes.

8. Settlement Patterns and Hillforts

Across Bronze Age Europe, communities typically consisted of small villages or scattered farmsteads. Over time, especially in the later phases, some groups constructed **hillforts**—defended enclosures on elevated terrain. These fortifications indicate a need for protection or a desire to control trade routes. Hillforts often featured wooden palisades, earthen ramparts, or stone walls. Within these walls, houses and granaries stored resources that local elites might have managed.

Hillforts became prominent in areas such as the Atlantic facade (parts of France, Iberia, and Britain) and Central Europe. They served as centers for craft production, trade, and possibly governance. While not as large or centralized as the palace cultures of the eastern Mediterranean, these sites showed that some European societies were moving toward more complex forms of organization. Bronze weapons—swords, spears, and axes—provided means for defense and aggression, reinforcing the status of a warrior class or chieftains who ruled from these strongholds.

9. Metal Hoards and Ritual Deposits

A striking feature of European prehistory is the **hoard**: collections of metal objects—axes, swords, ornaments—intentionally buried, often without evidence of retrieval. Some hoards may have been safe storages that people failed to recover. Others likely served a ritual purpose, offered to gods or ancestors. The location of certain hoards—such as bogs, riverbeds, or other liminal spaces—supports the idea of votive offerings.

Examples like the Eberswalde Hoard in Germany, containing gold bowls and jewelry, or the large bronze hoards in Scandinavia reveal substantial wealth deposited in the ground. These acts point to a belief that certain items needed to be returned to the earth or the divine realm. Alternatively, hoarding could signify a means of wealth accumulation, with metals functioning as a store of value. Either way, these caches underscore the prominence of bronze (and occasionally gold) in the social and religious spheres.

10. Long-Distance Exchange: Amber, Tin, and Salt

Trade was crucial for Bronze Age Europe. We have noted the importance of tin, but other commodities also bound distant regions. **Amber**, harvested from the

Baltic shores, traveled southward in exchange for metal tools or precious goods. Amber's translucent beauty and rarity made it a prized material for beads and amulets.

Salt was another valuable resource, essential for food preservation. Salt mines, such as those at Hallstatt in the eastern Alps (though Hallstatt culture is typically linked to the Early Iron Age, its roots in salt extraction run deep), suggest that salt trade routes were well established even in the Bronze Age. Meanwhile, maritime routes along the Atlantic allowed exchanges of copper, tin, and exotic goods between Iberia, Brittany, Britain, and Ireland. The network of cross-Channel contacts brought about cultural parallels in pottery styles, burial rites, and metal objects, revealing how open Europe was to long-distance interactions.

11. Weapons, Warfare, and Social Status

Bronze swords, spears, and shields became increasingly refined in the Middle and Late Bronze Age. European smiths developed leaf-shaped blades, decorative hilts, and functional tangs. A well-made bronze sword was a symbol of status and possibly a sign of a warrior's or chieftain's power.

Warfare likely occurred among rival groups competing for farmland, resources, or trade routes. Some skeletal evidence from Bronze Age burials shows trauma consistent with combat injuries. Hillforts also suggest the prevalence of conflict or the fear of raids. On a smaller scale, warfare might have consisted of cattle raids or personal feuds rather than massive battles. Nonetheless, the presence of prestigious weaponry in elite burials indicates that martial prowess and leadership in war contributed to higher social standing.

12. Bronze Age Farming and Livelihoods

While bronze weapons and ornaments draw attention, most people were farmers or herders. Agriculture relied heavily on cereals like wheat and barley, along with peas, lentils, and possibly new cultivars introduced through cultural contacts. Domesticated animals—cattle, sheep, goats, and pigs—provided meat, milk, wool, and leather. Horse domestication also became more widespread, aiding transport and warfare.

Bronze tools—axes, sickles, and plowshares—improved land clearing and crop harvesting. Early plows, still mostly wooden, were sometimes fitted with bronze tips for greater durability. Storage pits or granaries safeguarded surplus grain, enabling some communities to sustain specialized crafts or trade. Over generations, better farming techniques supported population growth, which in turn led to larger settlements or the development of hillfort communities.

13. Coastal and Riverine Settlements

Beyond hillforts, some Bronze Age Europeans built stilt houses or pile dwellings near lakes, rivers, or marshes. Famous examples appear around the Alpine lakes, where archaeologists (speaking only of ancient remains) have found preserved wooden structures, tools, and bronze items in waterlogged conditions. In coastal regions along the Atlantic or Mediterranean, settlements might be sited to take advantage of fishing, salt production, or maritime trade.

Boats and canoes played a role in communication and commerce. Logboats could ferry goods along rivers, while coastal craft navigated short sea routes. Although ships in Bronze Age Europe did not match the scale of Mycenaean galleys or Egyptian vessels, they still connected communities separated by water. The spread of certain pottery styles or metal objects across seas suggests that skilled seafarers ventured farther than just local waters, fostering cultural and economic ties.

14. Religion and Rituals in Bronze Age Europe

Religious beliefs likely varied by region, but common elements included reverence for ancestors, possibly a solar cult, and respect for natural forces like rivers, mountains, or groves. Megalithic monuments from earlier periods sometimes remained in use, adapted for new ritual practices. Ceremonial depositions of metal in watery places or the burying of hoards reflect an ongoing practice of making offerings to unseen powers.

Stone circles, henges, or wooden palisade enclosures might have served as communal gathering sites for rituals or seasonal festivals. Some researchers link the orientation of certain monuments to solstices or equinoxes, suggesting that Bronze Age Europeans tracked celestial events important for planting and harvesting cycles. Bronze objects with sun motifs—discs, wheels, or spiral patterns—could hint at a widespread solar symbolism that connected the cycle of the sun with agricultural fertility.

15. Artisans and Craft Guilds?

We lack written records for most of Bronze Age Europe, so the exact nature of craft organization remains speculative. However, the consistency in metal object forms and decorations across large areas suggests that specialist artisans shared techniques. Apprentices might have learned from master smiths who guarded the secrets of bronze alloying and casting.

Certain regions became famed for specific items—for instance, southwestern Britain for tin, or the eastern Alpine area for skillful swords. Craftspeople likely traveled or migrated, spreading styles and forging personal connections. Elite patrons rewarded skilled smiths with land, livestock, or precious gifts. This patronage system fostered innovation, leading to advanced designs in swords, shields, and personal ornaments. The success of these artisans shaped local economies, as communities traded surplus crops or raw materials for finished bronze goods.

16. Climatic Changes and Shifts in Settlement

Around the Late Bronze Age (roughly after 1200 BCE), parts of Europe experienced shifts in climate, possibly cooler and wetter weather. Such changes might have forced communities to relocate or alter farming practices. Hillfort construction could reflect a response to resource scarcity or social tensions, as groups competed for arable land.

In some areas, the once-thriving barrow burials gave way to **Urnfield** practices, where cremated remains were placed in urns and buried in groups. The Urnfield culture spread widely across Central Europe (roughly 1300–800 BCE), possibly linked to population movements or evolving religious beliefs about burial. Urnfield cemeteries indicate a more communal style of interment, contrasting with earlier barrow burials of elite individuals.

17. Changes in Trade and Cultural Interactions

The final centuries of the Bronze Age saw intensifying contact between different European regions and the Mediterranean world. Metalwork styles began to reflect influences from the Aegean, the Italian peninsula, and even the eastern Mediterranean. Conversely, goods from the interior—amber, furs, metals—flowed southward. This era also coincides with major upheavals around the eastern Mediterranean, such as the fall of palatial centers in the Aegean, but Europe's reaction was varied and not as catastrophic as in some parts of the Near East.

Nevertheless, certain European networks transformed. Some sea routes became riskier due to piracy, or alliances shifted as local leaders vied for control over precious resources. In the process, new cultural groups emerged, mixing older Bronze Age traditions with fresh innovations. The seeds of Iron Age communities—like the Hallstatt culture in Central Europe—were planted during these transitions, setting the stage for further developments.

18. Late Bronze Age Prestige Objects

As the Bronze Age in Europe matured, artistic expression reached high levels of sophistication. **Socketed axes** were not only functional but sometimes decorated with geometric patterns. Swords featured elaborate hilts, and shields were embossed with concentric rings or raised bosses. Some items appear purely ceremonial—too thin or delicate for real combat—implying that they served symbolic or ritual purposes.

Gold ornaments, such as twisted torcs, hair rings, and armlets, grew more common in certain wealthy communities. These items could be worn by high-ranking individuals, marking them as part of an elite. When placed in graves or hoards, they demonstrated the power and religious significance of metal, bridging the gap between practical use and spiritual or social display.

19. Toward the Iron Age

By the end of the second millennium BCE, iron technology began to make inroads in Europe. Iron offered advantages: once smelting and forging methods were understood, iron ore was more abundant than copper or tin. Early iron objects coexisted with bronze for a while, especially for high-status weapons or ornaments. However, iron swords eventually outperformed bronze in battlefield conditions, leading to a gradual shift.

This transition marks the close of what we call the Bronze Age in Europe. It did not happen overnight—some regions persisted with bronze for a long time, particularly for ceremonial or decorative items. But as iron spread, social structures changed. New trade routes opened for iron ore, and the old networks built around copper and tin adapted. The changes in warfare, settlement patterns, and material culture would usher in a new age of larger tribal confederations and proto-states.

CHAPTER 11: THE TRADE NETWORKS OF THE BRONZE AGE

Introduction

Trade was the lifeblood that connected Bronze Age civilizations, allowing them to obtain resources they lacked and distribute goods they produced in surplus. Although the world then did not have modern transportation or technology, peoples across vast distances managed to exchange metals, foods, luxury goods, and ideas. This process helped shape the development of cities, enriched local economies, and gave rise to new cultural contacts.

In this chapter, we will explore the complex trade networks that linked the ancient societies of Mesopotamia, Egypt, the Indus Valley, the Aegean, Anatolia, China, and Europe. We will see the role of caravans, ships, and overland routes, how various intermediaries handled delicate negotiations, and how elites in one region displayed exotic goods acquired from another. By understanding the mechanics of Bronze Age trade, we appreciate how interconnected these civilizations truly were and how trade shaped their fortunes.

---

1. Why Trade Mattered in the Bronze Age

During the Bronze Age, communities discovered that mixing copper and tin produced a stronger alloy—bronze—essential for tools, weapons, and ceremonial objects. However, copper and tin deposits were unevenly distributed. Many regions had one metal but needed the other. Some had no metals at all. Hence, trade became vital for securing these resources.

Beyond metals, people needed exotic goods for prestige, religious use, or simple curiosity—lapis lazuli, gold, frankincense, cedar wood, and fine textiles were among the coveted items. Rulers showcased these items as symbols of power. Temples might receive them as tributes to the gods. Meanwhile, the daily needs of growing cities—grain, oils, livestock—also entered the trade circuits. A city-state in a dry region might require imports of timber or agricultural products, paying with surplus craft goods or metal objects.

The Bronze Age did not have standardized currency in most areas. Instead, many transactions were based on barter or the exchange of weighed metals. Ingots of copper, tin, or silver could function like money, but local systems differed. Scribes in places like Mesopotamia developed record-keeping methods to track shipments and taxes. Along the Nile, Egyptian administrators managed large-scale expeditions to gather resources for the pharaoh. Trade networks, therefore, were not just lines on a map; they were lifelines that fueled armies, built temples, and kept economies dynamic.

---

2. Overland Routes: Caravans and Donkeys

Overland trade often relied on caravans of donkeys, mules, or later horses, traveling along established paths that cut across deserts, mountains, or plains. In Mesopotamia and neighboring regions, donkeys were the primary pack animals for hauling heavy loads of metals, grain, or textiles. Caravans marched slowly, stopping at fortified waystations or oasis settlements.

One famous system of overland trade grew between Assyria (in northern Mesopotamia) and various Anatolian city-states during the early second millennium BCE. Assyrian merchants established "karum" (trading posts), such as the one at Kanesh, to exchange tin and textiles for local silver and other goods. These merchants carried written contracts on clay tablets, detailing business deals and profits. A single journey could be long and dangerous: caravans risked robberies, rough weather, or political strife. Yet the gains were high, which fueled more caravans to embark on these routes.

In Central Asia, steppe peoples who domesticated horses might have served as intermediaries, linking distant farming communities with each other. Horses eventually became crucial for faster travel and chariot warfare, but in many parts of the Bronze Age world, the simple donkey remained a dependable backbone of land-based trade. Over time, these routes expanded into networks that crisscrossed entire regions, forming the basis of early "international" commerce.

---

3. Maritime Trade: Ships on Rivers and Seas

Rivers were natural highways during the Bronze Age. Cities along the Nile in Egypt depended on boats to transport grain, stone, and other supplies. In

Mesopotamia, the Tigris and Euphrates carried boats laden with dates, barley, and metals between city-states. Similarly, the Indus River connected inland settlements with coastal outposts, allowing products like cotton textiles or lapis lazuli to flow outward.

Seafaring trade also grew along coastlines and open seas. The Minoans on Crete became skilled mariners, using wooden ships to shuttle goods across the Aegean to mainland Greece, the Cyclades, and beyond. Mycenaean ships sailed as far as Anatolia, Cyprus, and the Levant. The Egyptians sent expeditions down the Red Sea, reaching Punt (an area possibly near the Horn of Africa) to acquire incense, ebony, and exotic animals. In the Persian Gulf, merchants traveled between Mesopotamian ports and Dilmun (modern Bahrain region), then onward to the Oman Peninsula or the Indus Valley.

Maritime traders had to master navigation, shipbuilding, and the management of cargo. Many ships were small by modern standards, relying on sails and oars. Crews faced storms, piracy, and unfamiliar coastlines. Still, the rewards were great: copper ingots, tin, precious stones, and luxury items fetched high value in foreign markets. Sea-based trade drastically shortened travel time compared to overland caravans, making coastal cities and island ports into thriving exchange hubs.

4. Main Trade Goods: Metals, Textiles, and More

The leading driver of Bronze Age trade was, unsurprisingly, metal. Copper traveled in ingot form from places like Cyprus (famed for copper deposits), Anatolia, or the Sinai, while tin might come from distant sources—Afghanistan, Central Asia, the Erzgebirge in Central Europe, or Cornwall in Britain. Bronze itself was not always transported as widely as its raw components, but some finished objects did move across regions.

Textiles also played a major role, especially woolen fabrics from Mesopotamia or linen from Egypt. Fine cloth could be traded for metals or sold to wealthy elites in smaller city-states. Timber and stone—crucial for building—were shipped across seas when local sources were scarce. For example, Egypt imported cedar from Lebanon to build boats and monumental structures. Fragrant resins, spices, and incense were prized in temples and elite ceremonies. Perfumed oils and cosmetics enhanced personal status, while certain precious stones or shells were carved into ornaments.

Foods, too, circulated along trade routes. Grain shipments might relieve famine-stricken areas, while wine or olive oil from the Mediterranean found markets in regions that did not grow grapes or olives. Livestock—such as cattle, sheep, or horses—could move as well, although the complexity of traveling with live animals meant only certain routes or short distances were practical. Yet these exchanges went beyond physical items: the movement of goods carried cultural ideas, art styles, and religious symbols.

5. Middlemen and Intermediaries

In many cases, the original producers of certain goods did not directly sell to the faraway consumer. Instead, there were middlemen—merchants or entire communities—that specialized in trade and acted as go-betweens. For example, the city of Dilmun in the Persian Gulf grew wealthy by acting as an intermediary between Mesopotamia and the Indus Valley. Ships stopped there to refit, pay tariffs, and exchange cargo.

Similarly, the Phoenicians (though best known in the Iron Age) may have had Bronze Age predecessors along the Levantine coast who facilitated maritime trade for Egyptian or Mesopotamian markets. In Central Asia, steppe nomads might have carried tin or precious metals between mining regions and the great river valleys. These middlemen charged fees or took a share of goods, making profit from their unique position. Over time, certain ports and caravan towns became major commercial centers, shaping the political power structures around them.

6. Impact on City-States and Empires

Trade contributed significantly to the rise of powerful states during the Bronze Age. For instance, Mesopotamian city-states like Ur, Uruk, and Babylon used trade revenues and resources to build monumental ziggurats and maintain armies. Egypt's wealth from trade expeditions—bringing in gold from Nubia, cedar from Lebanon, and exotic goods from Punt—boosted the pharaoh's prestige and financed grand temples.

The Minoans in Crete established palaces such as Knossos, partially funded by profits from maritime exchange. The Mycenaeans, with their strategic location on mainland Greece, expanded their influence across the Aegean by controlling sea routes, eventually surpassing Crete in the Late Bronze Age. Anatolian powers like the Hittites vied for control of trade routes that connected the copper- and silver-rich highlands to markets in the Levant or Mesopotamia. Even in the Indus Valley, the wealth from cotton textiles and bead-making contributed to the growth of urban centers like Mohenjo-daro and Harappa.

Wherever large-scale trade thrived, administrators grew more sophisticated, employing scribes to track inventories and taxes. Religious institutions also benefited, as temples or palaces often managed storehouses and collected tribute in the form of metals or grains. This synergy between trade, government, and religion laid the foundation for complex bureaucratic societies.

7. Diplomatic Exchanges and Gift-Giving

Formal trade was not the only way goods traveled. Diplomatic gift-giving played a huge role among Bronze Age elites. Rulers sent lavish gifts—fine textiles, precious metals, rare animals—to cement alliances or negotiate peace. The Amarna Letters from Egypt's New Kingdom mention correspondences with rulers in the Levant and beyond, discussing marriages, tributes, and gifts. These letters record that foreign kings expected gold from the pharaoh and offered goods like horses or precious stones in return.

Such exchanges were not purely economic. They were statements of status and power. A king who received fewer gifts than he sent might feel slighted. Diplomatic marriages often accompanied these exchanges, further linking royal houses. The movement of brides from one court to another also carried cultural influences, as they brought attendants, crafts, or religious practices. Thus, gift-giving functioned as a sophisticated version of trade, wrapped in diplomacy and personal relationships between royal families.

8. Transport Technology and Innovation

To facilitate trade, Bronze Age societies developed various transport innovations. As mentioned, donkeys and mules were primary pack animals, though the spread of horse domestication eventually revolutionized speed and efficiency. The invention or improvement of the spoked wheel enabled lighter carts and chariots, making some overland travel faster—though these vehicles often served military or elite ceremonial roles more than bulk transport.

Boat-building techniques advanced along major rivers and seas. Reed boats in Mesopotamia gave way to wooden hulls for heavier cargo. In the Aegean, ship designs evolved to handle open-water voyages, featuring keels that improved stability. Ports might have dock facilities, though often quite simple by later standards—stone quays, ramps, or beach landings. Some maritime trade used island-hopping routes that let ships resupply and avoid storms. Others ventured straight across large sea stretches, guided by the stars and coastal landmarks.

Storage containers also improved. Pottery jars with standardized sizes made measuring cargo easier, while large amphora-like vessels might hold oil, wine, or grain for sea transport. Overland caravans used leather sacks or woven baskets. Sometimes, metals traveled in standardized ingots, shaped like ox hides or rectangular bars. Each design simplified the counting, weighing, and division of shipments.

---

9. Trade and Cultural Exchange

Trade routes did more than move objects; they carried ideas, art styles, and sometimes entire technologies. A potter in the Aegean might see a new decorative motif on a foreign jug, adapt it, and pass it on to local consumers. A scribe in Mesopotamia might learn new words or script signs from a neighboring region, enriching local writing systems. Religious symbols could spread: an Egyptian symbol might appear on a seal found in Syria, or a Mesopotamian motif might decorate a Minoan fresco.

These interactions fueled cultural fusion. The Mycenaeans, for example, absorbed elements of Minoan art, religious iconography, and palace organization, blending them into a new Greek-speaking civilization. The Hittites in Anatolia borrowed gods and rituals from conquered peoples. The Indus Valley's bead designs influenced artisans in Mesopotamia. Meanwhile, smaller scale migrations—craftsmen traveling or settling in foreign lands—introduced local communities to new methods of metal casting or weaving.

Over the centuries, such exchanges helped shape more cosmopolitan societies along major routes, even as they left more isolated communities relatively unchanged. Elites often embraced foreign luxury items as proof of their wide connections. This gave impetus for further exploration and stronger trade links, forming an interlaced tapestry of shared knowledge across distant lands.

10. Security and Risks

Though trade was lucrative, it was also fraught with danger. Bandits might waylay caravans in remote stretches. Pirates or raiders could plunder ships near unprotected coastlines. Political shifts—like the rise of a new ruler hostile to foreign traders—might close off established routes or impose heavy tolls. Some city-states responded by building fortifications near major trade paths, offering caravans safe lodging for a fee. Powerful kings sometimes provided military escorts, hoping to encourage commerce and collect taxes.

Even natural disasters posed risks: storms could sink ships, floods might wipe out roads, and drought could devastate farmland, reducing demand for imported goods. A caravan that lost its pack animals in a sandstorm might never recover. Yet many traders were willing to take these gambles for the promise of high profits. Over time, these challenges prompted the development of treaties or alliances to protect caravans, maritime convoys, and strategic chokepoints. The creation of stable trade corridors often went hand in hand with the expansion of larger states or empires that could enforce peace along routes.

11. Regional Specialties in the Bronze Age

Different regions became known for specific products. Cyprus was famed for copper, crucial to the entire eastern Mediterranean. The Levantine coast provided cedar timber, purple dyes (from murex shells), and glass or faience items. Egypt exported grain, linen, and sometimes gold from Nubian sources. The Indus Valley specialized in cotton textiles, beads, and possibly large amounts of grain. Babylonia, in Mesopotamia, shipped barley, dates, and woolen cloth.

In the Aegean, Crete produced fine pottery (Kamares ware in earlier periods), while Mycenaean palaces exported decorated stirrup jars of oil or wine. In

Anatolia, tin deposits were not as plentiful, but silver and other metals like lead existed, plus local crafts like fine relief vases. Farther afield, in Europe, amber from the Baltic and tin from Cornwall found their way into the Continental trade system. Eastward in China, distinctive bronzes and possibly jade or silk might have trickled into Central Asia, though large-scale direct contact with the west was limited in early periods.

These local specializations generated a mosaic of trade flows, with caravans and ships carrying goods from one node to another, sometimes passing through multiple hands before reaching final destinations. Thus, a single piece of tin might have changed owners many times, each transaction adding a layer of profit or exchange.

12. Evidence of Trade: Archaeological Clues

How do we know about Bronze Age trade networks? Much of the evidence comes from archaeological findings:

1. **Shipwrecks**: Underwater excavations, like the famous Uluburun shipwreck off the coast of Turkey (Late Bronze Age), have revealed cargoes of copper and tin ingots, glass beads, ivory, and luxury goods from multiple cultures, showing the diversity of maritime commerce.
2. **Exotic Materials**: Items found far from their sources—like Baltic amber in Mediterranean tombs or Mesopotamian cylinder seals in Anatolia—prove that objects traveled great distances.
3. **Inscriptions and Tablets**: Written records, such as cuneiform tablets in Mesopotamia or the Amarna Letters in Egypt, mention trade expeditions, prices, and official business instructions.
4. **Standardized Objects**: Ingots shaped uniformly (e.g., oxhide ingots in the Mediterranean) or standardized weights for measuring metals point to established commercial practices.
5. **Changes in Craft Styles**: Sudden appearances of new pottery or decorative motifs in a region can indicate the arrival of foreign artisans or imported fashions.

Together, these clues let us reconstruct how Bronze Age peoples connected across seas, rivers, and dusty roads. Though incomplete, the picture that emerges is one of vibrant, far-reaching networks supporting both everyday needs and the grand ambitions of palace elites.

13. Role of Temples and Palaces in Trade

In many Bronze Age societies, temples and palaces served as economic hubs. In Mesopotamia, temple complexes stored surplus grain and employed scribes to administer trade transactions. These institutions might sponsor caravans or fleets, using their wealth to finance expeditions. Priests often oversaw the distribution of rations, gathering tithes from worshipers and turning them into tradable commodities.

In Egypt, the pharaoh's court directed large-scale expeditions. Royal officials led journeys to Sinai for copper or to Punt for incense and exotic items, returning with valuable cargoes for temples and the royal treasury. The Indus Valley's major cities likely had central storehouses controlling the flow of grain and craft products, although details remain unclear due to the undeciphered script. In Anatolia, Hittite kings regulated metal production and trade routes that crossed their territory.

By controlling trade, rulers and priests accumulated wealth, built loyalty among their supporters, and funded elaborate religious offerings. Temples might display foreign riches as evidence of divine favor. Meanwhile, local inhabitants benefited from the variety of goods available, though they were subject to taxes or tribute demands. This interplay between sacred and state power shaped the economic landscape of the Bronze Age.

14. Seasonal Patterns and Caravansaries

Weather played a huge role in when trade occurred. In regions with harsh winters or scorching summers, caravans had to time their journeys carefully to avoid impassable roads or scorching desert heat. River transport might rely on flood seasons or avoid them if the floods were too dangerous. Coastal shipping needed to dodge stormy months, so voyages might cluster in calmer seasons.

As routes grew more established, stopping points or caravansaries—places where traders could rest, feed their animals, and repair gear—emerged. These might be small forts, villages, or official posts run by local authorities. Traders paid fees or taxes to use the facilities but gained security and convenience in return. Over time, some caravansaries developed into bustling market towns. People from different ethnic backgrounds mingled, exchanging languages, customs, and knowledge about distant lands.

Thus, trade was not a random affair. It followed rhythms set by nature and politics. The cyclical movement of caravans and ships also meant that markets in major cities could anticipate seasonal arrivals of goods, adjusting prices and storage practices accordingly.

15. Barter, Metals as Currency, and Record-Keeping

Most Bronze Age trade did not rely on minted coins—that would come later in history. Instead, barter or the use of metals by weight prevailed. A merchant might offer a certain quantity of grain for an equivalent weight of copper or tin. People used scales and standardized weights made of stone or metal to ensure fairness. Silver bars or rings could also serve as a sort of proto-currency in parts of Mesopotamia, with records indicating how many shekels of silver a transaction required.

Scribes in larger polities kept track of shipments, sometimes on clay tablets, papyrus, or other writing materials. They recorded who delivered goods, how much was owed in tax, and which temple or palace storehouse would receive them. Diplomatic or commercial treaties might specify standard weights and measures to reduce disputes. Despite these systems, local differences persisted—what weighed "one unit" in one city could differ slightly from another, leading to negotiation or conflict when caravans arrived.

Record-keeping also reflected social hierarchies. Most peasants or small craftsmen dealt locally in goods or services, rarely leaving behind a written trail. High-level transactions—like shipments of metal ingots, lavish gifts to temples, or palace-led expeditions—were more likely to be documented. Therefore, the surviving records tend to focus on large-scale exchanges, overshadowing small-scale village trades that also formed the fabric of daily life.

16. Effects of Trade on Bronze Age Societies

Trade networks had many consequences for Bronze Age societies:

1. **Social Stratification**: The ability to control trade routes or metal supplies created wealthy elites. Merchant families and palace administrators who managed the flow of goods gained influence.
2. **Urban Growth**: Ports, caravan towns, and major cities prospered by taxing or facilitating commerce. This led to bigger populations, more specialized crafts, and the need for organized governance.
3. **Cultural Fusion**: As goods and ideas circulated, local art styles blended, new religious symbols appeared, and foreign words entered local languages. Diplomacy and intermarriage bound ruling families from distant lands.
4. **Economic Dependence**: Some regions became reliant on imports of crucial materials (like tin) or foods. Any disruption—political upheaval, blocked routes, or natural disasters—could destabilize a city-state or entire region.
5. **Warfare and Alliances**: Controlling trade could spark conflicts. Empires formed around strategic points, forging alliances to protect their commercial interests. Alternatively, they might fight wars to secure trade corridors.

In sum, trade was a powerful engine that drove growth but also introduced vulnerabilities. Societies had to balance their desire for exotic goods and metals with the risks of relying on far-flung networks.

17. Examples of Key Trade Corridors

Several notable corridors shaped the Bronze Age world:

- **Mesopotamia to Anatolia**: Donkey caravans carrying textiles and tin from Assyria in exchange for silver and local goods.
- **Egypt to the Levant**: Sea and land routes exchanging grain, linen, and gold for cedar wood, wine, and minerals.
- **Aegean to the Eastern Mediterranean**: Minoan and Mycenaean ships trading pottery, oil, and wine for copper from Cyprus, tin, and luxury items from Levantine ports.
- **Indus Valley to Mesopotamia**: Seaborne routes across the Arabian Sea and Persian Gulf, bringing cotton textiles, beads, and precious woods in exchange for metals, manufactured goods, and perhaps cereals.

- **China's Internal Routes**: Although more isolated, regional trade within early Chinese states or with steppe peoples for horses and metals contributed to the Bronze Age dynasties' growth.

Each corridor had unique hazards—mountains, deserts, stormy seas—and often needed a chain of intermediaries. Yet these paths formed the arteries that kept the Bronze Age world interlinked.

---

18. Collapse of Networks in the Late Bronze Age

Around the late second millennium BCE, many civilizations in the Eastern Mediterranean experienced turmoil. The Mycenaean palaces fell, Minoan Crete had already declined, the Hittite Empire collapsed, and Egypt faced invasions or internal strife. Historians debate the causes—earthquakes, drought, invasions by "Sea Peoples," or internal revolts. But one major consequence was the disruption of trade routes.

Without stable palatial authorities or secure shipping lanes, merchants hesitated to undertake long journeys. Tin supplies for bronze might have become scarce, pushing communities to seek local substitutes or adopt new technologies like iron. Ports were destroyed or abandoned, leading to a reduction in maritime commerce. This breakdown in connectivity contributed to what some call the "Bronze Age Collapse." In many places, it sparked a dark age where literacy and craft production diminished.

However, not all regions were equally affected. Some, like parts of the Near East, adapted or forged new alliances. In China, the transition from Shang to Zhou continued, with trade networks shifting but not completely collapsing. In Europe, the end of the Bronze Age paved the way for new cultural patterns and the eventual spread of iron. Still, the golden era of wide-reaching Bronze Age trade waned as these disruptions took hold.

---

19. Resilience and Continuity

Despite these upheavals, some trade routes endured or revived in new forms. The Levantine coast eventually saw Phoenician city-states flourish, continuing maritime commerce and founding colonies. In Mesopotamia, new powers like the Neo-Assyrian Empire rose, reasserting trade connections. Local markets adapted by focusing on shorter-range exchanges if long-distance routes became too risky. Craftspeople found ways to survive, though on a smaller scale until stability returned.

The lingering impact of Bronze Age trade remained evident in cultural syncretism, shared motifs, and the memory of previous prosperity. Scripts, administrative techniques, and certain religious ideas survived in local traditions, ready to resurface or evolve when new states formed. Moreover, the knowledge of maritime navigation and caravan organization did not disappear; it laid groundwork for future expansions in commerce once political conditions improved.

CHAPTER 12: RELIGIOUS BELIEFS AND RITUALS

Introduction

Religion in the Bronze Age was deeply intertwined with daily life, politics, and social structures. People across regions—from Mesopotamia to the Indus Valley, from Egypt to Minoan Crete—believed in gods, spirits, or cosmic forces that influenced harvests, health, and victory in battle. Rulers often claimed divine favor or even semi-divine status to legitimize their power. Priests and priestesses performed rituals to keep the gods content, and temples stood as grand symbols of communal devotion.

In this chapter, we will explore the diverse religious beliefs and practices of major Bronze Age cultures. We will see how they built temples, developed priestly hierarchies, and used rituals to maintain cosmic balance. We will also look at how religious ideas spread along trade routes, how different societies combined local traditions with foreign influences, and how religion shaped the art, architecture, and governance of the time.

---

1. The Role of Religion in Bronze Age Societies

For Bronze Age peoples, religion was not a separate domain but a fundamental aspect of how they viewed the world. Events such as floods, droughts, or eclipses were seen as signs from the gods. Good harvests implied divine favor, while disasters might mean the gods were angry. Rulers performed sacrifices and built monuments to appease or celebrate these powers, blending religious ceremony with political authority.

Daily devotions varied: household shrines, small altars, or local spirits might be invoked for protection. Larger communal rituals, led by temple priests, could involve offerings of animals, food, or precious objects. Public festivals marked seasonal changes, victories in war, or royal coronations. The process of dedicating expensive bronze or gold items to a deity also had economic and political meaning—demonstrating wealth, seeking blessings, and reinforcing social hierarchies.

2. Polytheism and Pantheons

Most Bronze Age cultures were polytheistic, worshiping multiple deities with specialized roles. In Mesopotamia, gods like Anu (the sky god), Enlil (lord of the wind), and Inanna/Ishtar (goddess of love and war) governed different aspects of life. City-states each had a patron deity, and the temple to that deity was the city's spiritual center.

Egyptians revered a vast pantheon, including Ra (the sun god), Osiris (god of the afterlife), and Amun (a creator god who rose to prominence in Thebes). Pharaohs claimed to be the gods' representatives on Earth. The Indus Valley civilization's religion is less understood, but art and seals suggest possible worship of mother goddesses, male figures (perhaps proto-Shiva), and sacred animals. The Minoans on Crete honored goddesses linked to nature, with the bull as a recurring symbol. Mycenaean Greeks recognized gods that may be forerunners to the classical Greek pantheon, as indicated by names found in Linear B tablets (e.g., Poseidon).

In China, the Shang and Zhou Dynasties worshiped ancestral spirits and high gods like Di or Tian (Heaven). Rulers acted as intermediaries, performing rituals to secure good harvests and victory. Even in Bronze Age Europe, though textual evidence is scarce, archaeological finds suggest devotion to sun deities or nature spirits, with megalithic sites possibly reflecting solar alignments.

Polytheism allowed for flexibility—new gods could be adopted if they proved powerful or if foreign influences entered the local scene. Mythologies also explained the origins of the world, legitimized rulers, and provided moral lessons through the deeds of gods or legendary heroes.

---

3. Temples and Sacred Architecture

Monumental temple construction was a hallmark of Bronze Age religion. In Mesopotamia, ziggurats rose above city skylines, serving as man-made mountains to bridge heaven and earth. Each ziggurat complex housed storerooms, priest quarters, and altars. Egyptian temples, aligned with celestial events, used massive stone columns and courtyards, culminating in inner sanctuaries where statues of the gods resided. Priests performed daily offerings, washing and clothing the deity's image.

Minoan palaces, such as Knossos, had central courts that may have hosted religious ceremonies, bull-leaping events, or communal gatherings. Shrines with horns of consecration and pillar crypts further hinted at the significance of nature-based worship. In the Levant, Canaanite cities built temples with cult statues and altars for offerings. The Hittites in Anatolia constructed large temple complexes in Hattusa, each dedicated to specific gods—some were originally local Anatolian deities, others borrowed from Hurrian or Mesopotamian traditions.

The Indus cities did not feature towering temples like Egypt or Mesopotamia, suggesting a different approach—perhaps more decentralized or domestic forms of worship. Nonetheless, structures like the Great Bath at Mohenjo-daro might have held a ceremonial function. In China, Shang palaces integrated ritual spaces, where oracle bone divinations and ancestral offerings took place.

In all these varied forms, temples symbolized communal devotion and political control. Building them required huge labor forces, demonstrating the power of priests or kings who managed them. The materials—stone, mudbrick, timber—reflected local resources, while the scale and craftsmanship reflected a society's devotion to its gods.

---

4. Priests, Oracles, and Divination

A formal priesthood developed in most Bronze Age civilizations. Priests guarded sacred knowledge, performed rituals, and interpreted divine will. They might come from elite families or be specially chosen by rulers. In Mesopotamia, the high priest (sometimes called an en or ensi if combined with rulership) mediated between gods and the city. Temples employed many functionaries: scribes, singers, cooks, brewers, and accountants, all supporting worship and temple economics.

Divination methods varied. Mesopotamians used sheep livers or other animal entrails to read omens. The Shang in China famously relied on oracle bones—scapulae of oxen or shells of turtles—heated until they cracked, with the cracks interpreted as answers from ancestors or high gods. Egyptian priests observed celestial movements, star alignments, or the flight of birds to glean divine messages. Ritual experts might also interpret dreams or cast lots.

These practices served practical ends: deciding on the best time for planting crops, launching a military campaign, or building a temple. Rulers never wanted to anger the gods, so they sought divine approval. Priests enjoyed high status because their role in reading signs, controlling temple wealth, and advising royalty on spiritual matters was crucial.

5. Sacrifice and Offerings

Central to Bronze Age religion was the act of sacrifice—offering animals, food, drink, or precious objects to deities. In Mesopotamia, daily temple rituals involved giving bread, beer, and incense to the god's statue. During festivals, large-scale sacrifices might feed the entire city, with the leftover meat distributed among priests and common people. Egyptians sacrificed cattle, geese, or other animals at temple altars, especially during major festivals honoring gods like Amun or Hathor.

The Minoans practiced bull sacrifice, as suggested by frescoes and bones found near shrines. Mycenaeans performed similar rites, sometimes burying the remains in pits near palatial complexes. The Hittites had elaborate instructions for offering bread, beer, and sheep or goats to their pantheon, which included storm gods, solar deities, and local mountain gods. In the Indus Valley, direct evidence of large sacrifices is less clear, but the presence of possible altars and animal remains suggests that offerings were made.

Beyond animals, precious metals or elaborately decorated bronze vessels were also dedicated. Temples accumulated vast treasuries that displayed wealth and piety. In some cultures, even human sacrifice might occur, as hinted by certain Shang dynasty royal tombs with human remains arranged in ritual patterns, or Mesoamerican parallels (though that's outside the Bronze Age Old World focus). Sacrifice was both religious devotion and a way for elites to demonstrate generosity or power.

6. Funerary Beliefs and the Afterlife

Across the Bronze Age world, beliefs about death and the afterlife shaped burial practices. Egyptians famously built pyramids and rock-cut tombs for pharaohs, equipping them with food, jewelry, and other goods to help them in the next life. The concept of preserving the body through mummification was linked to the journey of the soul to the Field of Reeds, a paradise that mirrored earthly life. The "Book of the Dead" guided the deceased through the underworld's trials.

Mesopotamians viewed the afterlife more somberly, as a dreary Underworld where spirits lingered. Nonetheless, burials often included personal objects, while some kings might be buried with attendants or lavish grave goods, as seen in the Royal Cemetery at Ur. The Indus Valley used both communal and individual burials; the precise religious meaning is unclear, but some graves show personal ornaments or pottery, suggesting belief in an afterlife needing such items.

In the Aegean, Minoans placed the dead in cave tombs or tholos tombs, sometimes with figurines or bronze weapons. Mycenaeans built shaft graves and tholos tombs, richly furnished with gold masks, weapons, and jewelry, revealing a strong concern for the afterlife. The Hittites, ironically, left fewer grand royal tombs, though they performed funerary rites that might involve cremation or inhumation, referencing the soul's journey to join ancestral spirits.

All these practices showed respect for the dead and fear or hope regarding what lay beyond. They also consumed vast resources—building tombs, burying valuables—that indicated the importance of ensuring a proper afterlife for influential individuals.

---

7. Mythology and Epic Traditions

Mythologies answered fundamental questions: how the world began, why natural phenomena occur, and how humans should behave. In Mesopotamia, tales like the "Epic of Gilgamesh" described gods, heroes, and the quest for immortality. Gilgamesh wrestles with divine powers, reflecting on life and death. The "Enuma Elish" explained how Marduk created order from chaos, justifying Babylon's religious supremacy.

Egyptian mythology recounted the death and resurrection of Osiris, offering hope for eternal life. Ra's journey across the sky symbolized daily renewal. The Indus script remains undeciphered, so we lack direct myths, but the later Vedic traditions in the Indian subcontinent inherited some Bronze Age elements, possibly including the worship of nature deities. In Crete, the myth of the Minotaur may reflect older Minoan bull-cult elements, though surviving references come from later Greek sources.

The Shang and Zhou in China recorded myths of divine ancestors and legendary sage-kings, who taught agriculture or controlled floods. Oracle bone inscriptions mention ancestor spirits regularly. In Europe, preliterate societies left fewer direct mythic texts, but rock art and burial rites hint at reverence for the sun, the changing seasons, and heroic feats. Over time, as writing spread, these myths were refined or replaced by new religious narratives. Nonetheless, the Bronze Age set the foundation for many traditions that evolved into classical mythologies.

8. Animal Worship and Sacred Symbols

Animals played prominent roles in Bronze Age religion. Bulls, for example, were revered in Minoan Crete, frequently depicted in frescoes and possibly linked to a male sky god or fertility principle. In Egypt, Apis the bull was worshiped in special rites, and many deities had animal heads—Horus (falcon), Anubis (jackal), and so on. Mesopotamian gods might be accompanied by symbolic animals—Adad or Ishkur with a bull, for instance.

Serpents, lions, eagles, and other creatures showed up in decorative motifs, temple reliefs, or guardian statues at gateways (e.g., the Lamassu in Mesopotamia had a bull or lion body, wings, and a human head, though that form became more iconic in the Iron Age). The Hittites revered stags and hawks in their art, while in the Indus Valley, unicorn-like figures or zebu bulls appear on seals. Such images likely held spiritual significance, whether as totems, protectors, or symbolic manifestations of divine strength.

Nature worship was also prevalent: rivers, mountains, or sacred trees might hold local importance, with small shrines built near them. Seasonal ceremonies might honor the return of rains or the rebirth of vegetation. In Bronze Age Europe, sun discs and boat symbols on rock carvings suggest a solar religion. Stone circles aligned with solstices also hint at sunrise or sunset rituals. All these practices reflect how closely Bronze Age societies connected the divine with the natural world.

9. Personal Piety and Household Worship

Not all Bronze Age religion was grand temple ceremonies. Common folk often worshiped at small household altars or local shrines. They might pour libations of beer or wine, burn incense, or recite prayers for good health and protection. Talismans, amulets, or small figurines were carried or placed in dwellings as guardians against evil spirits.

In Mesopotamia, each family might have protective household gods or spirits (lamassu or shedu in later texts). In Egypt, figurines of Bes or Taweret protected mothers and children. The Indus people may have used terracotta figurines of mother goddesses in domestic rites. Minoans had "snake goddess" figurines with upraised arms, suggesting household or local shrine worship. In the Chinese Shang dynasty, clan-based ancestor veneration was common, with each lineage remembering forefathers in personal or communal rituals.

This personal piety balanced the official religion. While major festivals and sacrifices demanded public participation, daily life included private acts of devotion. Farmers prayed for good rains, soldiers for victory, and mothers for safe childbirth. These simple yet heartfelt practices formed the bedrock of religious life for most people, overshadowed in the historical record by grand palace temples but vital to the spiritual fabric of Bronze Age communities.

---

10. Ritual Calendars and Festivals

Throughout the Bronze Age, societies developed calendars—often based on lunar cycles or solar observations—to schedule religious festivals. In Egypt, the rise of Sirius (the star Sopdet) before the annual Nile flood was a key marker, aligning with celebrations for the new year. Mesopotamian city-states held Akitu festivals to honor the new year or the sowing season. These events could last days, featuring processions of deity statues, music, feasting, and oracles.

Seasonal festivals tied to planting and harvest reminded people of their dependence on divine forces for survival. Priests ensured that the correct rites were performed at the right times, from sowing seeds in spring to storing grain in autumn. The entire community participated, reinforcing collective identity and shared beliefs. Minoan Crete's calendar might have revolved around agricultural cycles and maritime journeys, as indicated by some seals and possible references to bull-leaping events.

Large-scale festivals also displayed the wealth and might of rulers. Pharaohs or kings might sponsor lavish banquets, distribute food to the populace, and present gifts to the gods on behalf of the nation. Foreign dignitaries visiting during such festivals would see the grandeur of the host city, forging diplomatic ties and reinforcing the idea that the host's gods and rulers were favored by cosmic order.

11. Music, Dance, and Theatrical Elements

Music and dance were integral parts of Bronze Age religious rituals. Mesopotamian temples employed singers, harpists, and percussionists to accompany daily offerings. Egyptian tomb paintings show musicians performing with flutes, harps, and lutes during banquets or ceremonies. In Crete, frescoes depict dancing figures, perhaps part of bull-leaping spectacles or religious processions.

Elaborate performances might reenact mythological events, dramatizing a deity's triumph over chaos or the cycle of death and rebirth. The Hittites had complex rituals with recitations, songs, and possibly masked participants representing gods or spirits. In the Indus Valley, we have fewer direct details, but terracotta figurines of dancers or drum-like instruments suggest music played a role in communal gatherings.

Such performances created emotional bonds among worshipers, lifting them out of everyday life and into a shared spiritual experience. The pounding of drums, the chanting of hymns, and the swirl of dancers around a sacred fire or altar forged a collective identity. Rulers often sponsored these events, ensuring people saw them as favored by the gods who received the festival's devotion.

12. Religious Specialists: Shamans and Mediums

Outside of structured priesthoods, some regions also had shamans, mediums, or oracles who claimed direct contact with spirits or gods. They might enter trances, interpret visions, or heal the sick using herbal knowledge and spiritual rituals. In China, the Shang king himself performed oracle bone divinations, but local shamans may have existed, serving villages with cures and blessings.

In the steppes or peripheral areas, spiritual leaders guided clans in ancestor worship, nature veneration, and possibly ecstatic rites involving drumming or hallucinogenic substances. The limited textual evidence makes it hard to reconstruct these practices precisely, but archaeological hints—unusual burials, ritual masks—suggest such roles. These specialists often lived at the margins of official temple life, yet held importance for everyday communities.

At times, formal priesthoods and independent shamans coexisted or clashed. Rulers preferred to keep spiritual power centralized in official temples, but local traditions might trust wandering healers or mediums more. This tension highlights the diversity of Bronze Age religious expression beyond the polished ceremonies of major cult centers.

13. Syncretism and Borrowing of Deities

As trade networks linked distant lands, religious ideas traveled alongside goods. Gods from one region might be adopted into another's pantheon. The Hittites, for example, took in Hurrian and Mesopotamian deities, sometimes renaming them or equating them with local gods. Egyptian pharaohs occasionally recognized foreign deities if they believed they wielded genuine power—for instance, the goddess Astarte from the Levant found some acceptance in the Nile Delta.

In the Levant, Baal and other Canaanite gods had parallels in Mesopotamian or Egyptian forms. Mycenaean Greece might have absorbed Minoan goddesses into their emergent pantheon. Over centuries, these exchanges blurred boundaries, making religious beliefs more cosmopolitan in port cities or major crossroad settlements. Yet local cults still persisted, ensuring that religion remained a patchwork of overlapping traditions.

Syncretism smoothed diplomatic relations, too. If your neighbor's war god could protect your armies, why not build a small shrine in his honor? This attitude allowed multiethnic empires like the Hittites or Egyptians in foreign territories to maintain relative harmony by respecting local faiths, integrating them into official state worship where politically useful.

14. Oracles, Prophecies, and Political Decisions

Rulers rarely made critical decisions—like waging war or building a new palace—without seeking divine guidance. Oracle bones in China are a classic example, with the Shang king needing ancestral sanction for military campaigns. Mesopotamian kings might consult temple diviners, who interpreted omens from the flight of birds or the pattern of oil on water.

Prophecy, too, could shape politics. If a seer predicted victory in battle but demanded the king pay homage to a certain deity, that king might build a new temple or temple wing. At times, false or manipulated prophecies might serve political agendas. Rival claimants to a throne could cite divine messages for legitimacy. In Egypt, a new pharaoh might emphasize that the gods personally chose him, staging elaborate coronation rituals to prove it.

The result was a fusion of religion and governance. People believed that cosmic forces guided their leaders if they performed the right ceremonies. This faith could unify large populations under a single ideology. Of course, if disasters struck or wars went poorly, the ruler's spiritual authority might be questioned, paving the way for rebellion or new dynasties.

15. Art as a Reflection of Religious Ideals

Bronze Age art often served religious purposes. Temple walls and palace frescoes depicted gods, mythological scenes, or ritual ceremonies. Statues of deities, cast in bronze or carved in stone, received offerings or processional honors. Smaller amulets or figurines offered personal protection.

Symbols like the ankh in Egypt, the winged sun disc in Mesopotamia, or the double axe in Minoan Crete carried religious meaning. Artists stylized forms to convey divine power—Egyptian art, for example, maintained a formal canon to emphasize the eternal nature of gods and pharaohs. In China's Shang bronzes, the taotie motif might represent mythical beasts that bridged human and spirit worlds. In the Indus Valley, seals combined animal motifs with script, possibly representing clan totems or religious emblems.

Artworks displayed in shrines or tombs reminded worshipers of cosmic truths and the presence of higher powers. The labor and resources invested in these creations also underscored society's devotion. Scenes of worship or sacrifice in these images taught illiterate populations about official mythologies and the importance of respecting the gods.

16. Women in Bronze Age Religion

Women often played significant roles in religious life, though the extent varied by culture. In some Mesopotamian temples, women served as high priestesses (like the en-priestess of the moon god in Ur). These priestesses could hold real political influence, controlling temple wealth. In Minoan Crete, art shows prominent female figures in religious contexts—possibly priestesses or goddesses themselves—leading ceremonies or handling sacred snakes.

Egypt had "God's Wives of Amun," powerful priestesses who managed temple affairs and participated in state rituals. The Indus Valley's mother goddess figurines suggest that female fertility deities were revered. Even in Mycenaean or Hittite rites, women might sing hymns, brew sacrificial beer, or attend to altars.

Yet patriarchy still dominated many societies. Male priests or kings often held ultimate authority in state cults. Nonetheless, the presence of female deities, priestesses, or mediums indicates that women were not excluded from spiritual leadership. In some local shrines or domestic rituals, women may have been the primary practitioners, especially concerning fertility, childbirth, and household well-being.

---

17. Human Sacrifice and Controversies

The topic of human sacrifice in the Bronze Age is sensitive and debated. Some evidence suggests it occurred in certain societies. The Royal Tombs of Ur in Mesopotamia contain remains of attendants who may have been ritually killed to accompany their ruler in death. Shang tombs in China show skeletons arranged in ways that hint at sacrificial practices. Mesoamerican civilizations practiced human sacrifice extensively, but that is outside the Old World Bronze Age scope.

Interpreting these remains is challenging. They might reflect palace intrigue, forced suicides, or retainer burials rather than typical religious sacrifice. In many cultures, textual records do not openly describe such acts, or they have not survived. The practice, if present, would have been tied to beliefs in an afterlife where servants or warriors continued to serve a ruler.

Public tolerance for such sacrifice likely varied. Some societies might have seen it as an extreme expression of devotion or power, while others found alternative ways—like burying symbolic clay figurines or wealth objects. Regardless, the possibility of human sacrifice underscores the intensity of Bronze Age religious convictions and the extent to which elites exercised control over life and death.

18. Ritual Purity and Taboos

Many Bronze Age societies observed rules of purity—certain foods, behaviors, or physical conditions might be deemed unclean in a religious sense. Mesopotamian texts refer to purification rites before entering temples. Egyptian priests shaved body hair and wore clean linens, avoiding fish or beans in some periods for ritual reasons. In China, approaching ancestral shrines might require fasting or abstaining from certain activities.

Taboos could apply to places (holy grounds where ordinary people could not step), times (festivals with strict protocol), or actions (forbidden to break certain social or moral codes). Violations might be punished by the gods, leading to misfortune. To rectify mistakes, a community might offer extra sacrifices, fast, or perform cleansing rituals. This system of purity laws helped maintain social order, reinforcing the idea that cosmic balance depended on correct human behavior.

19. The Late Bronze Age Religious Transformations

As the Bronze Age approached its end in various regions, large empires or centralized palaces collapsed, causing shifts in religious structures. Temples were sometimes destroyed or abandoned. Priestly hierarchies might lose power if the monarchy that supported them fell. New groups or migrating peoples introduced fresh deities or cult practices.

For instance, in Greece, the fall of Mycenaean palaces led to the so-called Greek Dark Age. Many older rites continued in diminished form, setting the stage for the classical Greek religion that emerged centuries later. In the Levant, new political entities reorganized local cults. In Mesopotamia, successor states preserved some older gods but reinterpreted them under new dynasties. Egypt saw internal strife, but temples remained strong, adapting to each new regime.

While some religious aspects survived or evolved, others faded. Writing systems might disappear (as in the Aegean), erasing records of older beliefs. Over time, new religious movements or philosophies emerged from these transitional eras, building upon Bronze Age foundations but introducing distinctive changes in doctrine or worship.

CHAPTER 13: WARFARE AND WEAPONS

Introduction

Warfare in the Bronze Age was shaped by new metallurgical advances, emerging states, and shifting power dynamics. Although societies valued trade, religion, and diplomacy, conflict remained a defining part of human life. Kings and chieftains fought to control resources, trade routes, farmland, and sometimes the prestige that came from victory. Bronze weapons—spears, swords, daggers, axes—gave those who possessed them a significant advantage. Armies ranged in size from small raiding parties to organized forces with chariots and well-trained infantry.

In this chapter, we will explore how Bronze Age societies waged war, what weapons and tactics they used, how they organized their armies, and how warfare influenced politics, trade, and technological progress. We will look at major civilizations such as Mesopotamia, Egypt, the Aegean polities, Anatolia (Hittites), China, and parts of Bronze Age Europe, noting similarities and differences in their military practices. By understanding their approaches to warfare, we can see another dimension of how the Bronze Age shaped the course of history.

---

1. The Rise of Organized Armies

During the Stone Age, conflicts typically involved small-scale raids. But with the advent of bronze, farming surpluses, and growing populations in the Bronze Age, warfare became more organized and consequential. City-states and early kingdoms could field larger forces, supplying them with bronze-tipped spears and axes. Stored grain sustained troops on campaigns, while centralized governments coordinated conscription or professional warriors. Over time, some states developed sophisticated command structures and fortifications, establishing permanent garrisons to guard key locations.

In Mesopotamia, city-states like Ur or Babylon raised armies that included spearmen, archers, and perhaps early chariot contingents. The pharaohs of Egypt assembled forces to protect the Nile Valley and to expand into Nubia or the Levant. The Mycenaeans of Greece relied on well-armed warrior elites, as shown in their richly furnished tombs containing bronze swords and daggers. The Hittites in Anatolia deployed chariots and infantry, challenging rival powers such as Mitanni, Egypt, or local polities.

Wherever central authority was strong, warfare became a state-sponsored endeavor rather than just clan-based feuding. This shift had major impacts on political structures, social hierarchy, and economic demands, prompting the specialized manufacture of weapons, armor, and fortifications.

2. Bronze Weapons: Spears, Axes, and Daggers

Spears were among the most common Bronze Age weapons—simple to produce yet effective in close combat or thrown from a distance. A bronze spearhead fitted onto a wooden shaft could pierce leather armor or cause severe wounds. Spear size and shape varied by region. Some had broad, leaf-shaped blades, while others were slimmer, optimized for throwing.

Axes evolved from tools into deadly battlefield implements. Early axes had flat or slightly raised edges, but as bronze casting improved, smiths developed **tanged** or **socketed axes** that were sturdier. Warriors could strike powerful blows, sometimes splitting enemy shields or helmets. Axes also symbolized power in many societies—kings or high-ranking chiefs might carry richly decorated versions during ceremonial processions.

Daggers and short swords were smaller sidearms. Daggers were ideal for close-in fighting or as a last resort. Over time, as casting techniques advanced, smiths made longer blades that bridged the gap between dagger and sword. These "proto-swords" appeared in areas like the Aegean and Central Europe. Eventually, full-fledged bronze swords emerged, giving skilled warriors a lethal edge in single combat. The shape and length of these swords varied, from short thrusting weapons to longer slashing blades.

3. The Emergence of Bronze Swords

The sword was a game-changing weapon in the Bronze Age. Unlike spears or axes, which had earlier origins as hunting or farming tools, swords were purpose-built for fighting humans. Early examples often started as elongated daggers but soon took on distinct shapes suited to stabbing or slashing. They demanded more bronze to produce, making them costly. As such, swords were often status symbols signifying a warrior's prestige.

In Minoan Crete and Mycenaean Greece, swords became increasingly refined by the 16th century BCE. Some had "tang" handles riveted to the blade, while others featured complex hilts cast in one piece. Decoration might include inlaid gold or silver depicting scenes of hunts or mythic creatures. Warriors proud of their swords carried them into battle with spear or shield, confident in this symbol of elite rank.

Central Europe's **Unetice** culture and later **Tumulus** and **Urnfield** groups also made bronze swords, sometimes with leaf-shaped blades. Despite regional variations, the principle was the same: a skilled swordsman, armed with strong bronze, could inflict serious damage in melee combat. However, swords required advanced metallurgical knowledge to avoid weak points or breakage. Over time, repeated improvements in casting and metal composition allowed for longer, more resilient blades.

---

4. Defensive Equipment: Shields and Armor

While offensive weapons advanced, so did defensive gear. Shields made of wood, sometimes covered with leather, provided basic protection. A bronze boss or rim might reinforce the shield's center or edges. Rectangular or figure-of-eight shields appeared in the Aegean, while round shields with a central grip were known in other regions. Because bronze was expensive, all-metal shields were rare, although small bronze fittings were common.

Armor likewise varied. Early protective garments might be thick layers of leather or padded cloth. Over time, elites in some cultures wore bronze scale armor or plate pieces. The **Dendra panoply** from Mycenaean Greece (circa 15th century BCE) is a famous example of a full bronze cuirass, covering the torso with overlapping plates. Though highly protective, it was also heavy and somewhat restricting.

Helmets protected the head—a critical target in battle. Bronze helmets had shapes like conical caps or more elaborate designs with cheek guards. Some were made from hammered sheets, others from riveted plates. Feathers or horsehair crests could adorn the top, signifying rank or adding intimidation. Not everyone in a Bronze Age army could afford or obtain full protective gear, so heavily armored warriors were likely the noble or professional fighters, forming an elite corps on the battlefield.

---

5. The Chariot Revolution

One of the iconic images of Bronze Age warfare is the chariot. Pulled by horses (or sometimes onagers in early periods), chariots gave armies speed and shock value. Scholars debate whether chariots functioned primarily as mobile archery platforms, command vehicles, or frontal assault weapons. Different cultures used them in various ways:

- **Mesopotamia**: Early chariots might have been heavy, with solid wooden wheels. Over time, they evolved into lighter, two-wheeled versions for quick maneuvers.
- **Egypt**: The Egyptians refined chariots during the New Kingdom. They built them from lightweight wood, with spoked wheels and sturdy axles. Chariot crews typically had a driver and an archer, raining arrows on foot soldiers.
- **Hittites**: The Hittite chariot often carried three men—one to drive, one to fight with spear or bow, and another possibly for shield defense. This design gave them formidable presence, especially in open terrain.
- **China**: The Shang Dynasty introduced chariots later in the second millennium BCE, using them for prestige and battlefield advantage, though terrain constraints shaped their deployment.

Chariots needed skilled drivers, well-trained horses, and well-maintained roads or flat battlefields. They excelled on plains but struggled in mountainous or forested areas. Chariot warfare demanded coordination between charioteers and infantry. While only a fraction of an army might be chariot-borne, these vehicles became symbols of royal or noble status, featuring elaborate decorations. Battles like **Kadesh** (circa 1274 BCE) highlight how thousands of chariots on both Egyptian and Hittite sides could shape a major confrontation.

---

6. Infantry Tactics and Formations

Despite the glamour of chariots, the bulk of most Bronze Age armies consisted of infantry. Farmers, conscripts, or semi-professional warriors stood in lines or blocks, armed with spears, shields, and possibly bows. Commanders attempted to coordinate group movements, though exact details of Bronze Age battlefield tactics remain somewhat murky.

In Mesopotamia, steles and reliefs show ranks of spear-carrying soldiers behind large rectangular shields. Some city-states employed archers en masse, softening enemy lines before a charge. Egyptian reliefs depict armies marching in organized formations, each company led by a standard-bearer. The Hittites integrated infantry with chariot contingents, using foot soldiers to secure terrain or follow up after chariot assaults.

Logistics played a big role: feeding and supplying an army in the field required planning. Strong states, like the New Kingdom of Egypt, had administrative systems to mobilize and distribute rations, while smaller polities might rely on swift campaigns or looting to sustain forces. The discipline of a well-trained infantry could turn battles, but that discipline took time and resources to build. Many Bronze Age armies thus contained a mix of well-equipped elites and less-equipped masses, with variable morale and training.

---

7. The Importance of Fortifications

Defense was as crucial as offense, leading to the construction of fortified walls, gates, and citadels. In Mesopotamia, cities ringed themselves with mudbrick walls, sometimes adding towers or moats. The city gates might be heavily guarded, forcing attackers into choke points. Egypt's geography provided a natural defensive barrier in deserts and cataracts along the Nile, but on the eastern frontier, fortresses guarded key routes like the Sinai.

On Crete and mainland Greece, palace complexes or hilltop citadels had massive stone walls, for instance the so-called **Cyclopean walls** of Mycenae and Tiryns. Anatolia's Hittite capital, Hattusa, featured extensive fortifications with multiple gates, each adorned with reliefs of lions or sphinxes to intimidate invaders. In China, walled cities became common under the Shang Dynasty, giving elites a secure base from which to rule.

Siege warfare in the Bronze Age involved scaling ladders, battering rams, or attempts to breach gates. Prolonged sieges required cutting off water supplies or using sappers to undermine walls. However, advanced siege engines (like large catapults) were more typical of later eras. Still, controlling a strong fortress could deter invasion, forcing enemies to rely on starvation tactics or negotiation.

---

8. Naval Warfare

Although many Bronze Age societies engaged in maritime trade, large-scale naval battles were less common than land conflicts. Ships primarily served transport or raiding purposes. In the Aegean, Mycenaeans and Minoans patrolled sea lanes with swift vessels, sometimes clashing with pirates or rival states. The Egyptians had fleets on the Nile for troop movement and sometimes battled seaborne raiders at river mouths or along coasts.

Seafaring peoples like the possible ancestors of the Phoenicians might have used ships for coastal raids, though detailed accounts of Bronze Age naval engagements are scarce. The famous "Sea Peoples" who troubled the Eastern Mediterranean in the Late Bronze Age included maritime raiders from unknown origins, forcing states like Egypt to defend their shores vigorously. Some Egyptian reliefs show naval skirmishes, with archers shooting from ship decks.

Naval technology was still developing: hulls were mostly planked with wooden dowels or lashings, lacking the advanced mortise-and-tenon joints of later times. Bronze tools helped build stronger ships, but open-ocean voyages were risky. Crews used sails and oars, navigating by the sun, stars, and coastal landmarks. Where possible, seaborne invasions targeted lightly defended beaches or port towns. While not the primary dimension of warfare, control of maritime routes could yield strategic advantages in trade and resource access.

---

9. Strategy and Leadership

Leadership made a significant difference in Bronze Age warfare. Rulers who possessed charisma, strategic insight, and the ability to inspire loyalty could turn average armies into formidable forces. Written evidence such as the Amarna Letters or Hittite treaties reveals how kings negotiated alliances, threatened rivals, or mustered vassal troops. Egyptian Pharaohs, from Thutmose III to Ramesses II, claimed personal prowess in battle, leading chariots and boasting of victories on temple walls.

In Mesopotamia, some city-state rulers combined religious authority with military command. They performed rituals before campaigns, seeking divine guidance. The Hittite kings similarly invoked Storm Gods to bless their armies. The Mycenaean wanax (king) and lawagetas (possibly a war leader) coordinated palace resources to field well-equipped troops. In China's Shang Dynasty, the king was the chief diviner and war leader, forging campaigns against rebellious neighbors or nomadic threats.

Armies sometimes had specialized corps for archery, chariotry, or siege operations. Skilled officers might gain wealth and land from successful campaigns, reinforcing loyalty. Communication, however, was challenging—no quick ways to relay orders across miles of battlefield. Drums, horns, or standard-bearers helped direct troops. Meanwhile, logistic planning determined success: a well-led army with stable supply lines could outlast a larger but disorganized opponent.

10. Sieges and Conquests

Conquering fortified cities took a heavy toll, yet the rewards—access to trade routes, tribute from captured peoples, and political prestige—were great. The extended siege of a major city could last months, with attackers building camps and using sappers or battering rams. Defenders attempted to repair walls, sally out, or hold until relief forces arrived. Starvation was a frequent tactic—cutting off supplies and waiting for the defenders to exhaust food stores.

If a city fell, the victor might loot temples and granaries, carry off prisoners for slaves, or even raze the settlement as a warning. At times, the conquering king installed local vassals or governors, exacting tribute. Examples include the Hittite subjugation of northern Syrian cities or the Egyptian domination of certain Levantine towns. The Mycenaeans also sacked rival strongholds in the Aegean, exemplified by legendary conflicts like the Trojan War (whose exact historical basis is still debated).

Such conquests shaped political landscapes, forging early empires or hegemonic states. The victors not only gained resources but also integrated new cultural elements, sometimes adopting local gods or art styles. War, despite its destruction, thus served as a vector for cultural exchange, albeit through violence and coercion.

---

11. Raiders, Pirates, and Nomadic Threats

Not all warfare in the Bronze Age revolved around grand city conquests. Smaller-scale raiding was common, especially in border zones or along trade routes. Nomadic or semi-nomadic groups might harass settled areas, stealing cattle or goods. Pirates lurked on coastal waters, targeting merchant ships. Polities with strong navies or well-guarded caravans attempted to deter these attacks, but the wide expanses of sea and land made total security impossible.

In the steppes north of the Black Sea or in Central Asia, horse-riding tribes occasionally ventured south, trading or raiding. Their mobility and familiarity with horses could outmatch slower foot armies. These intermittent incursions disrupted stable states, forcing them to maintain frontier garrisons or negotiate tribute. Over time, some nomads might assimilate or become mercenaries in settled states. Others, more aggressive, contributed to the downfall of weakened empires during the Late Bronze Age collapses.

---

12. Rituals of War: Oaths and Sacrifices

Religion and warfare intersected in many ways. Before campaigns, leaders performed sacrifices to secure divine favor. Armies carried images of gods or protective symbols into battle. In Mesopotamia, the king might consult omens or oracles to pick an auspicious day for an attack. The Hittites had detailed instructions for war rituals, offering bread and beer to a pantheon that included the Storm God. Egyptians believed the pharaoh's success reflected the cosmic order upheld by Ma'at; thus, a victorious pharaoh was said to be chosen by the gods.

After victory, conquerors often dedicated captured arms or treasures to temples, attributing success to their deities. Prisoners of war might be sacrificed or enslaved, depending on local customs. Scenes on Egyptian temple walls show bound captives offered to Amun, while the Shang in China sometimes buried war captives around royal tombs. These acts displayed the victor's power and gratitude to the gods, reinforcing the notion that warfare was a sacred duty, not just a political tool.

13. Weapon Production and Craftsmen

Manufacturing bronze weapons required skilled artisans and a steady supply of metals. City-states or palaces might employ full-time smiths who specialized in forging spearheads, sword blades, or arrowheads. A smith's workshop contained clay or stone molds, furnaces for smelting copper and tin, and tools for hammering and polishing. Elite warriors often demanded personalized weapons with inscriptions or decorative inlays.

Metalworkers formed a respected profession, though they depended on a broader supply chain: miners, charcoal makers, transporters. In times of war, these supply lines became even more critical. If a city controlled major copper or tin mines, it enjoyed a strategic advantage. Conversely, a city lacking metals had to import them, leaving it vulnerable to blockades or market fluctuations. Over time, arms production became a core aspect of many Bronze Age economies, fueling both conflict and craftsmanship advances.

14. Gender Roles in Warfare

Men dominated most Bronze Age battles. Typically, armies and weapon production revolved around male warriors. However, some evidence suggests women might have occasionally fought or held martial roles. Myths and legends from various regions mention warrior goddesses (Ishtar in Mesopotamia, Anat in the Levant, possibly the Snake Goddess in Crete), symbolizing female power in combat. Egyptian queens like Ahhotep are depicted with ceremonial weapons, implying leadership in crises.

Still, the majority of references show men as front-line fighters, while women supported war efforts indirectly—managing farms, weaving textiles, or even forging arrow fletchings at home. Some elite women, especially in steppe cultures, may have known how to ride and use bows. Yet large-scale involvement of women in Bronze Age battles is not strongly attested in the archaeological or written record. The main role of warfare, from planning to fighting, belonged to men of the ruling or warrior classes.

---

15. The Psychological Aspect of War

Warfare in the Bronze Age, like any era, involved fear, morale, and psychological tactics. Armies might display captured heads or banners to intimidate foes. Mythic symbols on shields or chariots also heightened fear— for instance, large lion or bull motifs. The Hittites placed lion statues at city gates, projecting a powerful image. Egyptian reliefs depicting pharaohs smiting enemies reaffirmed their unstoppable might.

Rumors or omens could sway battles if one side believed the gods had abandoned them. A charismatic king who overcame adversity with perceived divine support boosted troop morale. Conversely, heavy losses or a string of defeats eroded confidence, triggering desertions or surrenders. Some leaders practiced limited mercy to lure opponents to surrender, while others used harsh punishments to deter rebellion. The fine balance between terror and clemency shaped how conquered peoples responded—resistance or integration.

---

16. Economy of War

Warfare was expensive. Bronze weapons and chariots cost substantial resources. Fielding large armies meant feeding and paying soldiers, forging gear, and maintaining supply lines. To finance campaigns, rulers levied taxes on peasants, demanded tribute from vassals, or seized loot from conquered territories. Temples might also contribute wealth or back certain military expansions if they gained from new territories.

In prosperous times, successful wars brought spoils—precious metals, slaves, or trade-route control—justifying the costs. Some states grew powerful by subjugating neighbors, building empires that spanned multiple regions (e.g., the Akkadian Empire, or later the Hittite Empire at its height). In lean times, however, prolonged war could bankrupt a kingdom or provoke internal revolts.

Overextension or reliance on mercenaries might strain finances. The cyclical nature of Bronze Age expansion and collapse often followed patterns where war fueled short-term gains but risked long-term instability.

17. Famous Battles and Campaigns

While many Bronze Age conflicts went unrecorded, some famous examples survive in fragments:

- **The Battle of Kadesh (circa 1274 BCE)**: Fought between Pharaoh Ramesses II of Egypt and King Muwatalli II of the Hittites near the Orontes River. Thousands of chariots engaged, with both sides claiming victory. A subsequent peace treaty is one of the earliest known.
- **Shang Campaigns (roughly 1600–1046 BCE)**: Shang kings in China launched repeated expeditions against rebellious states or nomads. Oracle bone inscriptions record appeals to ancestors for success.
- **Sargon of Akkad's Conquests (circa 24th century BCE)**: Regarded as one of the first empire-builders in Mesopotamia, Sargon defeated various city-states, establishing a realm that stretched from the Persian Gulf to the Mediterranean.
- **Mycenaean Raids and the Trojan War**: Though partly mythologized in later Greek epics, the Mycenaeans likely conducted seaborne raids against Anatolian coastal towns, culminating in a possible historical kernel behind the Trojan War legend.

These campaigns highlight how Bronze Age warfare could involve vast alliances, advanced tactics, and strategic maneuvers. They also reveal how states used propaganda—steles, temples, epic poems—to immortalize their triumphs or rationalize defeats.

18. The Transition to the Iron Age

By the later second millennium BCE, disruptions in trade and political systems (often termed the "Bronze Age Collapse") destabilized many regions. Tin supplies became unreliable, making bronze more expensive. Iron technology gradually emerged as a viable alternative. While smelting iron was initially tricky, once mastered, iron tools and weapons offered certain advantages—stronger edges, more abundant raw material.

The shift from bronze to iron did not occur overnight. Some areas continued using bronze for centuries, especially for ceremonial or decorative objects. But in warfare, iron swords and spears increasingly outperformed bronze rivals. The cost of equipping large armies dropped as iron ore was more widespread than copper-tin deposits. Thus, warfare in the Iron Age became more democratized, with bigger infantry forces overshadowing the elite chariot corps.

For the Bronze Age states that survived into this transitional era (like Assyria or Egypt), adopting iron tools was a strategic necessity. Others who could not adapt or who lost crucial resources vanished from history. Still, the legacy of Bronze Age warfare—its weapons, chariot traditions, and fortification techniques—continued to shape conflict in the centuries to come.

---

19. Cultural Impact of Warfare

Warfare left an indelible mark on Bronze Age cultures. Art and literature glorified heroes, kings, or gods who led armies to victory. Mythic cycles included war gods or champion warriors, reflecting communal respect for martial prowess. At the same time, repeated conflicts prompted technological leaps in metalwork, horse breeding, and logistics.

Cities evolved around citadels, storing weapons and organizing living spaces to accommodate soldiers or protect artisans. Writing systems might expand partly due to administrative needs—recording troop numbers, supply rosters, or treaties. The heroic ethos in some societies (like Mycenaean Greece) set a template for later epic traditions. Meanwhile, cultural identities formed around legendary battles, forging unity among diverse subjects under a victorious king.

Yet warfare also entailed destruction—burned cities, displaced peoples, enslavement. The cost in human life was high, though exact numbers are unknown. Some survivors migrated, carrying knowledge or crafts to new lands. Over time, these forced movements reshaped populations and introduced new cultural blends.

CHAPTER 14: DAILY LIFE IN BRONZE AGE SOCIETIES

Introduction

When we think of the Bronze Age, we often picture grand palaces, towering ziggurats, or heroic battles. Yet most people of that era were neither kings nor warriors. They were farmers tending crops, potters shaping clay, merchants haggling in bustling markets, or fisherfolk casting nets into rivers and seas. Understanding how they lived—how they ate, dressed, formed families, and practiced crafts—brings the Bronze Age to life on a human scale.

In this chapter, we will explore the daily life of Bronze Age communities across regions like Mesopotamia, Egypt, the Indus Valley, the Aegean, Anatolia, China, and parts of Europe. We will look at their homes, diets, social structures, gender roles, health, leisure activities, and the rhythms that defined ordinary existence. By focusing on these everyday details, we gain a more holistic view of a world shaped not just by monumental achievements but by the steady labor and creativity of countless individuals.

---

1. Settlement Patterns: Villages, Towns, and Cities

Most people in the Bronze Age lived in small villages, scattered around fertile lands or resource-rich areas. Farmers found soils near rivers like the Nile, Indus, Tigris-Euphrates, or Yellow River to be ideal. Over time, surpluses allowed some settlements to grow into towns or cities, with markets, administrative buildings, and possibly temples. The largest urban centers—like Babylon in Mesopotamia, Thebes in Egypt, Mohenjo-daro in the Indus Valley, Knossos on Crete, or Anyang in Shang China—could house tens of thousands of residents.

Urban planning varied. The Indus civilization had well-organized grids and drainage systems, while Mesopotamian cities expanded more organically, with winding streets and dense neighborhoods. In Minoan Crete, palace complexes formed the social and economic core. Hillforts in Bronze Age Europe might gather dwellings around a central fortress or citadel. Some regions saw homes built close together for mutual protection, while others spread out, each farmstead ringed by fields.

In these settlements, people of different professions clustered—potters near kilns, smiths in dedicated workshops, merchants near gates or harbors. Temples or administrative centers provided a focal point for trade and tribute collection. Despite local variations, a sense of community often revolved around shared rituals, markets, or civic gatherings.

2. Types of Houses and Building Materials

The style and materials of houses reflected local resources. In Mesopotamia, mudbrick was common, as timber was scarce and clay plentiful. Thick-walled homes offered insulation against scorching heat. Roofs might be flat, providing space to sleep on hot nights or to dry produce. Egypt also relied heavily on sun-dried mudbrick. Wealthier families might incorporate wooden pillars or stone door frames, though stone was typically reserved for temples and tombs.

In the Indus Valley, baked bricks were standard, especially in major cities. Houses often had multiple rooms, sometimes with an interior courtyard, wells, and rudimentary bathing areas. Aegean settlements—like Minoan towns—favored stone foundations with mudbrick or wooden upper floors. Some houses featured painted walls and even partial plumbing for drainage. The Mycenaeans built stone-walled homes, with plastered floors and thatched or tiled roofs.

In China's Shang period, rammed-earth walls were common, forming sturdy enclosures. Wooden posts and thatched roofs were typical for ordinary homes. Meanwhile, parts of Europe used wattle-and-daub (woven wooden strips daubed with clay) or timber-laced walls. Roofs might be thatch or wooden shingles, depending on local forests. Interiors were generally simple—a hearth for cooking, a few raised platforms for sleeping, and storage containers for grain. Furniture was minimal, often woven mats, wooden benches, or chests.

3. Family Life and Household Organization

Family structures in the Bronze Age varied by region but often revolved around extended kin. A household might include parents, children, grandparents, and sometimes unmarried uncles or aunts. In polygynous societies, a wealthy man could have multiple wives if it was culturally accepted, although that was not universal. Women typically managed domestic chores, cooking, and childcare, while men handled field labor or crafts. However, tasks could overlap, especially in small farms where everyone contributed.

Patriarchal norms prevailed in most Bronze Age cultures—fathers or eldest males held significant authority over household decisions. Daughters often married young and moved to their husbands' homes, forging alliances between families. Sons might inherit land or trades, continuing the family line. In some societies, women retained certain rights—Egyptian women, for example, could own property and initiate legal actions. In Mesopotamia, law codes recognized specific inheritance rights or obligations regarding marriage contracts.

Children learned responsibilities early. Boys might help in fields or workshops, while girls assisted with domestic tasks. Formal education was rare outside elites, except in cultures like Mesopotamia or Egypt, where scribal schools existed for those entering temple or palace service. Still, many children gained vocational skills from parents or local mentors. Marriage ceremonies varied widely, but often included gift exchanges, feasts, or religious blessings.

4. Farming and Food Supply

Agriculture remained the backbone of Bronze Age economies. Farmers cultivated cereals like wheat and barley in Mesopotamia, Egypt, and the Indus Valley. Rice became important in southern China, while millet dominated the north. In Europe, wheat and barley also prevailed, supplemented by rye or oats in certain regions. People planted legumes—lentils, peas, or beans—to enrich diets. Vegetables (onions, garlic, cucumbers) and fruits (dates, figs, grapes, melons) added variety. Olives and vines thrived around the Mediterranean.

Plow technology progressed with bronze-tipped shares, making it easier to break heavier soils. Irrigation systems, like canals in Mesopotamia or the Nile's annual flood channels, boosted yields. The Indus Valley's sophisticated water management and China's dike-building shaped farmland. In mountainous areas, terracing allowed hillside farming. Livestock—cattle, sheep, goats, pigs—provided meat, milk, wool, and manure. Horses gained importance for transport or chariot warfare but were less common as food sources.

Food security remained an ever-present concern. A single bad harvest could lead to famine. Communities stored surplus grain in granaries for lean years, though such reserves were sometimes siphoned by elites or lost in wars. Droughts or floods could devastate entire regions, forcing migrations or reliance on outside trade. Despite these risks, the agricultural cycle governed daily routines—plowing in early seasons, sowing seeds, tending crops, harvesting, and preparing for the next cycle.

---

5. Diet and Cooking

Diet varied by region and social class. In Mesopotamia, bread made from barley or emmer wheat was a staple, accompanied by beer, onions, and dates. Wealthy families ate more meat—mutton, beef, poultry—often boiled or roasted. Fish supplemented diets along rivers or coasts. Egyptians also loved bread and beer, with vegetables like lentils, chickpeas, lettuce, and sometimes fruit or sweeteners from honey or dates. The wealthy might enjoy more cattle or geese. Indus Valley diets included wheat, barley, peas, sesame, and perhaps fish or dairy from zebu cattle.

Around the Aegean, cereals, olives, and wine formed the trifecta, supplemented by sheep, goats, and seafood. Minoans and Mycenaeans used olive oil in cooking and preserved fruits in wine or honey. Meat was often associated with festivals or sacrifices, so day-to-day meals might rely more on grains and vegetables. In China, millet or early rice formed the staple, with possible additions of pork, poultry, and seasonal greens. Bronze vessels (ding, gui) used in feasts or sacrifices reflect shared communal meals. Europeans ate cereals like wheat and barley, along with dairy products, local fruits, and wild game.

Cooking methods included boiling in clay pots or cauldrons, grilling over open fires, and baking in simple ovens. Clay ovens or hearths were central to the house. Spices and herbs were known but less globally varied than later eras. Salt was precious; salt mines or brine evaporation sites fueled trade. Feasting was a communal event in many cultures, reinforcing social ties and distributing sacrificial meat.

6. Clothing and Textiles

Clothing reflected climate, available materials, and social status. In warmer regions like Egypt or Mesopotamia, linen was common, woven from flax. Simple kilts or wraparound skirts for men, and dresses or robes for women, kept people cool. The wealthy wore finer weaves, dyed or embroidered with patterns. In cooler areas—like parts of Europe or northern China—wool was the main textile, spun from sheep or goats. Cloaks, tunics, and leggings helped retain warmth.

The Indus Valley is famous for early cotton cultivation, which might have supplied comfortable fabrics for daily use. Dyes came from natural sources—madder for red, indigo for blue, saffron for yellow—though bright colors were rarer for ordinary folk. Silk was developing in China, but it was a luxury item often reserved for royalty or high nobility. Some textiles integrated decorative motifs or tassels. Looms ranged from simple upright frames to more complex weighted versions. Women typically handled spinning and weaving, passing skills down through generations.

Elites showed off status with jewelry—necklaces of gold, silver, or semi-precious stones; armlets or rings with intricate designs. In Mesopotamia, cylinder seals served both as personal identification and adornment. Minoans used gold hairpins or signet rings, while Mycenaean tombs yield diadems and beadwork. Even in humble households, a few beads or a small bronze pin might serve as cherished ornaments or fasteners for garments.

---

7. Occupations and Specializations

Beyond farming, Bronze Age societies relied on numerous craftspeople, traders, and professionals. Potters shaped clay into jars, bowls, and oil lamps. Smiths and metalworkers forged tools, weapons, and decorative items from bronze, occasionally gold or silver. Carpenters built wooden carts, furniture, and boats. Weavers spun and dyed cloth. Masons cut stone blocks for temples or city walls. Scribes maintained records, wrote letters, and oversaw trade agreements in literate cultures like Mesopotamia, Egypt, or among the Hittites.

Markets or bazaars within towns allowed merchants and artisans to display goods. Farmers might exchange surplus crops for pottery or metal tools. Trade specialists traveled to other cities or regions, bartering textiles, metals, or agricultural produce. Skilled craftsmen or scribes often enjoyed higher status, living near palaces or temple complexes. Apprenticeship systems ensured knowledge transfer: a young person might work under a master for years to learn the trade's secrets.

In larger states, administrative roles multiplied—officials collected taxes, managed storehouses, or supervised labor gangs for public works. Temple staffs included priests, scribes, musicians, bakers, and craftsmen producing ceremonial objects. Some individuals became long-distance traders or caravan leaders, forging cross-regional connections that enriched city coffers.

---

8. Gender Roles and Daily Tasks

While societies were patriarchal, women played essential roles in sustaining household economies. They fetched water, prepared food, spun and wove textiles, tended gardens, and cared for children. In agrarian families, women might also help in fields during planting or harvesting. Noblewomen in palatial centers might oversee female servants or manage estate accounts, especially if they were literate. Certain priestesses, like the en-priestesses in Mesopotamia or the "God's Wife of Amun" in Egypt, commanded wealth and influence.

Nonetheless, legal codes typically favored men in inheritance or divorce. Women's testimonies in courts might carry less weight. Arranged marriages were common, with dowries or bride-prices negotiated. Despite constraints, some women in merchant families engaged in trade or property transactions, especially if widowed. Societal norms varied—Egyptian women seemed to hold more legal independence than their counterparts in some Mesopotamian cities, for instance.

Children, regardless of gender, were expected to contribute to household tasks once old enough. Sons might accompany fathers to markets or workshops, learning the craft. Daughters aided mothers in weaving or cooking. Formal schooling (if available) was more accessible for boys of elite status, shaping their future roles as scribes or officials.

9. Health and Medicine

Living conditions in Bronze Age towns could be crowded, leading to issues with sanitation. Although some places, like the Indus cities, had drainage systems, waste management was still rudimentary. Contaminated water caused diseases. Life expectancy was lower than modern times, with high infant mortality rates. Nonetheless, communities developed basic medical knowledge. Healers used herbal remedies or performed simple surgeries—setting bones or lancing abscesses.

Egyptian papyri document treatments for wounds, eyes, or intestinal issues. Mesopotamian cuneiform tablets mention incantations blended with healing techniques. In China, early forms of herbal medicine might have existed. People recognized the importance of cleanliness—bathing or washing, especially in culturally advanced regions like the Indus or Minoan Crete. Still, epidemics or malnutrition could devastate populations if harvests failed or trade routes were cut off.

Religious practices often intertwined with healing. Temples functioned as centers of care where priests performed rituals to appease gods of health or used incantations to ward off evil spirits causing illness. Amulets might be worn to protect from disease. In the face of widespread ailments, families relied on home remedies, passing knowledge through generations. More severe cases might require specialized healers or temple-based interventions.

---

10. Leisure and Entertainment

In between labor and ritual obligations, Bronze Age people found ways to relax. Music played a prominent role—harps, lyres, flutes, drums, and rattles accompanied festivities. Dancing occurred at harvest festivals, religious ceremonies, or private gatherings. Board games and dice have been uncovered at various sites, indicating a fondness for strategy or gambling. The "Royal Game of Ur" from Mesopotamia stands as an early example of a structured board game.

Storytelling and oral recitation of myths or epics entertained families or communities on long evenings. Skilled bards or minstrels might travel, sharing tales of gods, heroes, or faraway lands. Public events like bull-leaping displays in

Minoan Crete or chariot races in some city-states offered spectacle. Feasts, often tied to religious or political celebrations, let people enjoy music, dance, and feasting together.

Children had simple toys—clay figurines, rattles, or miniature carts. They might gather for games of throwing pebbles or chasing each other through narrow alleys. In more complex societies, the elite indulged in hunting, with specialized hounds or trained huntsmen. Social drinking also existed—beer in Mesopotamia and Egypt, wine around the Mediterranean, fermented millets or rice in parts of Asia—fostering communal ties but sometimes leading to drunken brawls, as recorded in a few cautionary texts.

11. Religion in Everyday Life

Although Chapter 12 examined Bronze Age religion at length, it's worth emphasizing how deeply it permeated daily routines. Families placed small altars in their homes, offering bread, beer, or incense to household gods or ancestors each morning. Farmers prayed for good weather, fishermen invoked river or sea deities, and artisans sometimes dedicated a portion of their day's work to protective spirits. Seasonal festivals gave peasants a break from field labor to join in communal ceremonies—dancing, singing, and feasting.

Markets and streets might hold small shrines where travelers could make quick devotions. Oaths before deities sealed business contracts or political agreements. Divination was consulted for major decisions—marriage dates, planting times, journeys. Temple staff might walk city streets collecting alms or leftover grain from markets. Religion thus gave structure to time, with certain days set aside for worship, taboo tasks, or purification rituals.

12. Urban Markets and Long-Distance Trade

Everyday life also included trade interactions. Local markets sold fresh produce, fish, pottery, and textiles. Farmers brought surplus grains or fruits to barter for tools. Artisans displayed wares like metal knives, leather sandals, or dyed cloth. In major cities, caravans arrived with exotic goods—spices, incense, tin ingots, or precious stones. Ships docked at riverside or coastal ports, unloading cargo for sale.

Prices fluctuated with supply and demand. In literate cultures, scribes might record transactions on clay tablets or papyrus. Some regions used silver or weighed metals as a rudimentary currency measure; others relied on barter. Haggling was common. The atmosphere of these markets was lively—street performers, the smell of cooking food, the clamor of animals, and the chatter of travelers from distant lands.

For rural folk, heading to town for market day could be a highlight of the week or month, a chance to socialize, hear news, and glimpse foreign products. Meanwhile, wealthy elites might employ servants to handle shopping, or they attended specialized markets for luxury goods. This system fostered economic interdependence between countryside and urban centers, weaving a complex social fabric.

13. Social Hierarchies and Class Divisions

Every Bronze Age society developed social tiers. At the top sat rulers—pharaohs in Egypt, kings in Mesopotamia, or dynastic leaders in China—often claiming divine support. Below them were nobility or aristocrats who held land, commanded armies, or controlled bureaucracies. Priests enjoyed high status due to their religious roles. Scribes or merchants formed a literate middle stratum, crucial for administration and trade.

Artisans—metalworkers, potters, carpenters—ranked as skilled specialists, generally respected but still below the elite. Farmers formed the bulk of the population, taxed to support temples, palaces, or armies. At the bottom were slaves or indentured servants, sometimes war captives or debtors forced into labor. Slavery practices varied: in some places slaves could own property or buy freedom; in others, they faced harsher conditions.

These divisions shaped daily life. Elites lived in larger homes with multiple rooms, courtyards, and decorations. They wore finer clothes and ate more varied diets. They could afford advanced healthcare or amulets for protection. Commoners resided in simpler dwellings, worked longer hours, and had fewer luxuries. Social mobility was limited but not impossible—outstanding artisans or scribes might rise in favor with the palace. Still, birth status generally dictated one's opportunities.

14. Crime, Law, and Policing

Maintaining order in Bronze Age communities required some form of policing or legal system. Rulers issued edicts, while local officials or elders adjudicated disputes over land, trade, or family matters. In Mesopotamia, famous law codes (like Hammurabi's) outlined punishments for theft, assault, or malpractice. Egyptian records note local councils (kenbet) that heard cases, while temple authorities also intervened in moral disputes.

Punishments ranged from fines or restitution to corporal penalties. Execution or enslavement might be inflicted for severe crimes, though details varied by region. Laws often reflected social status—harm done to a noble might incur stiffer penalties than harm done to a commoner. Women's rights to property or divorce also appeared, though typically with restrictions. Policing was rudimentary: local watchmen or palace guards might quell disturbances. Large cities might have specialized squads that monitored markets or city gates.

Justice was sometimes entwined with religious concepts—swearing oaths before gods or oracles. Inconsistencies in evidence might be settled by trial by ordeal (plunging hands in hot water, for example) and seeing if the gods saved the innocent. Though far from modern legal frameworks, these systems helped regulate disputes, enabling social cohesion amid growing populations.

---

15. Childhood, Education, and Rites of Passage

Childhood experiences depended on social rank. Peasant children helped in fields from an early age, learning practical skills. Elite children had more leisure and could access formal instruction—scribal schools in Mesopotamia or temple schools in Egypt, focusing on reading, writing, arithmetic, and sometimes religious texts. The Indus script remains undeciphered, so it's uncertain how they taught literacy. In the Aegean or Europe, literacy was limited to palace scribes or a tiny fraction of the population.

Rites of passage marked the transition to adulthood. Puberty ceremonies might introduce youths into communal responsibilities. Boys in some warrior societies underwent training in weapons or survival. Girls prepared for marriage, acquiring domestic skills. Freed slaves or apprentices might hold a small ceremony to celebrate new status. Marriages themselves were pivotal milestones, forging alliances between families and reorienting the individual's social identity.

In times of turmoil—war, famine—children faced heightened risks of malnutrition or displacement. Extended families or village communities helped where possible. Infancy and childhood diseases claimed many lives, so each child surviving to adulthood was precious. This reality shaped fertility practices—families often had multiple children to ensure continuity, especially in an era lacking modern medicine.

---

16. The Role of Festivals and Community Gatherings

Communal gatherings energized social life. Seasonal festivals aligned with planting or harvest times. People wearing best clothes, merchants with special wares, and traveling entertainers converged on temple courtyards or city plazas. Feasts might include music, dancing, and distribution of sacrificial meat. Rulers could display generosity, giving away food or small gifts to curry favor. Religious processions showcased cult statues, reinforcing the link between divine powers and community welfare.

In the Indus Valley, large open courtyards in cities might have hosted communal events. Aegean cultures depicted processions in frescoes, sometimes carrying vessels or leading animals for sacrifice. Mesopotamian Akitu festivals celebrated the new year, with rituals ensuring cosmic renewal. In Egypt, festivals like Opet involved carrying the statue of Amun along the Nile, with public banquets and cheers.

Such festivities offered respite from daily toil, renewing communal bonds and shared identity. They also served political ends—rulers or priests used them to legitimize authority, resolve grievances, or gather tribute. People exchanged gossip, found marriage partners, or formed trade contacts. The joy of feasts offset the drudgery of agrarian routines, reminding everyone of the cultural and religious ties holding their societies together.

---

17. Travel and Communication

Bronze Age travel was slow and risky. Roads varied from dirt tracks to partially paved routes near major cities. Donkeys, mules, or oxen pulled carts laden with goods. Wealthy travelers rode in simple chariots or on horseback (in regions that had domesticated horses extensively). Overland journeys might be broken up by caravansaries or walled towns offering lodging and supplies. Merchants formed caravans for safety against bandits.

Rivers were crucial arteries—Egypt depended on the Nile for moving goods, Mesopotamia had the Tigris and Euphrates, the Indus peoples had their eponymous river, and China had the Yellow River system. Boats carried bulk cargo, linking internal settlements with coastal ports. Communication beyond local areas was limited to messengers or scribes carrying tablets, papyrus, or oral messages. Diplomatic letters might travel weeks before reaching a foreign court.

For many, life was spent within a day's journey of home. Only traders, soldiers, or officials traveled far regularly. This lent local cultures distinct flavors. Yet trade routes also brought strangers with new ideas, goods, or languages, gradually weaving diverse regions into a broader Bronze Age tapestry.

---

18. Crafts and Artistic Expression

Art and craft were omnipresent in daily life. Pottery decorated with geometric or natural motifs stored and served food. Jewelry makers shaped beads, pendants, and rings, often reflecting cultural symbols—spirals in Europe, lotus flowers in Egypt, mythical creatures in the Aegean, or taotie masks in Shang China. Textiles included dyed fabrics with patterns or embroidery, though few survive.

Public art, like frescoes or relief carvings, might decorate palace walls, temple gateways, or city gates. Scenes depicted hunts, religious rituals, processions, or mythological episodes. Some artisans specialized in figurines—small clay or bronze statues of gods or animals placed in homes or shrines. Items of daily use (combs, cosmetic boxes, weaving tools) might feature decorative touches, bridging function and beauty.

Guild-like structures sometimes existed, with master artisans training apprentices. In literate societies, scribes had pride in neat cuneiform or hieroglyphic inscriptions, turning writing into a visual craft. Glassmaking was still experimental, more advanced in some regions (like the Levant) for producing beads or small vessels. All these crafts not only fulfilled practical needs but also enriched cultural identity, signifying local style and status.

19. Coping with Hardships and Disasters

Life in the Bronze Age was not all feasts and creative pursuits. Natural calamities—drought, floods, earthquakes—regularly struck. Villages might be destroyed, forcing communities to rebuild or migrate. In the Aegean, volcanic eruptions like Thera's were catastrophic, altering trade routes and local economies. Disease outbreaks spread quickly in cramped city quarters. Warfare or raids could uproot entire populations, leading to enslavement or displacement.

Communities developed resilience strategies: storing grain for famine, building mudbrick levees against floods, forging alliances to deter invaders. Religious rites sought divine intervention or appeasement of angry gods. Families banded together, sharing resources or adopting orphans when disasters hit. Over centuries, repeated challenges shaped cultural emphasis on communal solidarity and spiritual explanations for misfortune. Yet these hardships also spurred innovation—improvements in irrigation, fortifications, or medical remedies.

CHAPTER 15: ART, ARCHITECTURE, AND CULTURE

Introduction

Art, architecture, and cultural practices in the Bronze Age reveal the creativity and values of societies ranging from Mesopotamia to the Indus Valley, from Egypt to the Aegean, and from Anatolia to Europe and China. While earlier chapters discussed daily life, trade, religion, and warfare, here we explore how people used materials, styles, and forms to express identity, uphold rituals, and showcase power. We will see how temples, palaces, sculptures, jewelry, and paintings became symbols of community pride or royal authority, and how cultural expressions evolved over time.

In this chapter, we will examine major architectural achievements like ziggurats and pyramids, consider the decorative motifs that defined distinct regions, look at how bronze casting shaped monumental art, and see how storytelling, music, and performance played into daily cultural life. By studying these cultural artifacts, we gain a deeper understanding of Bronze Age aesthetics, symbolic communication, and communal identity.

---

1. Defining Bronze Age Art and Architecture

"Bronze Age art" is a broad term. It includes all visual and decorative items from roughly 3000 to 1200 BCE (though timelines vary by region). Metal objects, pottery, frescoes, carved reliefs, statue-making, and architectural layouts all fall under its umbrella. The introduction of bronze, along with surpluses from improved agriculture, enabled more specialized artisans to emerge. Rulers and elites commissioned large-scale buildings—palaces, tombs, temples—that required coordinated labor and skilled design.

At the same time, everyday items like bowls, seals, and amulets carried artistic touches. Farmers might own painted pottery or small bronze figurines. Craftspeople adopted both local styles and influences from distant trade partners. In architecture, mudbrick or stone served as primary building materials, but the methods of shaping and decorating them varied. A grand temple in Mesopotamia might stand as a towering ziggurat, while in Egypt it took the form of colonnaded complexes leading to a hidden sanctuary. These architectural differences signaled diverse religious outlooks and cultural aesthetics, yet shared a common impetus: to embody communal values in lasting, impressive forms.

---

2. Mesopotamian Achievements: Ziggurats and Reliefs

Mesopotamia's architectural centerpiece was the **ziggurat**—a terraced, pyramid-like structure built of mudbrick. Each city-state had its own ziggurat dedicated to its patron deity. Examples like the Great Ziggurat of Ur (early second millennium BCE) rose in layers, each smaller than the one below, culminating in a shrine at the top. Ramps or staircases led upward, symbolically connecting heaven and earth. These towering monuments not only housed religious practices but also proclaimed the city's wealth and devotion.

The walls of temples or palaces might feature relief carvings or painted decorations. Over time, Mesopotamian rulers added narrative steles, such as the **Victory Stele of Naram-Sin**, depicting the king's conquests under divine auspices. Artists arranged human figures in registers (horizontal bands) or used hierarchical scaling—kings shown larger than subordinates. Cylinder seals also typify Mesopotamian art, intricately engraved with mythological scenes or repeated motifs. Pressed into clay, they identified owners and added a personal flourish to administrative documents.

Statues of deities or worshipers in a standing pose, hands clasped in prayer, reflect the strong religious orientation of the culture. Though initially simple, these statues evolved in style and detail, occasionally featuring inlaid eyes or inscriptions naming the donor. Stone was not abundant in the alluvial plain, so large sculptures were less common than in Egypt. Nonetheless, the combination of ziggurat architecture, relief steles, and cylinder seals underscores Mesopotamia's innovative flair in using art and monuments to assert civic pride and theological principles.

3. Egyptian Grandeur: Pyramids, Temples, and Tomb Art

Egypt's architectural feats are among the most iconic of the ancient world. Early in the Bronze Age (the Old Kingdom), builders erected **pyramids**—massive stone tombs for pharaohs. The most famous are at Giza: the Great Pyramid of Khufu, plus those of Khafre and Menkaure. Although the Old Kingdom might straddle the transition from the Stone Age to Bronze Age, these monuments set a lasting pattern for Egyptian architectural ambition. By the Middle and New Kingdoms (well within the Bronze Age), tombs evolved into cliff-cut complexes in the Valley of the Kings, and large-scale temples like Karnak and Luxor rose along the Nile.

Egyptian temples were built with stone columns, courtyard after courtyard, and sanctuaries hidden deep inside. Walls and columns carried carved reliefs celebrating the pharaoh's relationship with the gods—offering scenes, military victories, and hymns praising deities like Amun, Ra, or Hathor. Hieroglyphic inscriptions merged writing and art, depicting people and animals in a distinct style that emphasized profile views, balanced proportions, and a canon of bodily representation that endured for centuries.

Funerary art soared in complexity. Nobles commissioned rock-cut tombs with painted walls showing daily life, agriculture, feasting, or religious rituals. Art was not merely decorative but also functional: images of servants in tombs were believed to become real in the afterlife, ensuring the deceased's comfort. Statues—like the famous seated scribe or the bust of Nefertiti (slightly later in the Amarna period)—demonstrate Egyptians' skill at lifelike representation, especially for elite portraiture. While official art maintained formality, smaller pieces (amulets, personal figurines, cosmetic containers) showcased creative designs. Bronze, though overshadowed by stone in architecture, still contributed to tools and ceremonial objects—mirrors, statuettes, and elements of temple fittings.

---

4. The Indus Valley's Urban Planning and Artistic Subtlety

The Indus Valley civilization (Harappan culture) did not leave behind towering monuments like ziggurats or pyramids. Instead, they expressed sophistication through urban planning and smaller-scale artistry. Cities such as Mohenjo-daro and Harappa featured grid layouts, baked-brick houses, advanced drainage systems, and public structures like the Great Bath or large granaries. Though these might not match the colossal scale of an Egyptian temple, the uniformity and practicality of Indus cities reflect a strong communal aesthetic.

Indus art is visible in **seals**—small carved steatite or soapstone pieces bearing animal motifs (bulls, elephants, unicorns) and the still-undeciphered script. These seals, likely used for trade or administrative stamping, blend stylized animal imagery with precise carving. Figurines of dancing girls in bronze or terracotta mother goddesses further highlight personal or religious expressions. Pottery had geometric designs, sometimes featuring fish or leaf motifs, though the color palettes remained fairly simple.

Architecture centered on daily utility—houses with private wells, bathrooms, and uniform brick sizes. Public spaces included wide streets, drainage channels, and systematically spaced wells. While we lack grand palaces or temples, the consistent city design suggests a shared cultural identity. The relative absence of ostentatious royal monuments might hint at a more collective approach to power or religion. The Bronze Age artistry of the Indus civilization thus excels in subtlety and practicality over imposing architecture.

---

5. Minoan and Mycenaean Styles: Aegean Frescoes and Palaces

In the Aegean, the **Minoans** on Crete crafted sprawling palatial complexes, the most famous at Knossos. These structures incorporated multiple stories, storage magazines, central courtyards, and vibrant frescoes showing bull-leaping, processions, or marine life. Walls painted with swirling patterns of dolphins or flowers highlight the Minoans' fascination with nature and the sea. Architecture emphasized open spaces, light wells, and elaborate drainage—suggesting a culture oriented toward communal gatherings and lively aesthetics.

Mycenaeans on mainland Greece absorbed Minoan influences but developed more fortress-like palaces (e.g., Mycenae, Tiryns, Pylos). Massive "Cyclopean" walls ringed citadels, and a central megaron (great hall) served as the king's audience chamber. Frescoes in Mycenaean palaces depicted hunting scenes, chariot processions, or religious ceremonies, though the style was a bit stiffer than Minoan painting. Mycenaean goldsmiths produced exquisite funerary masks, diadems, and inlaid daggers (like those found in Grave Circle A at Mycenae), combining Egyptian or Near Eastern motifs with local tastes.

Both Minoan and Mycenaean pottery exhibit graceful shapes—beaked jugs, stirrup jars—decorated with marine or floral designs. Large storage pithoi lined palace storerooms, indicating a bureaucratic economy controlling food surpluses. The synergy of architecture, frescoes, pottery, and metalwork forged a distinct Aegean cultural identity that influenced later Greek art. By harnessing advanced bronze casting for weapons and tools, Aegean artisans could devote more energy to decorative arts in stone, faience, or gold.

6. Hittite and Anatolian Contributions

In Anatolia, the **Hittites** created impressive state buildings in their capital, Hattusa. Although overshadowed by stone-laden Egyptian temples or Mesopotamian ziggurats, Hittite fortifications spanned large areas, featuring multiple gates—like the Lion Gate or King's Gate—adorned with relief carvings of guardian animals or gods. Temples stood within these walls, built of stone foundations and mudbrick superstructures, housing altars and storerooms.

Hittite rock reliefs carved into cliffs or boulders (such as Yazılıkaya) depicted pantheons of gods or kings performing rituals. These outdoor sanctuaries merged the natural landscape with carved imagery, reflecting the Hittites' reverence for mountains, storms, and local deities. Administrative palace structures included courtyards, storerooms for tribute, and ritual spaces. Although the Hittites did not produce as many large freestanding statues as Egypt or Mesopotamia, their stone relief tradition was distinctive—heroic figures, gods wearing tall hats, and processional lines of deities.

Bronze craftsmanship thrived as well, especially in weapon-making. Some ceremonial swords or daggers had elaborate fittings, occasionally inlaid with silver or gold. Seals bearing cuneiform or hieroglyphic Luwian script combined practical stamping with artistic flair. Hittite artisans also borrowed motifs from conquered regions—Hurrian, Syrian, or Mesopotamian—creating a cultural blend that underscored their imperial reach.

7. Shang China: Bronzes and Ritual Vessels

Bronze Age China (particularly under the **Shang Dynasty**) is renowned for **bronze casting**, producing ritual vessels that rank among the world's most intricate metal artworks of the period. These vessels—dings, guis, liding, and more—served in ancestral rituals, holding offerings of food or wine for revered ancestors. The Chinese used a **piece-mold casting** technique, designing complex surface decorations often featuring the **taotie** mask (a stylized zoomorphic face) or other geometric patterns.

Large bronzes, sometimes weighing hundreds of pounds, symbolized royal authority. Only elites could commission such items, dedicating them in ceremonies and storing them in ancestral temples. Inscriptions on some vessels recorded achievements, genealogies, or dedications to ancestors. This intertwining of writing and art underscored the vessels' political-religious power. While stone or brick architecture of Shang cities was functional, it did not match the monumental scale of Egyptian pyramids. Instead, China's hallmark was metal artistry that combined technical mastery with spiritual significance.

Aside from bronzes, Shang-era jade carvings also displayed high craftsmanship, often shaped into discs (bi) or scepters (cong) used in rituals. Jade, prized for its purity and durability, carried symbolic weight as a link between heaven and earth. Ceramics, though simpler, still featured refined shapes and glazes. This focus on ceremonial objects reveals how Bronze Age Chinese culture prioritized ancestral worship, with powerful kings integrating politics, warfare, and spiritual practices through elaborate bronzes.

8. Bronze Age Europe: Megaliths, Hillforts, and Metal Art

In Bronze Age Europe (outside the Aegean), architectural expressions varied widely due to diverse cultures and geographies. **Megalithic monuments** (like Stonehenge in Britain or dolmens in Brittany) originated in Neolithic times but some were reused or adapted in the Bronze Age for burials or ceremonies. Barrows, or burial mounds, dotted landscapes in places like Central or Northern Europe, signifying prominent individuals laid to rest with bronze weapons or ornaments.

Hillforts emerged, combining defense with communal living. Their ramparts and ditches formed imposing silhouettes, though the internal structures often used timber or wattle-and-daub. Decoration was less uniform than in palace-based societies, but metalwork shone in jewelry—gold lunulae, torcs, and armlets. Sword-making in Central Europe advanced, showcasing leaf-shaped blades or complex hilt designs. Skilled bronze casters also produced **cauldrons, shields, and horns** (like the Scandinavian lurs used for ceremonies).

Rock art—carvings or paintings on cliff faces—depicted sun symbols, ships, and spirals, especially in the Nordic Bronze Age. These images possibly reflected solar cults or maritime activities. Although European Bronze Age art lacked the urban sophistication of Mesopotamia or Egypt, it expressed strong ties to nature, ritual, and social hierarchy, visible in barrow burials and hoards of metal objects. Cultural identity manifested through these distinctive local traditions, each shaped by environmental constraints and trade contacts.

---

9. Pottery Styles and Motifs

Pottery was universal in the Bronze Age, used for cooking, storage, and ceremonial tasks. Styles varied by region, but certain shapes or decorative motifs reveal cultural linkages or influences.

- **Mesopotamia**: Simple unpainted jars or bowls with occasional incised designs. Palatial contexts might show finer wares with geometric patterns.
- **Egypt**: Pottery included the well-known red-and-black slip ware, though more elaborate containers in everyday use were overshadowed by stone or metal vessels in elite contexts.
- **Indus Valley**: Red or buff ceramics with black painted motifs, often geometric or featuring stylized animals. Uniform across many sites, reflecting standardization.
- **Minoan Crete**: **Kamares ware** (Middle Bronze Age) used thin walls, swirling designs in white and red on dark backgrounds; later **Marine Style** depicted octopuses, fish, or seaweed.
- **Mycenaean Greece**: Stirrup jars, kraters, and amphorae with repeated shapes—spirals, waves, or stylized creatures.
- **Central Europe**: Cultures like Unetice or Urnfield produced simple, robust forms, occasionally with incised lines, knobs, or cord impressions.
- **Nordic regions**: Pots might show minimal ornament, but shape could reflect daily cooking or storage needs.

Craftsmen shaped, fired, and sometimes burnished pots, using coils or wheel-throwing. Painted or incised patterns indicated local tastes, often swirling or geometric. Pottery also served as a trade good. Meanwhile, special ritual vessels might be buried in hoards or graves, carrying symbolic significance for the afterlife or community ceremonies.

10. Sculpture and Figurines

Sculpture in the Bronze Age ranged from monumental stone statues to tiny clay or metal figurines:

- **Mesopotamia**: Statuettes of worshipers or deities, stone steles commemorating victories, and hammered reliefs on gates or palace walls.
- **Egypt**: Colossal statues of pharaohs (e.g., the seated statues at temple entrances), smaller personal sculptures for tombs, and impressive sphinx forms combining lion bodies with human heads.
- **Aegean**: Minoans had small terracotta or faience figures (snake goddesses), and Mycenaeans displayed carved stelae on grave circles or gold masks for the dead. Larger statues in stone were less frequent.
- **China**: Few large-scale stone statues survive from the Shang, but the bronze vessels themselves often took zoomorphic shapes or included relief decoration resembling masks, dragons, or birds.
- **Europe**: Large stone statues were uncommon except for megalithic monuments. People fashioned smaller figurines from clay or bronze. Some regions made "idols" with abstract shapes.

These sculptures performed religious, funerary, or political functions. Whether a life-sized pharaoh carved in granite or a modest clay mother-goddess figurine from a rural Indus home, each piece expressed communal beliefs. Style encompassed both realism and abstraction. Egyptian art strove for idealized portraiture; Mesopotamian might be more stylized with prominent eyebrows or large eyes. Aegean fresco-like figures extended into small sculptures with slender waists or fluid lines. Each tradition balanced symbolic meaning with aesthetic preferences.

11. Wall Paintings and Frescoes

Wall painting (or fresco) was especially notable in the Aegean. **Minoan** palaces at Knossos, Phaistos, or Zakros boasted vibrant scenes of bull-leaping, dancers, processions, and sea creatures. Colors included reds, blues, whites, and yellows. Artists employed fluid lines, giving figures a sense of motion. Mycenaean frescoes, influenced by Minoan styles, depicted hunting or battle scenes with bolder outlines.

In Egypt, tomb paintings used registers to portray daily life, funerary rituals, or the journey to the afterlife. The style maintained strict proportions and profile representation. Backgrounds often stayed plain, placing emphasis on the figures and hieroglyphic texts. Mesopotamia had fewer surviving wall paintings, focusing more on relief sculpture or baked-clay plaques. In the Indus Valley, if painting existed on walls, it has not survived well, although painted pottery suggests some skill in figurative painting.

Fresco technique involved applying paint to fresh plaster, melding pigment and surface. It required quick execution. Scenes often served a symbolic or narrative purpose—ritual, myth, or daily tasks. The choice of subject and style reflected cultural priorities: Minoans glorified nature and sports, Egyptians highlighted afterlife beliefs and pharaonic power, Mycenaeans celebrated hunts or warfare. All used color to create lively, engaging environments within palatial or sacred complexes.

12. Musical Instruments and Dance

Music and dance played key roles in Bronze Age culture, but we mainly infer their details from art, texts, or surviving instruments:

- **Mesopotamia**: Harps, lyres, pipes, drums. The Royal Standard of Ur (Early Bronze Age) features lyre players. Ceremonial ensembles likely accompanied temple rites or royal feasts.
- **Egypt**: Harps, flutes, lutes, sistrums (shaken instruments for ritual), and tambourines. Tomb paintings depict musicians entertaining banquet guests, with dancers in flowing outfits.
- **Aegean**: Frescoes show dancers, possibly accompanied by stringed instruments or pipes. Minoan music might have featured rattles or small drums for rhythmic bull-leaping events.
- **China**: Early bronze bells and chimes appear in subsequent dynasties, but seeds of that tradition began in the Shang era with potential small bells or percussive devices.
- **Europe**: Nordic Bronze Age lurs (long, curved bronze horns) found in bog deposits, likely used for ceremonies or processions. Simple drums, pipes, and possibly stringed instruments existed but are less documented.

Dances ranged from communal circle dances at festivals to specialized ritual movements. Minoan frescoes of graceful dancers or bull-leapers illustrate athletic and artistic expression, while Egyptian tomb art shows pairs or groups performing acrobatic routines. These cultural expressions served as entertainment, ritual devotion, and a way to mark festivals or communal gatherings.

13. Symbolism and Motifs: Animals, Nature, and Myth

Bronze Age cultures frequently used animals and nature-inspired imagery in their art. Bulls and lions symbolized strength, as in Minoan bull iconography or the lion gates of Mycenae and Hattusa. Eagles or falcons (in Egypt, Horus) embodied divine kingship. Serpents appeared in Minoan snake goddess figurines or in Mesopotamian incantations as potent symbols of rebirth or danger.

Nature motifs included spirals, waves, rosettes, or solar discs. The spiral pattern was widespread in Europe, carved into stones at passage tombs and on pottery. Minoans favored marine themes—octopuses, dolphins, starfish—reflecting their maritime lifestyle. Egyptian art abounded in papyrus plants, lotus flowers, or desert animals, linking the fertile Nile Valley with surrounding wilderness. Chinese bronzes often featured stylized dragons or monster masks, bridging mortal and supernatural realms.

Mythological creatures—griffins, sphinxes, or composite beings—appeared in the Aegean, the Near East, and Egypt. These hybrid forms might guard temples or palaces, signifying dominion over the natural world. Because writing was limited or lost in some cultures (Indus, preliterate Europe), we interpret these symbols through comparisons to later myths or from parallels in textual regions (Mesopotamia, Egypt). The recurring presence of certain animals or patterns underscores how deeply symbolic representation resonated with Bronze Age people in expressing power, religious belief, and cultural identity.

14. Urban Planning and Monumental Construction

Monumental construction in Bronze Age centers required advanced planning and labor coordination. Rulers mobilized peasants, slaves, or corvée labor for large projects like ziggurats, pyramids, or palatial complexes. Administrators planned irrigation canals, city walls, and temple expansions to keep pace with population growth. Skilled architects or overseers drew up designs, while scribes tracked materials and rations.

In Mesopotamia, city-states expanded around temples, with overlapping neighborhoods for merchants, artisans, and officials. Streets could be narrow, winding around courtyard houses. By contrast, Indus cities like Mohenjo-daro showcased near-rectilinear layouts, broad roads, and systematically placed wells—suggesting central oversight. Minoan palaces integrated storerooms, ritual spaces, and living quarters in labyrinthine plans that might have inspired later Greek myths of the Labyrinth. Mycenaean citadels favored elevated positions, ringed by massive stone walls.

In Egypt, monumental architecture peaked in both tombs and temples, aided by stone-quarrying expertise. The scale of these structures symbolized the pharaoh's cosmic authority. Shang China's capitals had large palace enclosures, rammed-earth walls, and carefully oriented gates. Bronze Age Europe, outside the Aegean, saw fewer city complexes but numerous defensive hillforts. Each region's layout reflected climate, resources, political structure, and religious emphasis, weaving architecture into the broader cultural narrative.

---

15. Patronage and Workshops

Behind every impressive palace or exquisite artifact lay systems of patronage. Rulers or high priests might commission massive temple expansions or elaborate funerary goods, employing entire workshops of artisans—scribes, metalworkers, stonecutters, weavers. Some workshops specialized in one material: a bronze workshop near palace foundries, or a stone-carving team near quarries.

Contracts or temple records might detail the rations assigned to craftsmen, the quality standards demanded, and deadlines for completion, especially for major events like coronations or building dedications. Skilled artisans sometimes traveled to foreign courts if they received better pay or if their homeland was conquered. This movement of craftspeople contributed to cross-cultural influences in style and technique.

Artisans also produced items for local markets—pottery, simple jewelry—catering to ordinary families. Elite patronage, though, spurred the greatest innovations, as lords competed to display more lavish, refined works. Temples might store precious metals for ongoing projects, recycling older objects or war booty into new sculptures. In doing so, they shaped cultural evolution, balancing tradition with innovation to impress patrons and the deities they served.

---

16. Cultural Exchanges and Hybrid Styles

Trade routes that carried metals and luxury goods also transported artistic ideas. Mesopotamia influenced the Levant and Anatolia, while Minoans inspired Mycenaean fresco techniques. Egyptian motifs, such as the sphinx or lotus, might appear on foreign objects, reflecting admiration or diplomatic gift exchanges. The Indus seals found in Mesopotamia show that Indus artisans borrowed some motifs or crafting methods while retaining local animal symbolism.

In some cases, foreign artisans settled abroad, merging local conventions with homeland aesthetics. The Hyksos in Egypt (during the Second Intermediate Period) introduced Levantine design elements, influencing Egyptian weapons and decorative patterns. Mycenaean pottery exported to Cyprus or the Levant introduced spirals or marine themes to local potters. The Hittites integrated Hurrian or Mesopotamian styles into their relief carvings, forging a unique Anatolian blend.

These cross-cultural fusions enriched Bronze Age culture, leading to "hybrid" objects with broad appeal. Because of shifting political alliances and wars, styles rose or fell in popularity. Yet the broader effect was a dynamic tapestry in which motifs and methods circulated, shaped by local preferences and powerful elites seeking novelty.

17. The Ceremonial and the Everyday in Culture

Not all Bronze Age art or architecture served regal or spiritual ends. Some items were purely domestic: a decorated ladle, a finely painted cup, or a wall painting in a simple home. These provided small joys or displayed the household's modest status. People might paint simple designs on house walls or craft homemade figurines for personal worship.

Meanwhile, major monuments overshadow daily structures, but they required support from the entire community. Farmers supplied food to feed laborers, metalworkers forged tools for stonecutters, and scribes managed records. Over time, a single statue or building might become a cultural landmark. Festivals or processions might revolve around such landmarks, turning them into communal meeting points.

Cultural identity, therefore, emerged on two levels: official or ceremonial expressions (palaces, temple art) and everyday customs (cookware, local crafts, family shrines). The interplay of both shaped how societies saw themselves, bridging grand ideals with practical living. People might admire a king's new temple façade but also cherish the pot they used for daily cooking, painted with familial or ancestral symbols. This layering of meaning gave Bronze Age culture resilience, weaving top-down initiatives with grassroots creativity.

---

18. Symbolic Functions of Art and Architecture

Art and architecture in the Bronze Age carried strong symbolic messages. A ziggurat represented cosmic order, bridging mortal and divine realms. An Egyptian temple's reliefs told of pharaoh's might, reassuring citizens that the gods blessed his reign. A Mycenaean fortress gate flanked by lion carvings warned enemies of the king's power. An Indus city's uniform brick size implied shared standards and communal identity. A Shang bronze vessel, covered in ritual motifs, declared the dynasty's link to ancestral spirits.

Symbolism also extended to funerary contexts: tombs and grave goods broadcast status in the afterlife. The mask of a Mycenaean noble or the gold objects in an Irish barrow signified prestige carried beyond death. Seals or signet rings identified personal authority, each motif revealing rank or profession. Even mundane items like weaving tools or cooking pots sometimes bore protective symbols.

These symbolic layers cemented social hierarchies, religious beliefs, and political propaganda. People reading or seeing such symbols reinforced communal narratives about cosmic harmony, rightful kingship, or the role of ancestors. Over centuries, repeated motifs gained deeper resonance, forging cultural continuity that endured even through crises like the Bronze Age collapse.

---

19. Late Bronze Age Shifts and Cultural Transformations

As the Bronze Age progressed toward its end (circa 1200 BCE in many regions), disruptions in trade and political structures affected art and architecture. Some palace systems crumbled, halting or altering large-scale building projects. In the Aegean, Mycenaean palaces burned, leading to a decline in fresco painting and large-scale sculpture. In Anatolia, the Hittite Empire fell, scattering local artisans. Egyptian art and architecture continued but faced challenges from internal unrest and foreign invasions.

These shifts did not erase cultural achievements overnight. Local craft traditions persisted or evolved. Refugees or itinerant artisans carried knowledge elsewhere, sparking new hybrid styles in emergent Iron Age polities. Certain motifs, like Egyptian decorative forms or Mesopotamian seal iconography, found echoes in later civilizations. The Indus civilization had already waned by this point, replaced by more local cultures, yet certain pottery or settlement practices lingered.

In some areas, monumental building gave way to smaller fortresses or new religious complexes. Art became simpler or adapted to iron-based economies and changing social structures. Yet the Bronze Age's cultural legacy lived on in myths, minor crafts, or the architectural ruins that later peoples revered. Over time, new kingdoms, like the Neo-Assyrian or early Greek city-states, built upon Bronze Age foundations, adopting or redefining older aesthetics.

CHAPTER 16: POLITICAL STRUCTURES AND GOVERNANCE

Introduction

The Bronze Age witnessed the formation and expansion of city-states, kingdoms, and early empires. These polities managed economies, waged wars, and forged alliances, all within a framework of evolving political institutions. Rulers claimed divine favor or ancestral legitimacy, gathering bureaucracies to tax, regulate, and govern expanding territories. Cities like Babylon, Thebes, Knossos, Anyang, and Hattusa became seats of power, overseeing regional trade and agriculture.

In this chapter, we will examine how Bronze Age societies organized themselves politically: the roles of kings, councils, or priesthoods; the structures of administration that managed resources; and the treaties and vassal relationships that held multiethnic empires together. We will see how leadership transitions and power struggles shaped entire regions, influencing everything from laws to foreign policy. By understanding these governance systems, we grasp the machinery behind the monumental achievements we have already seen—temples, armies, trade networks, and cultural innovations.

---

1. The Emergence of City-States and Chiefdoms

In the early Bronze Age, many societies progressed from tribal or clan-based leadership to more centralized chiefdoms or city-states. Surpluses from farming allowed certain families or leaders to accumulate wealth, sponsor public works, and organize labor. Towns with defensive walls or irrigation networks needed a guiding authority to mobilize effort and resolve disputes. Over time, certain strongmen or priestly figures assumed roles akin to kings, proclaiming themselves guardians of the land and mediators with the gods.

In Mesopotamia, city-states such as Uruk, Ur, and Lagash had **ensi** or **lugal** (kings) who oversaw temples, stored grain, managed water systems, and led armies. In the Nile Valley, small polities merged under a single ruler (the pharaoh), unifying Upper and Lower Egypt. The Indus Valley might have had multiple city centers (Harappa, Mohenjo-daro) each with local rulers or councils, though the exact structure remains unclear due to the undeciphered script.

Chiefdoms with palisaded villages or hillforts emerged in parts of Europe. Some areas, like the Aegean, formed palace-based polities in Crete or later mainland Greece, each controlling farmland and maritime routes. Such polities often balanced alliances and rivalries with neighbors, leading to shifting boundaries. The progression from local chiefdoms to state-level societies hinged on the ability to coordinate labor, handle disputes, and maintain religious legitimacy.

---

2. Royal Authority: Divine Kingship and Ancestral Claims

Many Bronze Age rulers claimed divine or semi-divine status, anchoring their authority in religious beliefs. **Egyptian pharaohs** styled themselves as gods' sons or living embodiments of Horus, bridging mortal life and the divine realm. Their position guaranteed order (Ma'at), which validated their decrees and construction of massive temples or tombs. Mesopotamian kings likewise invoked gods as patrons—some, like Sargon of Akkad, boasted that the gods personally chose them to subdue rival cities.

In China, Shang kings performed crucial ancestral rites, presenting themselves as the link between the living and powerful ancestral spirits. They oversaw oracle bone divinations, controlling messages from deities or the deceased. The Hittite kings, while not always claiming direct divinity, saw themselves as favored by storm gods or sun deities, forging treaties "in the sight of the gods." Even Mycenaean rulers might trace lineages to divine or heroic ancestors, gleaning prestige from epic traditions.

This notion of "divine kingship" legitimized high taxes, forced labor, and control over armies. If the ruler was perceived to fail or lose divine favor—evidenced by droughts, defeats, or social unrest—rebellions or palace coups could erupt. In turn, each new dynasty carefully proclaimed fresh divine sanction, continuing the cyclical pattern of rise and fall anchored in religious narratives.

---

3. Administrative Bureaucracies and Scribes

Managing a Bronze Age state required record-keeping and communication across multiple regions. Thus, scribes—trained in writing—formed the backbone of bureaucracies. Mesopotamia developed cuneiform on clay tablets, used by palace and temple officials to track grain, taxes, wages, and trade shipments. Egypt's scribes inscribed hieroglyphs on stone or wrote hieratic scripts on papyrus, logging harvests, building projects, and temple accounts. The Hittites had their own cuneiform as well as Luwian hieroglyphs.

In the Indus civilization, official administration is implied by uniform brick standards and city planning, though we cannot read their script. Minoan Linear A and Mycenaean Linear B tablets recorded palace inventories—oil, wine, wool, metals—managed by scribes. Shang China used oracle bone inscriptions for divination, but probably kept other records on bamboo or wood, now lost.

Bureaucracies oversaw labor corvées (public work duties), distributed rations to temple or palace workers, and enforced tribute from conquered areas. High officials acted as the king's agents, traveling to border towns or foreign courts with sealed letters. In large polities like Egypt or the Hittite Empire, multiple administrative tiers managed local, regional, and central tasks. This hierarchical system allowed states to organize large building projects, equip armies, or gather tribute. Yet it also demanded loyalty—scribes or provincial governors might rebel if they found alliances with rivals or local elites more profitable.

4. Temple and Palace Economies

In many Bronze Age societies, temples and palaces were economic hubs controlling farmland, herds, and craft workshops. **Mesopotamian** temples acted as redistributive centers: peasants gave grain or labor in exchange for protection, while temple officials allocated supplies for festivals, building, or trade caravans. Palaces gradually expanded, rivaling or overshadowing temples in managing surpluses. A strong monarchy might concentrate wealth in the palace, employing scribes and officials to direct resources.

In Egypt, the pharaoh's court directed large irrigation projects and commanded state workshops. Temples, especially in the New Kingdom, owned vast tracts of land, employing thousands of workers. Rulers often balanced palace authority with temple influence, awarding priests more land in exchange for religious support. The Indus cities appear to have had well-organized storehouses and standardized measurements, suggesting some central body directed resources. Minoan and Mycenaean palaces had storerooms for olive oil, grain, and wine, which they redistributed to palace officials or used for trade.

Such palace-temple economies reinforced elite power, but also required stable administration. If a palace lost control of routes or faced internal strife, local lords or merchants might seize power. Over time, some societies (like in Mesopotamia) swung between priestly dominance and royal dominance, depending on the vigor of particular dynasties or external threats.

5. Councils, Assemblies, and Noble Classes

Although kings held ultimate authority in many Bronze Age states, they seldom ruled alone. Councils of elders, nobles, or priests often guided policy or mediated conflicts. In Mesopotamia, references to assemblies—like the "puhrum" of elders—exist in early city-states. They might ratify decisions on war or major building projects. Egyptian society appeared more centralized around the pharaoh, yet high officials and powerful priests exerted influence behind the scenes.

In Mycenaean Greece, references to a *lawagetas* or a leading warrior figure next to the *wanax* (king) imply a structured hierarchy with multiple aristocrats overseeing provinces. Hittite kings negotiated with extended royal families and leading generals—factions could unseat a ruler if he lost support. In China, the Shang king might appoint relatives or trusted allies to govern outlying areas, creating a patchwork of local lords loyal (in theory) to the central court.

Social classes included nobles or aristocrats who owned land or led cavalry/chariot units, forming a separate stratum from commoner farmers or artisans. These aristocrats often gathered in councils to confirm succession or debate foreign policy. While the king might appear absolute, his success depended on balancing the interests of these elites. Overreaching royals risked assassination or palace coups, ensuring some checks existed even in monarchy heavy systems.

6. Law Codes and Justice

Codified laws emerged in literate Bronze Age societies to regulate disputes, property rights, and social conduct. The most famous example is **Hammurabi's Code** (circa 18th century BCE) in Mesopotamia, inscribed on a diorite stele. It delineated punishments for theft, assault, or fraud, often scaling severity by the victim's or perpetrator's social status. It also addressed marriage contracts, divorce, and labor disputes.

In the Hittite realm, tablets record legal provisions about land inheritance, debt, and personal injuries, though punishments were sometimes less draconian than earlier Mesopotamian codes. Egypt had no single extant law code in the same style, but scribal instructions and official edicts laid out principles. The concept of Ma'at (justice and cosmic order) guided judgments. Judges or local councils handled routine conflicts, sometimes requiring oaths or calling upon oracles.

Law codes served multiple functions: standardizing justice across regions, reinforcing social hierarchies, and projecting the king's benevolent or paternal role. People might appeal decisions or offer bribes to officials, underscoring that, in practice, corruption existed. Still, the presence of codified laws advanced the notion that certain regulations transcended personal whim, providing at least some consistency in governance.

---

7. Diplomacy and Alliances

As polities expanded, diplomacy became crucial. City-states and empires established treaties, alliances, or client-vassal relationships to manage conflict or secure trade. The **Amarna Letters** (14th century BCE) reveal correspondences between Egyptian pharaohs and rulers in Babylon, Assyria, Mitanni, and Canaan. They negotiated marriages (royal brides to cement ties), exchanged gifts (gold, horses, luxury goods), and discussed tributes.

Hittite kings also crafted treaties that placed conquered states or neighbors in vassal status. These treaties invoked gods as witnesses, threatening curses if either side broke the pact. Mycenaean rulers might secure Aegean ties through arranged partnerships or show forced subjugation if they conquered an island. Even smaller city-states used marriage alliances or trade agreements to stave off aggression from larger powers.

Diplomatic rituals included gift-giving, joint religious ceremonies, or public proclamations. Royal women married into foreign courts, carrying cultural influences. When alliances soured, wars erupted. Yet throughout the Bronze Age, diplomacy acted as a stabilizing mechanism, allowing long-distance trade and relative peace for certain intervals. The interplay of competition and negotiation shaped a dynamic political landscape.

8. Military Control and the Role of Garrisons

Securing territories demanded military presence. Rulers established fortresses or garrisons at strategic points—river crossings, mountain passes, or trade hubs. Soldiers stationed there collected tolls, monitored local populations, and deterred raids. In Mesopotamia, city-states might place outposts along caravan routes. Egypt stationed troops in Nubia or the Sinai to safeguard gold mines or copper resources. The Hittites built fortress cities throughout Anatolia and northern Syria.

These garrisons reported to a regional governor or viceroy, who in turn answered to the king. Supply lines needed to feed and arm these outposts. If local rebellions brewed, the garrison either quelled them or called for reinforcements. Over time, some garrison towns evolved into provincial capitals, hosting administrative offices. Soldiers might integrate with local communities, adopting or blending cultural practices.

Maintaining an extensive network of garrisons was costly, requiring taxes or tributes from the populace. In return, the state offered "protection," though that might feel more like occupation to some local inhabitants. When central power weakened, these outposts could be cut off, either abandoned or taken over by local strongmen. This cyclical rise and fall of garrisons reflected the broader tensions of empire-building in the Bronze Age.

---

9. Managing Resources: Taxes and Tribute

Collecting resources from local populations was fundamental to sustaining a Bronze Age government. Methods included:

- **Taxes in Kind**: Peasants surrendered a portion of their harvest, livestock, or craft goods to temple or palace storehouses.
- **Labor Corvée**: Citizens had to work a set number of days on public projects—irrigation canals, palace building, or city walls.
- **Tribute from Vassals**: Conquered regions delivered metals, grain, or luxury items, acknowledging the overlord's power.
- **Commercial Taxes**: Merchants paid tolls at city gates or seaports. Official weigh stations and scribes enforced these fees.

Scribes recorded receipts, stored them on tablets or papyrus. Officials allocated these revenues to feed palace personnel, equip armies, fund construction, or conduct trade. Some states, like those in Mesopotamia, allowed local assemblies to decide tax rates, though ultimately the king or temple authorities ratified them. In large empires—Egypt, Hittites, Shang China—tribute from outlying zones formed a huge portion of central wealth.

If taxes became too burdensome or local elites felt exploited, revolts flared. Rulers often balanced extraction with some measure of public works or religious legitimacy, claiming that taxes funded the gods' temples or protected farmland from invaders. Still, heavy tribute demands occasionally collapsed local economies, feeding the cycle of unrest or fragmentation that marred Bronze Age polities.

---

10. Succession and Palace Intrigue

Rulership in the Bronze Age was often hereditary, but transitions could be tumultuous. A dying king might designate a son or relative, but rival claimants could challenge that choice. In Mesopotamia, dynastic changes sometimes brought entire new families to the throne if the old line faltered. Egyptian tradition aimed for direct father-to-son succession, but pharaonic lines occasionally broke, leading to intermediate periods of competing claimants.

Intrigue brewed in palaces, with queens, princes, generals, or priestly factions maneuvering for power. Poisonings, conspiracies, or orchestrated assassinations appear in some historical or semi-legendary records (like the Hittite annals or certain Egyptian texts). Foreign intervention also influenced successions—one power might back a claimant in a neighboring kingdom to secure an alliance or a puppet regime.

In stable times, a new king staged elaborate coronations to affirm divine sanction. Temple ceremonies, feast distributions, and perhaps mass debt remissions or prisoner releases won popular support. The monarchy would reinforce ties with nobles through gift-giving or marriage alliances. Yet even these measures did not guarantee security; strong personalities among local lords or military leaders sometimes overshadowed weaker royals. The precariousness of succession was a recurring source of political upheaval.

11. Women in Power

Although Bronze Age governance was largely male-dominated, certain women rose to prominence. In Egypt, queens like Hatshepsut governed as pharaoh in the 15th century BCE, commissioning monumental building projects and claiming royal titles. The position of **God's Wife of Amun** carried significant influence over temple holdings. Mesopotamia had priestesses who oversaw temple estates—Enheduanna, daughter of Sargon of Akkad, was a high priestess and the earliest known named author.

Hittite queens sometimes acted as regents if the king was absent or a child inherited the throne. Diplomatic marriages brought foreign princesses to new courts, where they might champion their homeland's interests. In the Aegean world, evidence suggests Mycenaean queens oversaw palace workshops or religious ceremonies, but clear records are sparse. China's Shang dynasty might have had powerful consorts or female generals—Fu Hao's tomb, for instance, indicates she led military campaigns and held large landholdings.

Despite these examples, female governance was not the norm. When it occurred, it often relied on extraordinary circumstances—a lack of male heirs or a strong personal network. Even then, male officials frequently tested or challenged a woman's authority. Nevertheless, these prominent women influenced policy, managed resources, and patronized cultural projects, leaving a mark on Bronze Age governance.

---

12. Vassalage and Empire Building

Some Bronze Age states transcended city-state boundaries to form empires. The Akkadian Empire, under Sargon and his successors, united much of Mesopotamia. The Assyrian and Babylonian states later pursued similar expansions. Egypt's New Kingdom conquered Nubia and extended into the Levant. The Hittites controlled large swaths of Anatolia and northern Syria. Mycenaeans might have formed a loose hegemony over parts of the Aegean, though it is debated. Shang China consolidated territories along the Yellow River, subduing neighboring chiefs.

Empire-building meant imposing vassalage: local rulers kept power but paid tribute, provided troops, and acknowledged the emperor's supremacy. Often, hostages or royal marriages solidified loyalty. Garrisons and roads integrated conquered lands. If vassals rebelled, punitive campaigns followed, or new puppet rulers were installed. Diplomacy played a role, with large states negotiating alliances among themselves to contain threats.

At their height, these empires facilitated trade and cultural exchange, bringing stability across vast zones. Yet they also sparked constant warfare, as rival powers contested borderlands. A single setback—like a major defeat, drought, or internal revolt—could unravel control, returning regions to local leadership. This cycle of expansion and contraction characterized Bronze Age geopolitics, with a handful of "great powers" overshadowing smaller polities.

---

13. The Hittite-Egyptian Rivalry and Treaties

A prime example of Bronze Age geopolitical complexity was the conflict between the Hittite Empire and New Kingdom Egypt over Syria. Both powers sought control of trade routes and resources. The **Battle of Kadesh** (circa 1274 BCE) was a massive confrontation, with thousands of chariots on both sides. Although Ramesses II of Egypt claimed victory in his inscriptions, the outcome was likely inconclusive.

Subsequently, the two states negotiated one of the earliest surviving peace treaties. Carved on clay tablets in cuneiform and in Egyptian hieroglyphs, it established spheres of influence and mutual defense pacts, sealed by a royal marriage. This treaty stabilized the Levant for a time, enabling trade caravans to move with less fear of raids, while each empire could focus on other frontiers. It underscores how diplomacy and political maturity could quell large-scale conflict, albeit temporarily.

The Hittite-Egyptian rivalry (and eventual accord) exemplifies Bronze Age international relations, complete with espionage, alliances with local princes, and symbolic gift exchanges. Their peace agreement set a precedent for future treaties, showing that warlike Bronze Age societies also recognized the benefits of negotiated settlement when mutual exhaustion or new threats arose.

14. The Mycenaean Palace System

On the Greek mainland, Mycenaean palaces at Mycenae, Pylos, Tiryns, or Thebes functioned as administrative centers. Tablets in **Linear B** script detail rations for workers, inventories of weapons, or tribute from local districts. The *wanax* (king) presided over the megaron (throne room), with a *lawagetas* possibly managing military affairs. Smaller officials oversaw flocks, farmland, or craft production.

The palace directed the storage of olive oil, grain, and textiles, some for local consumption, some for export. Artisans produced high-quality pottery and metal goods, distributed through palace networks or to foreign markets. Mycenaeans likely extracted tribute from coastal towns, controlling trade across the Aegean. Evidence of fortifications suggests competition with each other or external foes.

This centralized system collapsed around 1200 BCE, with fires destroying key sites. Whether internal strife, external invasion, or broader disruptions caused it remains debated. Post-collapse, Greece lost writing for centuries—the so-called "Greek Dark Age." The memory of palace-based governance survived in epic tradition, forming a mythical backdrop for classical Greece. This story illustrates how Bronze Age governance could flourish rapidly under strong palatial systems yet unravel due to interconnected crises.

---

15. The Role of Priests and Temples in Governance

Religion and governance were deeply interwoven. Temples held large tracts of land, employed workers, and sometimes clashed with royal authority over resource control. In Mesopotamia, early city-states might have been temple-centered theocracies, gradually transitioning to more secular monarchy. Still, the high priest or priestess remained influential, sanctifying the king's rule.

Egypt's temples, particularly in the New Kingdom, accumulated enormous wealth. The cult of Amun in Thebes rivaled the pharaoh's treasury, prompting occasional reforms or power struggles. The Indus Valley's lack of monumental temples suggests a different religious-political structure, though we can guess that some collective authority coordinated city planning. Minoan palaces featured shrines, while Mycenaean tablets mention offerings to gods, indicating a priestly role within the palace administration.

Temple bureaucracies might handle land leases, grain distribution, and artisan workshops. They also arbitrated moral or legal matters, reflecting the gods' will. Rulers who neglected or offended major cults risked losing legitimacy. Conversely, temple endorsements could bolster a new dynasty. This dynamic tension shaped policy—kings had to maintain good standing with powerful priesthoods, or risk rebellions cloaked in religious discontent.

16. Local Governance: Town and Village Life

Beyond grand palaces and capital cities, local governance often relied on elders or minor officials who kept order, coordinated irrigation, and collected taxes. In a typical Bronze Age village, the headman or council might settle minor disputes, ensure communal water sharing, or relay instructions from higher authorities. People rarely interacted directly with the distant king, but they felt the king's reach through tax agents, soldiers, or traveling scribes.

If raiders threatened, a local official might send messengers to the nearest fortress for assistance. Village shrines or small temples offered spiritual guidance. In return, peasants contributed labor to palace building or temple expansions, seeing it as both civic duty and religious devotion. Periodically, caravans or a royal inspector visited, checking compliance and gathering information. This grassroots layer gave the realm stability, for if villages were discontent, larger uprisings could brew.

Local autonomy varied. Some regions had a strong tradition of communal self-regulation, while others faced tighter control from central bureaucracy. Environmental factors (mountains, deserts) sometimes limited direct palace oversight, letting local chiefs hold sway. Meanwhile, frontier zones might see overlapping claims from multiple states, fueling confusion or conflict. These complexities highlight that Bronze Age governance was not monolithic but layered, with local, regional, and central powers constantly negotiating authority.

17. Warfare's Influence on Government

Earlier chapters described warfare and its ties to weapon development. But warfare also shaped governance profoundly. Rulers who excelled in battle gained prestige, distributing loot to supporters. Conquest expanded territory, forcing new administrative layers to manage vassals. Constant militarization meant states invested in arms production and fortifications. This militaristic focus sometimes overshadowed the well-being of common folk.

Alliances formed among threatened cities—like Levantine coalitions against Egyptian expansion or Mycenaean alliances for Aegean dominance. The presence of strong armies and chariot corps required stable taxation and bureaucratic efficiency. In some polities, the warrior class formed a parallel power structure, challenging or supporting the king. Overly militarized states risked wearing out resources, inciting rebellions, or ignoring trade and agriculture. Yet a kingdom that neglected defense risked being overrun by ambitious neighbors.

Thus, warfare prompted both centralization and potential strains on governance. Some kings tried to balance conquest with internal development, building roads and fostering trade. Others spiraled into near-constant campaigns, draining labor and wealth. The success or failure of these military policies often decided a dynasty's fate, culminating in either regional empires or abrupt collapses.

18. Interactions with Nomadic or Non-Urban Societies

Not all Bronze Age communities built cities or recognized kings. Nomadic or pastoral groups roamed steppes or deserts, occasionally interacting with agrarian states via trade or raids. This forced settled polities to adopt strategies of diplomacy (offering gifts or marriage ties) or building frontier forts. In Central Asia, horse-riding peoples might supply horses or serve as mercenaries, shaping the balance of power.

Peripheral highland communities (e.g., in Anatolia's mountains, the Zagros range near Mesopotamia, or remote corners of Europe) sometimes had tribal structures with chieftains. They traded metals, timber, or other resources to lowland states, maintaining partial independence. Political structures there might revolve around clan councils rather than centralized kings. Yet, as large states expanded, they might impose vassal treaties or forcibly incorporate these communities.

These interactions highlight the diversity of political models in the Bronze Age—ranging from sophisticated palace economies to clan-based confederations. Where large states met nomads or highlanders, borders became zones of cultural blending, commercial partnership, or violent clashes. Over time, such contact spurred the flow of ideas like horse-chariot warfare or new metallurgical techniques, influencing how both sides governed themselves.

19. The Decline of Bronze Age States and Political Fragmentation

Around 1200 BCE (though dates vary regionally), many established powers collapsed or shrank. Mycenaean palaces burned, the Hittite Empire disintegrated, and Egyptians retreated from the Levant. Mesopotamia faced internal upheavals, though new states like Assyria would later rise. In the Aegean, literacy vanished, trade declined, and smaller communities replaced palatial centers. In China, the Shang fell to the Zhou around 1046 BCE, continuing Bronze Age traditions but also introducing changes in governance and culture.

Causes for these declines include natural disasters, droughts, migrations (like the "Sea Peoples"), or economic strains from disrupted trade routes. Once-powerful polities could no longer maintain garrisons, pay armies, or quell internal dissent. Local rulers or newcomers took advantage of the power vacuum. Administrative systems that once coordinated large populations broke down, leading to a "dark age" in some regions, or simply a reorganization under new leadership in others.

Yet many administrative, cultural, and legal practices survived in fragmentary form. Later Iron Age kingdoms inherited knowledge of writing, law codes, fortification strategies, and diplomatic norms. The Bronze Age meltdown, in essence, reset political structures, paving the way for fresh experiments in governance—like Neo-Assyrian expansion, Zhou feudalism, or the rise of smaller Greek polis-states. It was an end, but also a turning point, in global political history.

CHAPTER 17: THE BRONZE AGE COLLAPSE

Introduction

The term "Bronze Age Collapse" refers to a period around the late second millennium BCE (roughly 1200–1100 BCE), when numerous powerful states in the Eastern Mediterranean and Near East either fell or underwent profound upheaval. Empires and kingdoms that had dominated international trade and politics for centuries—like the Mycenaeans in Greece, the Hittites in Anatolia, and many city-states in the Levant—crumbled or contracted drastically. Egypt also struggled against waves of invaders and internal crises, though it continued in altered form. Meanwhile, large-scale disruptions took place in regions ranging from the Aegean to Mesopotamia.

In this chapter, we will examine the nature and causes of this collapse. We will look at the main powers before the crisis, explore theories about why so many societies experienced simultaneous declines, and consider the consequences for trade, culture, and governance. Historians debate the extent to which "invasions," "climate change," "systems failure," or "internal rebellions" contributed. The collapse was likely multifaceted, emerging from an intersection of environmental pressures, diplomatic breakdowns, and social strains. By understanding this collapse, we discover how fragile the interconnected Bronze Age world could be, and how its downfall set the stage for new epochs in the Iron Age.

---

1. The World Before the Collapse: A Brief Overview

Just before the collapse, the Eastern Mediterranean was home to multiple "great powers" that often interacted through trade, diplomacy, and occasional warfare:

1. **Mycenaean Greece**: Palace-based polities (Mycenae, Pylos, Thebes, etc.) dominated the Greek mainland and influenced the Aegean. They engaged in maritime commerce, shipping pottery and olive oil while importing metals and luxuries. Their Linear B tablets record palace administration, with elites controlling farmland and craft production.
2. **Minoan Crete**: Already weakened from earlier crises, Crete had fallen under Mycenaean influence. Some Minoan traditions persisted, but the main power had shifted to Mycenaean centers.

3. **Hittite Empire**: Centered in Hattusa (Anatolia), it spanned large parts of Anatolia and northern Syria. Treaties with Egypt, Babylon, and smaller polities stabilized the region, though repeated wars with Assyria and local rebellions tested its resources.
4. **New Kingdom Egypt**: Rulers like Ramesses II oversaw an empire stretching into Canaan and Nubia. Egypt's wealth came from controlling trade routes and exploiting gold mines in Nubia. A strong bureaucracy and large standing army supported pharaonic rule.
5. **City-States of the Levant**: Including Ugarit, Byblos, and others, these coastal and inland towns thrived on maritime trade, linking Mesopotamia, Egypt, Cyprus, and the Aegean. They were often vassals to bigger powers, paying tribute but retaining local autonomy.
6. **Mesopotamia**: Kassite Babylon, Assyria, and Elam contended for influence. Assyria expanded gradually, Babylon focused on internal development, and Elam periodically intervened in Mesopotamian politics.

This system was surprisingly interconnected, with letters (like the Amarna Letters) detailing gift exchanges, diplomatic marriages, and peaceful or hostile relations. We find Mycenaean pottery in Anatolia or the Levant, Hittite treaties referencing Egyptian campaigns, and so forth. Despite frequent conflicts, these powers also maintained a broad equilibrium. This interplay created a "globalized" Bronze Age economy that thrived for centuries.

---

2. Signs of Tension and Instability

Even before the final collapse, pressures accumulated. Some city-states faced internal rebellions by disgruntled vassals or rival factions. Trade routes, so crucial for tin and copper, had grown more complex to maintain. The Hittite Empire suffered from occasional famine or plague, forcing it to rely heavily on imports of grain from places like Egypt. Egypt, too, began seeing cracks—pharaohs after Ramesses II struggled to maintain control in Canaan, and tomb robberies indicated unrest at home.

Across the Aegean, Mycenaean palaces sometimes vied for control of the same islands or sea routes, leading to local warfare. A few Linear B tablets mention emergency measures or "defensive mobilizations." Archaeological layers show some palaces experiencing destruction events even in the 13th century BCE, prior to the final wave around 1200 BCE. Meanwhile, in Mesopotamia, Assyria rose in strength, challenging older states like Babylon or the Hittites for territory. These simmering rivalries set the stage for a more drastic meltdown.

A crucial factor was the reliance on long-distance trade for metals. If tin or copper shipments were disrupted by wars or piracy, entire bronze industries could falter. Lacking metals, states found it harder to equip armies or maintain lavish building projects, fueling domestic strife. We also see possible climate fluctuations—periods of drought or cooler temperatures—that might have reduced harvests, straining palace economies. This web of interconnected stressors was poised to unravel once severe shock events occurred.

3. The Role of the "Sea Peoples"

One of the most debated aspects of the Bronze Age Collapse is the role of the so-called "Sea Peoples"—a loose term used in Egyptian records to describe naval raiders or migrating groups who appeared in the eastern Mediterranean around the late 13th and early 12th centuries BCE. Pharaoh Merneptah and Ramesses III record battles against these peoples who attempted invasions by both land and sea. They included groups named by the Egyptians as Peleset, Tjekker, Shekelesh, Denyen, and others.

Initially, scholars proposed that the Sea Peoples were the prime cause of destruction across the Aegean and Anatolia. They supposedly sacked the Hittite capital and rampaged along the Levant, toppling city-states and eventually being repulsed by Egypt. However, newer perspectives suggest that these groups were themselves uprooted populations—either due to famine, climate issues, or displacement by earlier conflicts—who moved en masse searching for new lands.

Archaeological evidence shows multiple cities burned around 1200 BCE, some with signs of violent destruction consistent with raids or invasions. Ugarit, a major Levantine port, was destroyed and never fully reoccupied. Hattusa also appears to have been abandoned, though the details are murky. Mycenaean palace sites show burn layers, though it's unclear if "Sea Peoples" or local rebellions were primarily responsible. In any case, these maritime or land-based migrations added to the turmoil, intensifying the collapse rather than acting as its sole cause.

4. Climate and Environmental Factors

Climate change has emerged as another possible catalyst for the Bronze Age Collapse. Proxy data (like pollen analysis, sediment cores) in the eastern Mediterranean and Near East suggest episodes of drought or cooler temperatures around 1200 BCE. Reduced rainfall would severely affect agriculture in marginal zones. Empires such as the Hittites and Mycenaeans, dependent on stable harvests, might have faced famine or economic strain.

In the Levant, recurrent crop failures would undercut city-states reliant on local farmland. Nomadic or semi-nomadic groups might have been forced to migrate for survival, exacerbating tensions. If palace centers could not feed their populations or armies, loyalty would falter, making them vulnerable to raids. While climate shifts alone might not cause total collapse, they could amplify existing fractures—like fueling migrations or uprisings from starving communities.

Furthermore, external trade for grain became riskier if weather disrupted shipping or if other regions also experienced shortages. The system's interdependence meant that a widespread climate downturn could undermine multiple states simultaneously. Crop failures would undermine tax revenues, hamper armies, and push states to scramble for resources, sometimes leading to military conflicts or abrupt dissolution of central authority.

---

5. Economic and Trade Disruptions

The Bronze Age "globalized" economy hinged on metals, especially tin for bronze alloy. Tin was scarce and often had to be imported over long distances (e.g., from Central Asia, the Erzgebirge in Europe, or Cornwall in Britain). If persistent warfare blocked caravans or if maritime routes were compromised by pirates or invading fleets, metal supply chains broke down. Artisans could not produce enough bronze weapons or tools, hindering a state's capacity to fight or maintain infrastructure.

Simultaneously, the flow of luxury goods—like high-quality ceramics, gold, ivory—was disrupted. Elites who depended on foreign luxuries to sustain status lost a key resource. This could spark internal discontent if aristocrats felt the central power failing to deliver prestige goods. Traditional alliances also crumbled: treaties requiring tribute in metal might go unfulfilled, prompting conflict or rebellion. Over time, major ports such as Ugarit were destroyed, so goods from Cyprus or the Aegean no longer arrived. The entire system of interregional exchange that had flourished in the late Bronze Age essentially collapsed, driving polities into more localized, self-sufficient modes.

6. Sociopolitical Upheavals: Rebellions and Class Tensions

In many Bronze Age states, governance rested on a small elite controlling surpluses. Farmers and artisans bore heavy tax burdens. While stable conditions might have been tolerated during times of prosperity, crises could spark uprisings. If harvests failed or leadership lost credibility, internal revolts might break out. Palaces or bureaucratic centers often became targets of looting by local populations fed up with exploitation.

In Mycenaean Greece, the final destruction layers at sites like Pylos or Mycenae might reflect both external invasions and local insurrections. Some evidence suggests entire administrative apparatuses were overthrown. Similarly, in the Hittite realm, subject peoples or local nobles could have rebelled once the central king's grip loosened. Temple or palace storehouses full of grain or bronze goods offered tempting spoils for disaffected groups.

Such internal strife meant states could not respond effectively to external threats like the Sea Peoples or other migrant groups. Garrisons deserted, or soldiers turned against the ruling class. As the "system" of centralized palace control fractured, multiple smaller factions or local warlords emerged, hastening the meltdown. This social dimension reveals that the Bronze Age Collapse did not come solely from outside invaders but also from discontent within.

7. The Hittite Empire's Sudden Fall

Among the great powers, the Hittite Empire's disappearance was particularly dramatic. Around 1200 BCE, Hattusa was abandoned. The empire, once spanning large parts of Anatolia and northern Syria, fragmented. Texts from the empire's final years are scant but hint at famine, invasions, or internal betrayals. Later traditions mention the arrival of new groups in Anatolia, including the Phrygians, though exact timing is debated.

Some Hittite nobles or vassal kings survived, establishing so-called Neo-Hittite city-states in southeastern Anatolia and northern Syria. These smaller polities carried on aspects of Hittite culture—Luwian hieroglyphs, art motifs—but the grand imperial structure was gone. Factors like poor harvests, shifts in trade routes, and external raids from the west or the Gasga tribes in the north are all implicated. The fate of the last known Hittite king, Suppiluliuma II, remains unclear. It is possible he died in battle or fled.

This collapse undermined the entire Anatolian trade network. Regions once dependent on Hittite-protected routes found themselves isolated or forced to pay tribute to local warlords. The vacuum allowed new powers—like early Iron Age polities or even Assyria from the east—to eventually expand. In a matter of decades, a once-formidable empire that had rivaled Egypt became a patchwork of smaller states or deserted ruins, exemplifying how sudden and total the Bronze Age Collapse could be.

---

8. The Mycenaean Downfall in Greece

The Mycenaean world likewise crumbled around 1200 BCE. Palaces that had administered farmland, crafts, and trade were destroyed by fire. Linear B writing disappeared, indicating the bureaucracy dissolved. Large-scale building projects ceased, replaced by simpler living arrangements. Over time, population levels shrank or relocated. Some sites show signs of partial rebuilding, but the distinct Mycenaean "palatial culture" ended.

Reasons for this downfall may include seaborne raiders, internal rivalries among palaces, or general economic breakdown. The storied "Dorian Invasion" of Greek tradition might reflect migrations or a later mythologized memory of northwestern Greek groups moving south. Archaeology suggests multiple destructions over decades, not a single event. Trade with the eastern Mediterranean fell sharply, so Mycenaean elites could no longer secure metals or exotic goods, weakening their power.

A "Dark Age" followed, in which writing vanished and material culture became less elaborate. Many people moved inland, favoring defensible highland sites. Over centuries, new groups (Ionians, Dorians, Aeolians) shaped regional identities, sowing seeds for the later rise of the Greek city-states (poleis) in the

Iron Age. The memory of Mycenaean heroes endured in epic poetry, like the Homeric tales, but the centralized palace system never reemerged in the same form.

---

9. Egypt Under Pressure: From Merneptah to Ramesses III

Egypt was one of the few major Bronze Age powers to withstand the immediate collapse, though it emerged weakened. Pharaoh Merneptah (late 13th century BCE) recorded victories over Libyans and "Sea Peoples," but internal strife simmered. A generation later, Ramesses III (20th Dynasty) faced major invasions by sea and land. His mortuary temple at Medinet Habu depicts pitched battles against these mysterious groups. While Egypt prevailed, the cost was high—resources drained, and the empire in Canaan largely lost.

Furthermore, evidence points to economic troubles and labor strikes (like the famous Deir el-Medina strike) in Ramesses III's reign. The priesthood of Amun grew powerful, controlling large estates. The grand days of universal empire were over. Although the pharaoh still claimed cosmic authority, dynastic instability and corruption undermined royal power. Egypt retreated from Asia, focusing on internal matters.

For centuries, Egypt had anchored a stable system of trade and tribute. Now with the Levant in chaos and the Hittites gone, Egyptian commerce declined. Freed from Egyptian oversight, local rulers in Canaan or Syria formed small independent states or fell under new influences. As the Bronze Age ended, Egypt remained a recognizable entity but lost its extended empire. In the Iron Age, new challengers, like the Libyans or Nubians, frequently tested the Nile Valley from the west and south.

---

10. Mesopotamia: Power Shifts and the Assyrian Rise

Mesopotamia fared differently than the Aegean or Anatolia. Around 1200 BCE, Kassite Babylon was weakening, and Elam seized the moment to invade, plundering Babylon's treasures. The Kassite dynasty fell, replaced by new local rulers. In the north, **Assyria** was on the rise, though it also faced challenges. The broader trade disruptions affected Mesopotamian commerce, but the region's strong agricultural base ensured many cities persisted.

In time, Assyria overcame its rivals, establishing a new imperial phase in the Iron Age. The older Bronze Age city-states of the middle Euphrates, some of which might have recognized Hittite or Babylonian suzerainty, collapsed under warfare or migrations. Population shifts forced a reorganization of the political map. Although not as dramatic as the Mycenaean or Hittite disappearance, the transformations in Mesopotamia were significant—an older balance gave way to new powers, setting the stage for the Neo-Assyrian Empire.

The impetus behind these changes included the knock-on effects from the Mediterranean collapse. Fewer goods arrived from the Aegean or the Levant, undermining local industries reliant on raw materials. Political elites also shifted alliances. In short, Mesopotamia remained a crucial cultural core, but the world around it changed drastically, leading to a reconfigured network of states by the turn of the Iron Age.

---

11. The Levant and Coastal Cities: Ugarit's Demise

No region better illustrates the abrupt nature of the collapse than the **Levant**, where coastal ports thrived on maritime trade. A prime example is **Ugarit**, a wealthy city-state in modern Syria. Famous for its cuneiform tablets in multiple languages (including an early alphabetic script), Ugarit was a cultural and commercial nexus. Around 1190–1180 BCE, the city was destroyed, likely by seaborne raiders or local conflicts. The palace archives show letters left unsent, ovens unextinguished—evidence of sudden calamity.

Ugarit's fall severed a key link connecting Hittite Anatolia, Cyprus, Mesopotamia, and Egypt. Similar fates befell other cities along the coast, some recovering under new rulers while others vanished. The Phoenician cities (Tyre, Sidon, Byblos) might have survived by adapting to new conditions, eventually rising in the Iron Age as maritime traders. But the older Bronze Age networks, reliant on stable alliances with Hatti or Egypt, crumbled. With the Hittites gone and Egypt in retreat, the Levantine political landscape fragmented.

The destruction of these ports meant an end to many scribal and cultural traditions. The libraries and archives were buried in ash, while any local elites who fled or died took with them the memory of integrated Bronze Age diplomacy. Survivors reorganized into smaller city-states or migrated inland. A transitional period followed, leading to the emergence of new polities—Aramaean tribes, early Israelite communities, and eventually the Phoenician city-states that shaped Iron Age commerce.

12. Collapse in Europe Beyond the Aegean

While the meltdown in the Aegean is most famous, broader Europe also experienced shifts around this era. In parts of Central Europe, cultures like the Urnfield tradition (c. 1300–800 BCE) continued, evolving from earlier Bronze Age groups (Unetice, Tumulus). Some regions saw expansions of hillfort building, possibly due to insecurity or population movements. The Atlantic coast, including Britain and Ireland, also displayed changes in settlement patterns, though not as stark as the Mycenaean downfall.

Farther north, the Nordic Bronze Age ended around 500 BCE—so it didn't align exactly with the 1200 BCE crisis. Yet some disruptions in amber trade or local power structures may have coincided with the Mediterranean meltdown. The overall interconnectedness was not as intense as in the East, so while influences arrived from the Aegean or the Near East, local cultures might have adapted more gradually.

Nevertheless, the collapse of Mycenaean palatial centers impacted maritime links. Fewer Mycenaean trade vessels reached the western Mediterranean or the Atlantic. Overland contacts with the Balkans also changed, as the Greek world entered a "Dark Age." This shift, in turn, shaped the trajectory of early Iron Age cultures in Europe, which developed more localized identities, forging new connections once Phoenician or later Greek colonists appeared in subsequent centuries.

13. China's Parallel Developments (Shang to Zhou)

China's Bronze Age disruptions took a different path. Around 1046 BCE, the Shang Dynasty fell to the Zhou. This shift did not coincide precisely with the eastern Mediterranean collapse timeline, but it did represent a major transition in Chinese political structure. The Zhou introduced the Mandate of Heaven concept, claiming the Shang lost divine favor due to tyranny.

This transition was violent but also somewhat orderly in the sense that the Zhou retained many Shang cultural practices (bronze casting, ancestral worship) while reasserting them under a new feudal system. The Shang capital, Yin (Anyang), might have faced sacking, but the broader region quickly adapted to Zhou rule. Bronze technology continued to flourish, and the Zhou managed to build a network of vassal states.

Thus, China's Bronze Age transformation was more internal and ideological than the catastrophic meltdown seen in the Aegean. China was less integrated with the Near Eastern trade networks, so the "Bronze Age Collapse" in the West had little direct effect. The Shang-to-Zhou shift underscores that "collapse" need not be universal or identically timed. Regional contexts mattered greatly in determining how a Bronze Age society navigated transitions into new eras.

14. Systemic Failure: Complexity Theories

Some scholars propose that the Bronze Age societies grew so complex—economically and politically—that they became vulnerable to cascading failures. When one pillar collapsed (like a major trade route or a key resource), the entire system began to fall. A city reliant on distant tin supplies that suddenly vanished could not maintain its bronze-dependent army, leading to defeats or revolts.

Additionally, the palace economies demanded constant inflows of prestige goods to keep elites loyal. If external crises halted these imports, elites might lose faith in the central administration. The multiplicity of alliances and dependencies meant small shocks could amplify. A single destructive raid might topple a city, forcing refugees to flee, who then stressed neighboring regions, creating further instability.

This perspective sees the Bronze Age as a "complex system" with tight interlocking parts. The more globalized it became, the more a single failure could spread. This does not negate the roles of climate, invasions, or local rebellions; rather, it integrates them, explaining how the synergy of factors resulted in widespread collapse. Once disintegration began, states were too intertwined and specialized to revert smoothly to simpler modes, leading to centuries-long disruptions.

15. Archaeological Traces of Catastrophe

Archaeologists unearth tangible signs of the collapse: burned layers in major palaces (Pylos, Mycenae, Hattusa, Ugarit), abrupt ends to local pottery styles, hoards of valuables hastily buried and never retrieved, half-finished letters or shipping tablets, and destruction debris containing arrowheads or sling stones. In some cities, these layers are thick with rubble, collapsed walls, and charred timbers, indicating violent or accidental fires.

In other places, we find skeletal remains suggesting massacre or hasty burials. The disappearance of certain goods—like Mycenaean fineware in the Levant or Cypriot copper ingots in the Aegean—signals broken supply lines. The once-lively port at Ugarit shows no reoccupation. In Greece, population data from settlement patterns confirm that many lowland palace sites were abandoned, with people moving to defensible hilltops.

These traces confirm a major rupture. But they do not always clarify cause. A burned palace could result from foreign attackers, local revolt, or accidental fire amid general unrest. The timeline sometimes spans decades, so "collapse" might have been a drawn-out process with multiple waves of destruction. Nonetheless, the archaeological record collectively points to the disintegration of the vibrant Bronze Age system that had thrived for centuries.

---

16. Refugees, Migrants, and Cultural Mixing

When cities fell, survivors scattered. Some may have joined marauding groups labeled "Sea Peoples," while others fled to safer regions. This led to cultural mixing: exiles carried traditions from Mycenae or Ugarit to new settlements. Pottery or decorative styles can appear far from their homelands, suggesting diaspora communities. Another example is the presence of "Mycenaean-style" swords in Cyprus or the Levant even after Mycenaean palaces were gone.

Such migrations often triggered local tension. Host communities might fear newcomers, leading to skirmishes or assimilation. Over time, small pockets of immigrants formed new polities or integrated with locals. In the Iron Age, we see evidence of such blended communities. Some might have formed the biblical Philistines (linked to the "Peleset" of Egyptian records), bringing Aegean customs to Canaan's coast. This partially explains the distinct cultural layers visible in post-Bronze Age archaeological contexts.

While displacement was traumatic, it also catalyzed innovation. People adapted to new environments, forging fresh alliances. Skills like bronze-smithing or seafaring survived, albeit on a smaller scale. Over decades or centuries, these pockets of migrants shaped the cultural mosaic of the early Iron Age, retaining echoes of their old Bronze Age heritages.

---

17. The Aftermath in Different Regions

By about 1100 BCE, the immediate storm of destruction had passed, but the political landscape was drastically altered:

- **Greece**: Entered the "Greek Dark Age," a period with reduced population, loss of literacy, and simpler material culture. Over centuries, new social structures emerged, eventually giving rise to the Archaic Greek city-states.
- **Anatolia**: Fragmented into Neo-Hittite or Syro-Hittite states in the south, while new groups like the Phrygians or Lydians emerged in the west. The once-central Hittite monarchy vanished.
- **Levant**: Coastal cities either destroyed or reorganized. Phoenician polities rose, focusing on maritime trade. Inland, new tribal groups (Aramaeans, Israelites, others) formed small kingdoms.
- **Egypt**: Survived but entered a slow decline. The New Kingdom ended, giving way to the Third Intermediate Period, with weaker central power and strong regional factions.
- **Mesopotamia**: After some turmoil, new powers like the Neo-Assyrian state took shape. Babylon continued under different dynasties.
- **Cyprus**: Suffered destruction at key sites, then saw migrations of Greek speakers, leading to a blend of cultures in the early Iron Age.

In each region, the central Bronze Age palatial model gave way to more localized systems. Trade networks changed hands or shrank in scope. Overland or sea routes eventually revived but with new players—Phoenicians, Aramaeans, smaller Greek communities, and so forth. The old empire alliances never returned; the Bronze Age "global" culture was gone, replaced by more fragmented, evolving Iron Age societies.

18. Scholarly Debates: Single Cause vs. Multicausal Approaches

For decades, researchers argued over a single prime cause—were the Sea Peoples solely responsible? Or was climate the key factor? More recently, consensus leans toward a "multicausal" approach. The collapse was not an overnight invasion but a confluence of forces:

1. **Climate Stress**: Droughts or temperature shifts undermined agriculture.
2. **Invasions/Migrations**: Displaced groups attacking or resettling in the Eastern Mediterranean.
3. **Internal Revolts**: Subjects overthrowing palace elites or seizing surpluses amid crises.
4. **Trade Disruption**: Metal shortages crippling militaries and economies.
5. **Systems Complexity**: Interdependence amplifying local crises into regional collapse.

While not every region experienced every factor equally, the synergy of multiple stresses caused widespread transformations. The differing timelines or intensities reflect local resilience. Some pockets endured or adapted—Egypt resisted invasions for a time, Assyria rebuilt an empire in the Iron Age. But for many, the synergy spelled the end of centuries-old traditions. This broad perspective clarifies why we call it a "collapse" rather than a simple shift—major political, economic, and cultural pillars fractured almost simultaneously.

---

19. Cultural Memory and Myths of a Heroic Age

Long after the dust settled, later civilizations preserved memories or myths of a lost "heroic age." In Greece, poets like Homer or Hesiod recounted tales of mighty Mycenaean kings (Agamemnon, Odysseus) who fought epic wars (Trojan War) and interacted with gods. These stories likely blurred real Bronze Age events with legend, forging a romantic narrative that influenced Greek identity.

In Anatolia, echoes of Hittite grandeur lingered among Neo-Hittite states, though direct continuity was partial. Mesopotamian scribes remembered the Kassites or older city-states as part of a grand lineage, weaving historical kings into genealogical lists. Egyptians wrote about past glories under Ramesses II or earlier pharaohs, even as they recognized their empire had retracted.

CHAPTER 18: AFTERMATH OF THE BRONZE AGE COLLAPSE

Introduction

After the upheaval of the Bronze Age Collapse, many regions experienced depopulation, cultural shifts, and a decline in long-distance trade. But human societies adapt. Over the 12th to 10th centuries BCE, survivors rebuilt settlements, forged new alliances, and introduced technological or social changes that marked the dawn of the Iron Age. The end of old palatial structures did not mean an end to civilization; rather, it spurred a complex process of reorganization that varied by region.

In this chapter, we will explore how different areas—Greece, Anatolia, the Levant, Egypt, Mesopotamia, and beyond—navigated this transition. We will examine population movements, the spread of iron technology, shifts in governance, and the development of new cultural identities. Though the immediate aftermath might appear as a "dark age," it laid critical foundations for emerging empires and city-states that would define later antiquity. Understanding this recovery phase shows us how communities overcame crisis, blending old traditions with innovations that shaped the Iron Age world.

---

1. Defining "Aftermath" and Recovery

The decades following the Bronze Age Collapse—roughly 1200 to 1000 BCE—are sometimes labeled a "dark age," particularly in the Aegean, due to reduced literacy, simpler material culture, and the breakdown of prior state structures. Yet the term "dark age" can be misleading. While many palaces lay in ruins and large-scale building ceased, smaller communities continued to function. People did not vanish; they simply reorganized politically and economically.

Recovery varied in speed. Some sites were reoccupied quickly, with partial continuity in craftsmanship or local governance, while others lay abandoned for generations. New or expanded settlements emerged in more defensible locations—cliff edges, hilltops, or easily fortified peninsulas—reflecting ongoing insecurity. Over time, population levels rebounded, local trade resumed, and new elites formed. Gradually, iron tools and weapons began to replace bronze, opening fresh possibilities in agriculture and warfare.

The immediate aftermath thus entailed a patchwork of local revivals and ongoing crises. Each region had unique conditions—Egypt maintained some continuity under later dynasties, while Mycenaean Greece lost literacy. We can see this transitional era as an essential bridging period, sowing seeds for future polities like the Neo-Assyrian Empire, the Phoenician city-states, or the classical Greek poleis.

---

2. Greece: From Palaces to "Dark Age" Communities

In Greece, the collapse of Mycenaean palaces triggered a centuries-long transitional era (c. 1100–800 BCE). Writing (Linear B) vanished, trade networks shrank, and many sophisticated crafts declined. Large building projects stopped, replaced by modest homes of wood and stone. Key sites, such as Mycenae or Tiryns, might have retained some inhabitants, but they no longer displayed monumental architecture or elaborate burials.

Population movement was significant. People migrated to regions like Ionia (western Anatolia), possibly explaining Greek legends of Ionian settlements. Others retreated to isolated upland zones. Archaeological evidence shows a simpler pottery style—often called "Sub-Mycenaean" or "Protogeometric"—replacing the flamboyant Mycenaean ceramics. Over time, the Protogeometric style evolved into Geometric, marking a slow cultural revival.

Socially, power shifted from centralized palaces to local chiefs or clan leaders. Without a strong bureaucracy, communities made decisions collectively or under minor local dynasties. Yet these centuries laid down future frameworks: small, autonomous communities that would later become city-states (poleis). By around 800 BCE, literacy returned in the form of a new Greek alphabet (adapted from Phoenician), and trade with the Near East reawakened. The "dark age" ended as Greece entered its Archaic period, forging the path to classical civilization.

While the collapse was traumatic, this period fostered social and political experimentation. Freed from palace constraints, some communities developed egalitarian tendencies or new forms of leadership. Epic poetry—like the Iliad and

Odyssey—preserved memory of the Mycenaean past, fueling a heroic ethos that influenced the evolving Greek identity.

3. Anatolia: Neo-Hittite States and New Ethnic Groups

The fall of the Hittite Empire left Anatolia fragmented into smaller polities. Former Hittite territories in southeastern Anatolia and northern Syria became **Neo-Hittite** or Syro-Hittite city-states, such as Carchemish, Melid, and Gurgum. Though independent, they preserved aspects of Hittite language (Luwian) and iconography, carving reliefs on city gates and producing inscriptions in Luwian hieroglyphs. Some recognized each other's kings in loose alliances or short-lived confederations.

In western and central Anatolia, new or previously minor groups rose to prominence. The **Phrygians**, possibly related to peoples who migrated from the Balkans, established a kingdom with Gordium as a center. Their traditions included tumulus burials reminiscent of earlier barrow practices, and they eventually developed a distinctive Iron Age culture. Further south, the Lydians also emerged as a notable power in the Iron Age.

Archaeological remains show a shift from the grand Hittite palatial structures to smaller fortified sites. The scale of building shrank, but creativity endured. Neo-Hittite rulers commissioned basalt reliefs depicting hunts or religious scenes, merging old Hittite motifs with local tastes. Over time, these states contended with Aramean expansions and eventually faced the might of the Neo-Assyrian Empire, which in the 9th–8th centuries BCE would conquer or vassalize many. Thus, Anatolia's post-collapse identity was a mosaic of small polities, each blending Hittite legacy with new influences.

4. The Levant: Rise of Phoenician and Aramaean Polities

With the destruction of Ugarit and other coastal centers, the Levant entered a transitional phase where the old Bronze Age city-state system gave way to smaller, more flexible polities. Among the survivors, **Byblos**, **Tyre**, and **Sidon**—cities the Greeks later called "Phoenician"—rose to new prominence. Freed from Hittite or Egyptian oversight, they exploited maritime trade routes, venturing westward to establish outposts that foreshadowed the great Phoenician colonization in the Iron Age (like Carthage in North Africa, later on).

In inland regions, **Aramaean** tribes consolidated power, founding new kingdoms (Damascus, Hamath, Zobah). These states controlled caravan routes and farmland, sometimes building city walls and palaces reminiscent of older traditions but on a smaller scale. The biblical narratives record the emergence of Israelite tribes in Canaan, though evidence is still debated among archaeologists. Moab, Ammon, and Edom likewise formed local kingdoms. This patchwork replaced the older system of vassals under major empires, making the Levant a hotbed of smaller, fiercely independent realms.

Iron weapons began appearing in increasing numbers, giving some advantage to states that mastered smelting and forging techniques. Phoenician traders also introduced an **alphabetic** writing system, derived from earlier local scripts, which would profoundly shape literacy across the Mediterranean. Thus, while the Bronze Age collapse destroyed older centers, it paved the way for a dynamic Iron Age Levant, known for maritime enterprise, linguistic innovation, and new political forms.

---

5. Egypt's Third Intermediate Period

Egypt, though it repelled the Sea Peoples under Ramesses III, emerged from the crisis weakened. The 20th Dynasty ended in turmoil as priestly and military factions vied for control. The New Kingdom gave way to the **Third Intermediate Period** (c. 1070–664 BCE). Different families or lineages, some with Libyan roots, controlled the Delta region, while Thebes in Upper Egypt often fell under the authority of high priests of Amun.

No longer able to maintain a buffer in Canaan or extensive trade outposts, Egypt retreated within its borders. Tomb building scaled down from grand complexes to smaller chapels or burials. Art and architecture continued but lacked the unified, lavish style of earlier dynasties. Over centuries, petty dynasties rose and fell, sometimes uniting parts of the country. Meanwhile, external powers—like the Nubian kingdom of Kush—took advantage, even ruling Egypt for a time during the 25th Dynasty.

Though the pharaoh's cosmic role persisted in religious ideology, real power was fragmented. This intermediate era underscores that survival did not guarantee prosperity. Egypt endured as a cultural entity but lost the imperial might it once wielded. Trade revived eventually—Phoenicians plied the Mediterranean, Greek merchants arrived in the Delta—but the old Bronze Age ways of direct Egyptian hegemony in Asia were gone. In time, new alliances formed, setting the stage for eventual confrontation with rising Near Eastern empires.

6. Mesopotamia's Transformation: Babylon, Assyria, and Elam

In Mesopotamia, the Kassite rule in Babylon ended around 1155 BCE when Elamite forces sacked the city. Subsequently, Isin and other local dynasties attempted to restore Babylonian might, but it was a slow process. Over the following centuries, Babylonia remained culturally rich—scribal traditions, religious temples continued—but politically it was overshadowed by Elam or Assyria.

Assyria, despite some initial struggles, capitalized on the power vacuum. By the 10th and 9th centuries BCE, it embarked on conquests that built the **Neo-Assyrian Empire**, arguably the first "superpower" of the early Iron Age. The region's strong agricultural base, combined with the legacy of cuneiform bureaucracy, allowed for a more rapid reestablishment of centralized authority. The old Bronze Age city-state model gave way to imperial provinces governed by Assyrian officials.

Elam, in southwestern Iran, played a role in Babylon's affairs and occasionally clashed with Assyria. Although Elamite culture retained distinct language and traditions, it also adopted or adapted Mesopotamian influences. Over time, Elam itself faced conquests by the Neo-Assyrians. Thus, Mesopotamia's post-collapse epoch saw the consolidation of larger territorial states, a departure from the patchwork of Bronze Age polities. This was a new era shaped by iron weaponry, militarized expansions, and evolving administrative structures.

7. Cyprus and the Shifts in Maritime Trade

Cyprus, known for copper (the island's name may derive from "copper" itself), was a vital supplier during the Bronze Age. It had close ties to Mycenaean Greece and the Levant, hosting mixed Greek-Anatolian communities by the 13th century BCE. The collapse impacted Cyprus severely—some port towns show destruction layers, though not always as abrupt as in Ugarit. Nevertheless, the old trade patterns faltered, forcing communities on Cyprus to adapt or relocate.

In the later 12th and 11th centuries BCE, a wave of Greek-speaking settlers likely arrived, merging with local populations to form distinct city-kingdoms. This blending introduced new pottery styles (e.g., "Cypro-Geometric") and social forms. Over time, Cyprus reestablished maritime links, this time more strongly connected to the emerging Phoenician networks. Eventually, the island boasted a patchwork of small polities (like Kition, Salamis) with Greek or Phoenician influences.

So, while Cyprus lost its Bronze Age position as a metal-trade linchpin, it emerged in the Iron Age with renewed importance as a cultural crossroads. The legacy of copper exploitation continued, but the scale and nature of commerce changed, reflecting the broader shift in Eastern Mediterranean power.

---

8. Shifts in Material Culture: Iron Replacing Bronze

One of the hallmark changes in the aftermath was the gradual adoption of **iron** in tools and weapons. Initially, iron smelting was labor-intensive, requiring high temperatures and specialized forges. Yet iron ore was far more common than tin or copper. As knowledge spread, iron production became cheaper, enabling local communities to arm themselves without depending on distant tin sources.

By the 10th century BCE, iron swords, spearheads, and farming implements began to outnumber bronze in many regions, from the Levant to Greece and Mesopotamia. This transition varied—Egypt, for instance, continued using bronze for certain ceremonial items, and high-quality steel making was still centuries away. But the widespread availability of iron changed power balances. Smaller states that previously lacked reliable metal supplies could now manufacture or acquire weapons more readily, fostering new military opportunities.

The shift also affected craft organization. Bronze-smithing workshops adapted or closed, while blacksmiths rose in importance. Artisans sometimes combined iron for functional edges with bronze or decorative metals for handles or ornamentation. This new technology encouraged local independence from the grand trade networks of the Bronze Age, though it took time to perfect forging techniques that matched the strength of well-made bronze. Over generations, iron would prove a decisive factor in the ascendancy of new empires like Assyria, forging an Iron Age world order.

---

9. Language, Writing, and Literacy Changes

The collapse saw disruptions in scribal traditions. **Linear B** vanished from Greece, leading to centuries without writing. Hittite cuneiform ended with Hattusa's abandonment, though Luwian hieroglyphic scripts persisted in Neo-Hittite states. Egyptian hieroglyphic continued, but usage shrank during internal strife. Mesopotamia kept cuneiform, though Babylonian and Assyrian dialects shifted over time. The Indus script was already defunct, as that civilization had declined earlier.

Concurrently, new writing systems or adaptations emerged. Phoenician scribes refined an alphabetic script that used fewer symbols than cuneiform. This script eventually influenced Aramaic, Hebrew, Greek, and beyond, revolutionizing literacy. Aramaic spread across the Levant and later became a lingua franca in the Near East, partly because of its simplified alphabet. Greek, once reintroduced with an alphabet derived from Phoenician letters around the 8th century BCE, soared in usage and cultural expression.

Literacy also took new social forms. Instead of being confined to palatial bureaucracies, reading and writing might become more accessible to merchants or local officials. This shift foreshadows the Iron Age emphasis on alphabets as opposed to the older syllabic or logo-syllabic systems. Thus, while the collapse ended or reduced some scribal cultures, it indirectly paved the way for new scripts that democratized literacy in subsequent centuries.

---

10. New Political Experiments and State Forms

With the old palace-based states dismantled, survivors experimented with alternative governance. In Greece, small tribal or clan-based units eventually crystallized into early poleis, each with distinct customs and leadership structures. Some formed oligarchies led by local aristocrats; others had a "basileus" (chief/king) with limited power. Over time, these city-states revived trade and set up colonies abroad, culminating in the Archaic Greek civilization.

In the Levant, local dynasties—Aramaean, Phoenician, Israelite, etc.—organized city-kingdoms or tribal confederations. They balanced negotiations with rising empires, forging vassal treaties or short-lived alliances. Egypt navigated the Third Intermediate Period through a patchwork of local dynasties. Mesopotamia saw the resurgence of strong monarchies in Assyria. Anatolia fostered numerous petty kingdoms with Hittite cultural roots or new ethnic identities.

This proliferation of political diversity contrasts with the Bronze Age, where a few major powers overshadowed smaller states. The fragmentation allowed for more regional autonomy, though it also invited conflict. Some historians argue this era laid the groundwork for dynamic development in the Iron Age—smaller states might innovate militarily or economically to survive. Over centuries, certain powers (Assyria, in particular) reimposed large-scale empire building, but the spirit of local governance and alliances shaped the new world.

---

11. Social Structures: From Palace Elites to Local Chieftains

During the Bronze Age, palaces had concentrated power among royal families, priests, scribes, and warrior elites. The collapse disrupted these hierarchies. Many palace elites lost their privileges if they couldn't maintain shipments of exotic goods or lavish building projects. Freed from palace taxes, some rural communities might have found new forms of leadership—local chieftains or councils that replaced the old bureaucracy.

However, social inequality did not vanish. Ambitious warlords or tribal chiefs rose in the power vacuum, controlling farmland and forging small-scale aristocracies. Over time, these elites consolidated, leading to new "kingdoms" or city-based leadership. Yet these polities often had smaller scale than the former Bronze Age states, focusing on local alliances or defense.

For peasants, life could be harsh: frequent raids, uncertain harvests, and less centralized protection. Some found new opportunities to migrate, seeking better farmland. Craftspeople adapted by producing simpler goods for local customers, though a fraction specialized in forging iron. The social pyramid was somewhat flattened compared to palace times, yet inequalities persisted. Gradually, fresh aristocracies emerged, often referencing "heroic ancestors" or forging genealogies connecting them to older traditions, thus maintaining some continuity in status-based societies.

12. Cultural Memory and Oral Traditions

With the loss of writing in places like Greece, or the decline of older scribal institutions in the Levant and Anatolia, oral tradition became a key vessel for preserving history and myths. Epic poems, genealogies, and heroic sagas were recited by bards or storytellers, shaping communal identity. The stories of Trojan heroes, the voyages of Odysseus, or local mythic battles stemmed from these centuries of retelling.

In the Near East, literate centers like Assyria or Babylonia continued some scribal lines, but even there, older archives were lost or scattered. The Hittite script was all but forgotten outside a few Neo-Hittite enclaves. Egyptian priests archived temple records, but with limited new expansions, historical inscriptions focused on local events. Over generations, legends about the once-great bronze societies turned into foundational myths or cautionary tales.

Such oral traditions could unify emerging communities. For instance, the biblical narratives of exodus or conquest might partially reflect Bronze Age migrations and collapse experiences, though shaped by later theological frames. Greek bardic traditions provided a sense of shared heritage for scattered communities, eventually culminating in the Homeric epics. These cultural memories bridged the gap between the lost Bronze Age polities and the reemerging Iron Age societies.

13. Trade Revival in the Early Iron Age

Though the immediate decades after 1200 BCE saw trade decline, new networks slowly formed. The **Phoenicians**, in particular, seized maritime opportunities by the 10th and 9th centuries BCE, sailing far west to establish colonies like Gadir

(Cádiz) in Iberia. They traded purple dye, cedarwood, glass, and metal goods. Greek traders later joined in, founding their own colonies around the Mediterranean. These Iron Age expansions partly replaced the old Bronze Age route system, but with new centers and players.

Assyria, once it consolidated, also sought to rebuild overland routes, forcibly integrating the Levant, parts of Anatolia, and Babylonia. Meanwhile, local markets in each region adapted to iron-based economies, though bronze remained for decorative or ceremonial objects. Some earlier trade goods—like Aegean pottery or Cypriot copper—resurfaced in new forms, reflecting changed tastes and production techniques.

This revival was not a simple restoration of Bronze Age systems. The political and cultural environment was now different. City-states or petty kingdoms negotiated individually, forging alliances or paying tribute to bigger powers like Assyria or, in the west, emerging states in Italy. Over centuries, robust networks did reappear, fueling the famed "Orientalizing" influences on Archaic Greece and the broader Iron Age leaps in cultural exchange.

---

14. Technological and Agricultural Adjustments

Aside from iron-making, agriculture also evolved post-collapse. Some populations introduced or refined new strains of cereals, or adapted terraced farming in marginal areas. Freed from the heavy palace demands, smaller communities experimented with different cropping patterns or livestock rearing. In the Levant, for example, hill-country settlements improved orchard cultivation (olives, figs) that supplemented cereals.

As population densities fell in some zones, farmland reverted to pasture or forest. This might have aided the recovery of soils but also reduced overall surpluses. Over time, communities that stabilized often reinvested in modest irrigation or drainage systems, less grand than Bronze Age canal works but sufficient for local needs. This decentralization allowed for resilient local food production.

Craftsmen learned to handle iron for plowshares, eventually boosting productivity. In tandem, simpler polities demanded fewer massive building projects. The shift from large palace consumption to smaller local markets changed supply chains. Production and consumption realigned, but it took generations to fully exploit iron-based agriculture and toolmaking. By the 9th or 8th century BCE, many societies saw revived populations, improved yields, and new social structures that harnessed these innovations.

---

15. Religious Continuities and Transformations

Religious beliefs often proved resilient amid collapse, but practice adapted to new circumstances. In Greece, the worship of gods like Zeus, Hera, or Poseidon might trace back to Mycenaean times under different names or forms. Local shrines replaced palatial sanctuaries. Over centuries, Greek religion evolved, eventually developing the pan-Hellenic pantheon recognized in the Archaic and Classical eras.

Egypt preserved many temple cults, though the Third Intermediate Period diluted centralized priestly control. The Hittite pantheon lingered in Neo-Hittite states, morphing into local forms. The Levant saw continued devotion to Baal, El, Astarte, and other deities, though smaller city-states might highlight particular local gods. Aramaean or Israelite religious developments introduced monolatrous or monotheistic trends, culminating in the Hebrew tradition.

Ritual objects and temple building scaled down or took new shapes. In some areas, we see continuity in burying the dead with grave goods, but on a smaller scale than the opulent Bronze Age tombs. New types of cultic symbols emerged, reflecting either migrations or syncretism with indigenous beliefs. Overall, religion remained a cornerstone of identity, bridging old and new. People still prayed for harvests, offered sacrifices for protection, and recast their pantheons to fit the Iron Age environment.

---

16. The Birth of New Identities: Aramaeans, Israelites, Philistines

In the Levant, the power vacuum allowed tribal or migrant groups to forge new polities:

- **Aramaeans**: Originating from northern Syrian and steppe regions, they established city-states (Damascus, Hamath). Their Aramaic language spread widely, eventually becoming a lingua franca.

- **Israelites**: According to biblical tradition, tribes coalesced in Canaan after the collapse. Archaeology suggests hill-country villages expanded, showing local distinct pottery and architecture. By the 10th century BCE, they formed early monarchies (Saul, David, Solomon).
- **Philistines**: Possibly linked to the Peleset of Egyptian records, they settled coastal Canaan (Gaza, Ashkelon, etc.). Their pottery styles show Aegean influences, and they quickly adapted to local Levantine culture.

These groups reconfigured local politics, displacing older city-states or blending with them. Their languages, settlement patterns, and religious rites drew on diverse heritages—some from the Bronze Age, others from new migrations. By the Iron Age, the Levant was no longer overshadowed by Hittite or Egyptian empires, but alive with smaller states forging distinct identities that shaped biblical-era history and beyond.

17. The Neo-Assyrian Emergence

While many old powers vanished, **Assyria** reemerged as a formidable empire in the early Iron Age (circa 10th–9th centuries BCE). Building on leftover knowledge from Bronze Age scribal and military traditions, Assyria systematically conquered neighboring lands, from Babylonia to Syria-Palestine. This expansion contrasted with the older Bronze Age pattern of multiple great kingdoms; the Neo-Assyrian Empire eventually dwarfed its predecessors in scale and administrative sophistication.

The reasons for Assyria's success included iron weaponry, a professional army, siege engineering, and advanced logistics. It also reasserted cuneiform record-keeping and introduced new forms of imperial governance, appointing provincial governors loyal to the king. The memory of Bronze Age complexities helped shape Assyrian policies on tribute, trade, and diplomacy. They recognized that controlling metals, harvests, and roads was vital.

In effect, the Neo-Assyrian state represented a "next generation" empire, forging an Iron Age order that replaced the old Bronze Age interplay of multiple, similarly scaled powers. It systematically subjugated or destroyed smaller polities, from the Levant to parts of Anatolia. This milestone signaled that the world after the collapse was not "less civilized," but rather on a trajectory toward new forms of large-scale imperial rule, culminating in even mightier Iron Age empires like the Neo-Babylonian and Persian states.

18. Influence on Later Civilizations

The rebuilding and reorganizing of societies after the Bronze Age Collapse laid important cultural and institutional foundations. For instance:

- **Greek Civilization**: The recolonization and reintroduction of writing (the Greek alphabet) in the 8th century BCE led to the birth of classical Greek literature, philosophy, and the polis system. Concepts of citizenship, law, and civic identity arguably trace back to earlier local governance that crystallized after the collapse.
- **Levantine Trade**: Phoenicians honed maritime commerce, founding colonies throughout the Mediterranean. Their alphabet shaped scripts from Greek to Aramaic, becoming a cornerstone of Western literacy.
- **Mesopotamian Empire-Building**: The success of the Neo-Assyrians, followed by the Neo-Babylonian and Persian Empires, drew on knowledge gleaned from older states but reorganized it for the new political environment.
- **Biblical Traditions**: Israelite identity, shaped in the centuries following the collapse, influenced religious texts that form the basis of major world faiths.
- **Cultural Memory**: Myths of a lost "heroic age" in Greek epic or the Hittite imperial memory among Neo-Hittite states framed how later peoples viewed the past, eventually documented by classical historians.

Thus, while the Bronze Age world ended, its remnants and transformations seeded the cultural and political growth of the early Iron Age. The new societies integrated older heritage with fresh innovations, eventually giving rise to hallmark civilizations of the first millennium BCE.

---

19. The Long Shadow of Collapse

The Bronze Age Collapse remains a case study in the fragility of complex societies. It shows how extensive trade and interdependencies can lead to prosperity but also to systemic vulnerability. Modern scholars draw parallels with contemporary globalization, noting that external shocks—environmental crises, mass migrations, supply chain disruptions—can produce cascading effects if not managed.

Ancient communities tried to adapt: some with defensive measures, others with new alliances or local resilience strategies. They show that after catastrophic decline, reconstruction is possible, though it can take centuries and yield quite different socio-political structures. The Iron Age saw fewer giant, near-equal powers; instead, single massive empires (like Assyria) or localized city-states rose. That shift underscores how collapses can reshape geopolitics in unpredictable ways.

The Bronze Age memory lingers because of the starkness of the meltdown. The richly interwoven trade networks that had spanned from Greece to Mesopotamia, from Egypt to Anatolia, were severed. The scale of destruction at places like Mycenae or Ugarit is haunting, reminding us that even advanced systems are not immune to breakdown. Yet from these ruins, the seeds of future empires, alphabets, and religious traditions sprouted—signifying that collapse can also be a catalyst for reinvention.

CHAPTER 19: LEGENDS AND MYTHS FROM THE BRONZE AGE

Introduction

Myths and legends formed a key part of how Bronze Age peoples understood their world—how they related to gods, explained nature's forces, justified royal authority, and commemorated heroic deeds. Much of what we call "myth" today was once living religious narrative, interwoven with daily rituals. Though many Bronze Age texts are lost or remain partially known, surviving epics, hymns, funerary writings, and archaeological clues help us reconstruct some of these stories. From Mesopotamia's Gilgamesh epics to fragments of Minoan or Mycenaean lore, from Egyptian cosmic myths to the ancestral tales of China's early dynasties, these narratives shaped identities and moral values.

In this chapter, we will explore the major mythic traditions of the Bronze Age: their cosmic themes, heroic journeys, gods' roles, and how legends influenced cultural self-perception. While certain motifs (flood stories, heroic quests) recur across regions, each society tailored them to local beliefs and political needs. Myths also fueled legitimacy for kings who claimed divine descent or heroic ancestry. By studying these stories, we glean how Bronze Age people made sense of existence—bridging the earthly realm of crops and conflicts with the mysterious domain of gods and supernatural powers.

---

1. The Nature of Myth in the Bronze Age

"Myth" in the Bronze Age served multiple functions. It was not merely entertainment but a vehicle for explaining natural phenomena (floods, droughts, plagues), legitimizing social structures, and defining moral or ritual norms. Priests and scribes recorded some myths in temple archives, reading them during festivals or inscribing them on steles or tablets. Other stories survived in oral form, told by traveling bards, local elders, or families during communal gatherings.

Because writing systems were new or limited to elite circles in many places, myths circulated widely through performance, dance, and recitation. Temple rituals might dramatize a deity's victory over chaos, ensuring cosmic balance.

Mythic symbols—like the Egyptian solar boat or the Mesopotamian winged figure—appeared in art, reaffirming the presence of gods in daily life.

Importantly, myths often overlapped with epic traditions. A poem praising a king's deeds might blur lines between historical fact and divine sanction. Characters in these narratives—heroic warriors, wise kings, monstrous creatures—carried moral lessons. Over centuries, repeated retellings shaped collective memory. Even after Bronze Age polities fell, their myths endured, influencing later cultures (for example, Greek epic songs or biblical narratives possibly reflecting older Levantine or Mesopotamian themes). Thus, Bronze Age myths were both culturally rooted and historically impactful, bridging religion, tradition, and identity.

2. Mesopotamian Myth: Gilgamesh and Creation Epics

One of the oldest known epics is the **Epic of Gilgamesh**, with roots in early Bronze Age Sumerian poems that were refined in later Akkadian or Babylonian versions. Gilgamesh, a semi-divine king of Uruk, embarks on quests to defeat monsters, meets his companion Enkidu, and ultimately confronts the reality of mortality. While the standard version we have is from later second millennium BCE tablets (Middle-to-Late Bronze Age), the story's core was shaped by earlier Sumerian tales.

The epic weaves themes of friendship, heroism, arrogance, and the quest for eternal life. Gilgamesh, two-thirds god and one-third human, tyrannizes his city until the gods create Enkidu, a "wild man," to challenge him. After battling, they become friends and embark on heroic journeys—slaying the guardian Humbaba in the Cedar Forest and defying the Bull of Heaven. Enkidu's eventual death drives Gilgamesh to seek immortality, only to learn from Ut-napishtim about the flood that almost ended humanity and the futility of defying mortal fate.

Mesopotamian myth also includes creation stories like the **Enuma Elish**, which enshrines Marduk as the champion who defeats the chaotic goddess Tiamat. By forming the world from Tiamat's body, Marduk establishes cosmic order, and humans are created to serve the gods. These myths justified the political primacy of Babylon, as Marduk was Babylon's deity. Ritual recitations during the New Year festival reaffirmed the cosmic legitimacy of the king. Such narratives show how mythic drama reinforced social and divine hierarchies in Bronze Age Mesopotamia.

3. Egyptian Myth and the Quest for Cosmic Order

Egyptian myth revolved around maintaining **Ma'at**—the principle of cosmic harmony. Texts like the Pyramid Texts (Old Kingdom) and the Coffin Texts or Book of the Dead (Middle and New Kingdoms) preserve theological and mythic elements. Deities Ra, Osiris, Isis, and Set were central in explaining creation, kingship, and afterlife. Pharaohs claimed to embody Horus while living and become Osiris after death.

A prominent myth is the **Osiris-Isis cycle**: Osiris, a righteous king, is murdered by his jealous brother Set. Isis, Osiris's wife/sister, reassembles his body and conceives Horus, who later battles Set to avenge his father. Osiris becomes lord of the underworld, judging souls, while Horus rules the living. This story symbolized rebirth, tying it to the Nile's cyclical floods. It underscored the notion that rightful kingship must triumph over chaos.

Another key theme is Ra's daily journey across the sky and nightly passage through the underworld. Egyptians interpreted sunrise and sunset as Ra's continual victory over dark forces. Religious texts read during funerary rites guided the deceased's spirit, paralleling the myths of gods who overcame obstacles for rebirth. Pharaoh's role in upholding Ma'at was mythically validated: he was the pivot ensuring cosmic regularity. Temple rituals reenacted these myths, merging theology with governance.

Hence, Egyptian myths both comforted believers—promising an orderly cosmos and eternal afterlife for the righteous—and legitimized the ruling class. Scenes on temple walls depicted these narratives in stylized, formal art, reminding worshipers that the gods, monarchy, and cosmic cycles were inseparably linked.

---

4. Minoan and Mycenaean Tales: Echoes in Greek Myth

While Minoan Crete and Mycenaean Greece left few direct mythic texts (Linear A is undeciphered, and Linear B tablets mostly record inventories or administrative notes), later Greek myths contain possible echoes of these Bronze Age cultures. The **Minotaur** story—King Minos of Crete locking a bull-man creature in the Labyrinth—may reflect Minoan bull-leaping rituals and labyrinthine palace architecture at Knossos. The tale of Theseus slaying the Minotaur could symbolize mainland Greek resistance or infiltration into Minoan power.

Similarly, Mycenaean palaces worshiped deities that appear as proto-forms of the classical Greek pantheon. Some Linear B tablets mention "Posedeia" (Poseidon), "Diwia" (Zeus's consort?), or "E-re-u-ti-ja" (perhaps Eileithyia, a childbirth goddess). This implies that heroic figures in later epics, such as Agamemnon, Menelaus, or Achilles, might trace roots to real Mycenaean kings or warriors. The Trojan War saga, as described in Homer's *Iliad* (written centuries later), may reflect a memory of Mycenaean conflicts with Anatolian cities like Troy (Wilusa in Hittite records?).

Thus, Minoan-Mycenaean mythic content survived indirectly through Greek oral tradition. After the Bronze Age Collapse, traveling bards recounted heroic genealogies, weaving them into narratives that crystallized in the Archaic era (8th–7th century BCE). The gods' involvement in mortal affairs—a hallmark of Greek myth—mirrors older Near Eastern patterns. In effect, the "mythic tapestry" inherited by classical Greece carried strands from the palatial Bronze Age, reimagined through centuries of oral retelling.

---

5. The Indus Valley: Elusive Myths and Cultural Memory

The Indus Valley civilization, centered on Harappa and Mohenjo-daro, left seals and figurines that hint at a mythic worldview—unicorn motifs, horned deities, mother-goddess figures—but no deciphered texts describing their gods or heroic legends. Later South Asian religious traditions in the Iron Age (the Vedic culture) provide some parallel references to earlier traditions, but direct links to the Indus remain debated.

Some scholars propose that certain Indus seals depicting a seated, horned figure surrounded by animals might be an early form of the god Shiva or a proto-Pashupati ("lord of creatures"). Figurines of female deities or animals could represent fertility cults or mother goddesses. However, without readable texts, we cannot confirm a narrative akin to Gilgamesh or Osiris. It is possible that oral myths flourished among Indus communities, telling stories about creation, floods (like later Vedic references to a cosmic flood?), or local heroes.

When the Indus urban centers declined (c. 1900 BCE, earlier than the Late Bronze Age meltdown in the Mediterranean), local traditions may have dispersed among rural or migrating groups. Over centuries, these might have merged with incoming Indo-Aryan myths. Later Hindu epics (the *Mahabharata*, *Ramayana*) and Puranic tales contain faint echoes of ancient structures, but the direct continuity from Indus myths remains speculative. While we lack explicit Indus legends, the civilization's art and religious artifacts suggest a mythic dimension that shaped daily life, overshadowed by the ephemeral nature of non-literate traditions.

---

6. Hittite and Anatolian Myth: Storm Gods and Kings

The Hittites in Anatolia compiled extensive mythic-cultic texts in cuneiform, including adaptations of Hurrian, Luwian, or Mesopotamian stories. Central to Hittite religion was the **Storm God** (often named Tarhun or Teshub in Hurrian contexts), who fought chaos monsters or overcame rebellious mountains. Another deity was the **Sun Goddess of Arinna**, representing order and sovereignty. The Hittite king performed rituals to appease these gods, often reciting mythic narratives that recounted cosmic battles ensuring seasonal fertility.

One notable Hittite text is the **"Illuyanka" myth**, where the Storm God battles a serpent (Illuyanka). The serpent initially triumphs, but the Storm God, with help from a mortal, later defeats it. This cyclical myth of gods fighting serpents echoes Mesopotamian Tiamat vs. Marduk or the Canaanite Baal vs. Yam, suggesting cross-cultural mythic influences. Another cycle involves the vanished god Telipinu, whose disappearance causes famine until the gods track him down, symbolizing the return of fertility after drought.

Hittite mythic texts also show the empire's absorptive approach. They incorporated Hurrian epics about Kumarbi, who fathered gods like Teshub, reminiscent of an older Near Eastern pattern of succession among deities. In these stories, cosmic struggles mirror the Hittite emphasis on a king's role to maintain stability. Ritual instructions often accompanied myths, specifying offerings or recitations for festivals. This integration of myth into state religion strengthened the monarchy's bond with the divine realm, a hallmark of Bronze Age Anatolia.

---

7. Chinese Early Dynastic Legends: Sage Kings and Ancestral Spirits

In China, the Shang Dynasty used oracle bones, inscribed with questions to ancestral or celestial powers. While direct mythic narratives on these bones are sparse, later Chinese traditions reference prehistoric "sage kings" who tamed floods or invented agriculture—like Yu the Great, who controlled flooding, or Shen Nong (the Divine Farmer). Such stories reflect an older stratum of myth that might date to the late Neolithic or early Bronze Age.

Ancestral worship was central. The Shang king served as the chief intermediary, ensuring the ancestors supported the living. Clan-based genealogies linked current rulers to semi-mythic forebears. These genealogies sometimes included episodes of miraculous births or heroic feats that established the clan's legitimacy. Though not epic poems in the Mesopotamian sense, these traditions functioned similarly—to unify the community under a sense of divine lineage.

With the Zhou conquest of the Shang around 1046 BCE, new concepts emerged, like the **Mandate of Heaven**, which retroactively framed Shang's downfall as a moral failing. Yet older mythic elements—sacrificial rites, references to sky or storm deities—persisted. Later Chinese texts from the Zhou and beyond recount legendary rulers (Huangdi, Yao, Shun) who preceded the Shang, crediting them with moral and technological leaps. While some tales formed after the Bronze Age, they likely drew on older oral motifs that had circulated among early dynasties, bridging myth with historical memory.

---

8. European Legends: Megalithic Echoes and Proto-Indo-European Themes

In Bronze Age Europe, beyond the Aegean, literacy was scarce, so myths remain mostly speculative. Yet megalithic monuments (from earlier Neolithic phases) often continued in ritual usage, potentially tied to local creation or ancestral myths. Barrow burials might have spawned heroic legends around the person interred. Rock carvings in Scandinavia depict sun wheels, ships, or spirals, suggesting a solar or fertility cult.

Later Iron Age Celtic or Germanic traditions contain certain recurring motifs: sky gods fighting giants or serpents, ancestral heroes traveling by boat. Some anthropologists suggest these could reflect long-standing Indo-European mythic themes (like "the thunder-god vs. serpentine chaos"), with local Bronze

Age societies elaborating them in oral sagas. In the absence of direct text, we rely on iconography (spiral patterns, weapons in hoards) to guess that narratives of heroic deeds or cyclical cosmic battles existed.

When classical Greek or Roman authors encountered northern Europeans, they recorded glimpses of tribal myths about ancestors descending from gods, or nature spirits dwelling in forests and rivers. These stories may have Bronze Age roots, having evolved for centuries in preliterate societies. The fact that many such motifs (the heroic dragon-slayer, divine twins, or a mother goddess) appear widely across Indo-European cultures suggests a deep shared mythic heritage, shaped by local Bronze Age contexts.

---

9. Flood Myths and Shared Story Patterns

A striking motif across multiple Bronze Age cultures is the **flood myth**. In Mesopotamia, Ut-napishtim's story in the Gilgamesh epic parallels the earlier Sumerian tale of Ziusudra or the Akkadian Atrahasis myth—where the gods flood the earth, but one righteous man is warned to build a boat, saving humanity and animals. This resonates with later biblical accounts of Noah's ark, indicating a widespread flood tradition in the Near East.

Ancient Chinese legends also include flood-controlling heroes (like Yu), though the details differ. Some scholars see a common recognition of devastating floods along major rivers as the impetus for these stories. In each version, the flood myth cements a moral lesson: the favored hero's piety or diligence wins divine mercy, restarting civilization under new terms.

Such parallels reflect more than chance. Trade routes and migrations allowed myths to migrate, or else human societies spontaneously developed flood lore from real flood experiences. Either way, these stories offered theological explanations for water disasters and gave rulers a heroic precedent for taming chaos. By the late Bronze Age, scribes in Mesopotamia had standardized the Gilgamesh flood narrative, which likely spread through Levantine connections, eventually influencing post-Bronze Age traditions in the region.

10. Heroes and Divine Ancestry in Bronze Age Genealogies

Across Bronze Age polities, rulers boasted genealogies linking them to gods or legendary heroes. Egyptian pharaohs traced lineage to Ra or other primeval gods. Mesopotamian kings might claim descent from Gilgamesh or city-patron deities. The Hittite monarchy invoked the Storm God's backing, and Mycenaean elites claimed heroic forefathers—like Perseus or Heracles in later Greek tradition. In China, the Shang royal clan traced ancestry to mythical founder-heroes, ensuring rightful dominion.

These genealogies served a propaganda function, reinforcing hierarchical authority. If a king was literally or symbolically "son of the sky god," disobedience became sacrilege. Temples or scribes produced official genealogical lists, sometimes spanning centuries, to legitimate continuity. Such lists might include improbable lifespans or miraculous births, further elevating the monarchy above ordinary folk.

Sometimes, local or rival dynasties constructed competing genealogies. For instance, in Mesopotamia, each city-state might highlight a different heroic founder or sponsor deity. The existence of multiple versions of Gilgamesh's line or differing accounts of certain ancestral gods reveals that mythic genealogies were malleable political tools. Over time, these genealogies merged into epic cycles (like those known from the Greek epics) or official "king lists" in Mesopotamia or Hittite annals. This melding of myth and recorded history shaped how Bronze Age societies conceptualized authority and tradition.

---

11. Mythic Rituals: Dramatizing Cosmic Battles

Bronze Age temples often staged ritual performances reenacting mythic battles—like the Mesopotamian New Year festival (Akitu), where priests recited the Enuma Elish, dramatizing Marduk's defeat of Tiamat. The communal retelling underscored the cyclical renewal of cosmic order. Similarly, Egyptian festivals might involve carrying statues of gods in processions to depict a victory over Seth's chaos or the journey of the sun through the underworld each night.

Such theatrical or ceremonial enactments engaged participants beyond mere listening. Processions, music, dance, and offerings made the myths tangible. In some Minoan contexts, bull-leaping events could be read as symbolic confrontations with primal forces, though textual evidence is scant. The Hittites had detailed instructions for festivals, including references to reciting heroic or creation myths to reaffirm the Storm God's guardianship.

Ritual objects—bronze weapons representing a god's power, or figurines embodying mythic characters—reinforced these dramas. By witnessing or joining these rites, citizens felt connected to the cosmos. This fused myth with social identity: the ongoing cosmic struggle paralleled daily challenges of farmland fertility, stable governance, and protection from enemies. Mythic rituals thus bridged religious belief and communal experience, forging solidarity in the face of uncertainties that defined Bronze Age life.

---

12. Oracles, Omens, and Mythic Authority

Throughout the Bronze Age, leaders turned to oracles or diviners for guidance, often referencing mythic precedents. In Shang China, oracle bones explicitly mention seeking ancestral or divine approval for hunts, battles, or harvest times. The interpretive process might evoke mythical tales of how ancestors overcame adversity with help from high gods. In Mesopotamia, extispicy (reading sheep livers) drew on the cosmic framework where gods signaled their will.

Myths justified why certain omens mattered. A favorable sign could mean the king mirrored Gilgamesh's success or the Storm God's triumph. Unfavorable omens might recall stories of a hero undone by hubris, urging caution. Egyptian priests performed dream interpretations or star-watching, relating them to the cosmic journeys of Ra or Osiris. Hittite kings asked oracles about war campaigns, perhaps reciting lines from the Illuyanka myth if the threat was serpentine or from an enemy region known for rebellious "chaos."

Thus, mythic authority undergirded oracular decisions. When priests declared a sign aligned with heroic tradition, the king or generals complied. Myth became an active force shaping policy. If an expedition succeeded, it validated both the mythic parallel and the diviner's skill. Over time, the boundary blurred between real political events and their mythic framing, ensuring that every major Bronze Age endeavor carried a narrative weight linking mortal actions to the cosmic tapestry.

13. Cultural Exchange of Myths Across Regions

Just as goods traveled among Bronze Age polities, so did story motifs. Hittite texts incorporate Hurrian and Mesopotamian myths. Canaanite deities like Baal appear in Egyptian references. Mycenaean traders might have heard tales of Gilgamesh in Levantine ports or recounted their own heroic lore in foreign courts. The shared flood motif suggests possible diffusion or parallel invention.

Diplomatic marriages, like those documented in the Amarna Letters, could bring foreign priestesses or scribes who carried home legends of their gods. Traveling artisans or mercenaries might share local myths around campfires, planting seeds of cross-cultural motifs. Over generations, these seeds could sprout hybrid stories—such as the assimilation of Mesopotamian dragon-slaying images into Hittite or Greek contexts.

Archaeological finds—cylinder seals with foreign divine symbols in Mycenaean graves, or Egyptian scarabs in Syrian temples—indicate an exchange of religious or mythic iconography. While language barriers slowed full textual adoption, visual representations or partial retellings could still spread. By the late Bronze Age, the Eastern Mediterranean was a patchwork of overlapping mythic influences, each site adapting borrowed tales to suit local needs. This fluid network set a foundation for the multi-cultural storytelling that blossomed in the Iron Age, bridging older mythic traditions with newly formed epics or scriptures.

14. Mythic Resonances with the Bronze Age Collapse

As the Bronze Age ended, mythic themes of cosmic upheaval and heroic struggle took on new resonance. A city destroyed by unknown enemies might be likened to a god punishing a rebellious realm, fitting older tropes of divine wrath or inevitable fate. Survivors invoked older heroic myths to rationalize adversity or inspire hope in rebuilding.

Later accounts of the Trojan War, for example, reflect a memory of Mycenaean conflicts, recast through a mythical lens that overshadowed purely historical detail. The "Sea Peoples" invasions could be reinterpreted as primeval chaos forces raging against the old order, paralleling myths where gods or heroes tried to hold back destructive floods or monstrous armies. Even genealogies might shift, linking post-collapse leaders to prior heroic lines to reaffirm continuity.

In places like Mesopotamia or Egypt, scribes recorded the downfall of neighbors as divine punishment for hubris, reinforcing moral themes in myth. Hittite fragments suggest a final attempt by kings to appease the gods through elaborate rituals, reminiscent of earlier cosmic battles. Once the dust settled, new polities molded these myths to justify their rise—promoting the idea that they alone had the gods' favor after a universal purge. The Bronze Age Collapse thus provided real-world chaos that mythic narratives could interpret, melding historical crisis with cosmic drama.

15. The Enduring Legacy of Bronze Age Myths

Long after Bronze Age societies vanished or transformed, their myths persisted, either through direct textual transmission (like Gilgamesh in cuneiform libraries) or via reworked oral epics. Greek epic tradition gave us the *Iliad* and *Odyssey*, capturing echoes of Mycenaean legendary material. The biblical texts of the Iron Age contain flood references, genealogies, and narratives possibly shaped by earlier Canaanite or Mesopotamian influences. Egyptian religion, in diminished form, continued until the Roman era, still referencing Osiris or Ra.

Assyrian and Babylonian scribes preserved and copied older Sumerian and Akkadian myths, ensuring Gilgamesh, Atrahasis, and Enuma Elish reached libraries like that of Ashurbanipal in Nineveh. When archaeologists rediscovered these tablets in the 19th century CE, the modern world learned that biblical stories, Greek hero tales, and other traditions had antecedents in Bronze Age narratives. This revelation shaped comparative mythology, opening vistas on cultural diffusion.

Today, Bronze Age myths capture the imagination through retellings in popular culture—novels, films, or fantasy works inspired by Gilgamesh or Minoan labyrinths. Scholars appreciate them as primal templates for later heroic cycles, cosmic dualities, and moral parables. They remind us that ancient peoples, across thousands of miles, grappled with universal questions about mortality, creation, and the interplay of chaos and order. The Bronze Age myths remain a living testament to how stories forge communal identities, bridging the ephemeral to the eternal.

CHAPTER 20: LASTING LEGACIES OF THE BRONZE AGE

Introduction

The Bronze Age, spanning millennia and encompassing vast regions of Eurasia and North Africa, ended long ago. Yet its achievements in metalworking, urban organization, writing systems, trade networks, and cultural expressions profoundly influenced subsequent epochs. Even after the Bronze Age Collapse, many innovations—like the fundamentals of scribal bureaucracy, monumental architecture, religious traditions, and social hierarchies—continued, transforming but never vanishing. Later civilizations, from classical Greece to the Neo-Assyrian Empire, from Iron Age Europe to the Shang-Zhou transitions in China, built on Bronze Age foundations.

In this final chapter, we will explore the **lasting legacies of the Bronze Age**: the inventions, institutions, and ideas that endured or evolved in the Iron Age and beyond. We will discuss how states inherited bureaucratic practices, how literacy advanced from earlier scripts, how cultural memory of heroic or divine genealogies shaped identity, and how trade patterns adapted. By tracing these legacies, we see that the Bronze Age was not an isolated "primitive era," but a formative period whose imprint resonates through ancient history—even influencing aspects of our modern world.

---

1. The Invention and Spread of Metallurgy

The defining feature of the Bronze Age was the discovery and mastery of bronze—an alloy of copper and tin (with occasional arsenic or lead). This technology revolutionized tools, weapons, and craft production. Even after iron supplanted bronze for everyday implements, bronze's role in decorative, ceremonial, or specialist objects continued. In many cultures, bronze casting remained central for statues, ritual vessels, or high-status items.

The piece-mold casting technique in Shang China influenced later Chinese metalworking traditions, producing elaborate bronzes for centuries. In the Mediterranean, bronze coinage eventually appeared (though more common in the Iron Age), building on earlier metal-weighing practices. The knowledge of smelting, alloying, and mold-making pioneered in the Bronze Age paved the way for iron smelting breakthroughs. Metallurgy expanded regionally—nomadic tribes gained forging skills, smaller communities accessed simpler forms of metal production.

Beyond the technical realm, the social and economic infrastructure around metal—mining, trade caravans, workshops—remained critical. Even as states collapsed, local blacksmiths or bronze-smiths preserved core knowledge, ensuring a continuity of metal expertise. The sophistication of Bronze Age metallurgical networks laid the groundwork for the Iron Age expansion, demonstrating that once humankind mastered metal, the path toward more advanced forging was inevitable.

2. Urban Planning and Architectural Templates

Bronze Age societies advanced in constructing planned cities, monumental temples, and palaces. The Indus civilization's grid layouts, baked-brick architecture, and drainage systems informed later South Asian urban design. Mesopotamian traditions of city walls, ziggurat temples, and canal-based infrastructures influenced subsequent empires like the Neo-Assyrian or Neo-Babylonian states, which still built on older city foundations (Nineveh, Babylon).

Egypt's knowledge of stone building, gleaned from erecting pyramids and massive temple complexes, continued well into the Late Period and Ptolemaic times. Similarly, the Aegean palatial style—central courtyards, storerooms, elaborate drainage—echoed in smaller Iron Age city layouts, though adapted to new defensive concerns. The Mycenaean megaron concept (a large hall with a central hearth) may have influenced later Greek temple ground plans (a main cella or naos preceded by columns).

In Anatolia, Hittite construction of multi-gate fortifications and integrated temple-palace districts provided a model for later Neo-Hittite or Aramaean polities. Even Europe's hillfort expansions in the Iron Age might reflect lessons from Bronze Age fortification knowledge. Thus, while some grand structures fell to ruin, the architectural logic they embodied—walled enclaves, storerooms for surplus, designated ritual areas—remained essential for new polities reorganizing after the collapse.

3. Bureaucratic and Administrative Practices

The Bronze Age introduced sophisticated record-keeping to manage surpluses, labor, and trade. **Cuneiform** in Mesopotamia and the Hittite realm, **hieroglyphics** and **hieratic** in Egypt, **Linear B** in Mycenaean Greece, and **oracle bone script** in Shang China all represent early bureaucratic writing. Even if some scripts disappeared post-collapse, the notion of systematically tracking resources or correspondences endured.

In Mesopotamia, cuneiform remained the official record medium for centuries, forming an unbroken chain of administrative tradition. The concept of written law codes—exemplified by Hammurabi—reappeared in subsequent monarchies, emphasizing the king's role as lawgiver. Egypt's scribal class, though battered during intermediate periods, revived with each dynasty, continuing temple and state documentation.

When new scripts emerged—like the Phoenician alphabet—they built on the impetus for literacy established by Bronze Age scribes. The idea that writing was essential to legitimate governance, manage tributes, and formalize treaties came from centuries of palace-temple practice. Even Greek city-states, once they reacquired writing in the 8th century BCE, used it for law codes, dedicatory inscriptions, and official decrees, echoing older patterns of administrative literacy. Hence, the Bronze Age's scribal bureaucracy laid a universal template for state functioning in the ancient world.

---

4. Religious Continuity and Temple Structures

Despite the Bronze Age Collapse, many religious sites and beliefs persisted into the Iron Age, evolving rather than vanishing. In Mesopotamia, venerable temples to gods like Ishtar, Marduk, or Shamash remained functional. New dynasties rebuilt or enlarged them, referencing older inscriptions or mythic precedents. Egyptian temples dedicated to Amun, Ptah, or Ra continued usage, albeit sometimes under separate local authorities.

The Hittite pantheon survived in Neo-Hittite city-states, albeit localized. Storm God shrines still dotted Anatolia, if on a smaller scale. Bronze Age figures like Teshub (Hurrian Storm God) or Kubaba (a mother goddess) had cults that endured for centuries. In the Levant, Canaanite deities transitioned into

Phoenician or Aramaean worship, with Baal, El, and Astarte continuing as central gods. Even in the Aegean, smaller shrines to local or Mycenaean-derived deities eventually contributed to the classical Greek pantheon.

Temple architecture might adapt to Iron Age aesthetics, but the concept of a sacred precinct for communal worship and sacrifice remained. Priestly roles also carried over, albeit with different political alignments. The mythic traditions these temples preserved shaped how Iron Age peoples approached divinity. Thus, the Bronze Age gift of large, organized religious institutions survived, bridging the collapse and reemerging in various forms.

5. Heroic Ideals and Epic Traditions

A major cultural legacy is the heroic tradition. Myths and epic poems from the Bronze Age formed seeds for later works that shaped entire literary canons. The Mesopotamian **Epic of Gilgamesh** persisted in libraries, re-copied by scribes in the first millennium BCE. Greek epic cycles grew from Mycenaean heroic lore, eventually culminating in Homer's *Iliad* and *Odyssey*. These epics served as cornerstones of Greek identity, inspiring ethics, education, and political discourse.

Such hero narratives often glorified virtues like bravery, loyalty, cunning, or piety. They also reminded audiences of the impermanence of even mighty palaces. Ties to Bronze Age genealogies gave Iron Age elites a sense of antiquity—rulers might claim descent from Achilles or Gilgamesh-like figures, harnessing ancient mystique. Poetry recitations in public gatherings kept these legends alive, bridging preliterate Bronze Age wonders with textual Iron Age societies.

Though details changed over centuries of retelling, the fundamental concept that "there was once a greater age of heroes, tested by gods and epic battles" shaped cultural memory. Philosophers or prophets might critique or reinterpret these stories, but the heroic ethos remained embedded in art, political propaganda, and religious festivals. This underscores how Bronze Age legends became keystones for identity formation well into classical eras.

6. Trade Routes and Cross-Cultural Influences

The Bronze Age created extensive trade networks, linking copper from Cyprus, tin from distant mines, precious stones from Central Asia, and manufactured goods from palace workshops. While the Late Bronze Age meltdown disrupted these routes, many re-emerged in the Iron Age under new control. Phoenicians took the lead in maritime trade, forging ties with North Africa, Iberia, and beyond, drawing partly on the maritime experience of Minoans and Mycenaeans.

Assyrian conquests consolidated overland routes, establishing safe corridors for merchants from the Persian Gulf to the Mediterranean. This revived markets for metals, textiles, and luxury items. Over time, Greek traders also joined, bridging the Aegean, Levant, and eventually the Black Sea. The impetus for large-scale exchange, begun in the Bronze Age, did not vanish—it reconfigured, with different states seizing opportunities.

Moreover, cultural influences piggybacked on commerce. New alphabets spread from the Levant to Greece, possibly influenced by older cuneiform-based systems. Artwork or religious motifs, like the griffin or solar disk, might appear in new contexts. Iron Age societies refined or re-contextualized Bronze Age forms, fostering the ongoing diffusion of styles. Even centuries later, the memory of Bronze Age wealth (like the "gold-rich Mycenae" in Homer) propelled explorers or merchants to seek out old trade routes or rumored resources. The concept of long-distance commerce as an engine for prosperity traced back to Bronze Age precedent.

---

7. Feudal and Vassal Models in Post-Collapse States

Many Bronze Age states practiced a form of overlordship over vassal territories—most famously the Hittites, who used treaties to bind local kings. This diplomatic approach, anchored by tribute and mutual defense, set a pattern for Iron Age expansions. The Neo-Assyrian Empire also used vassal treaties with strict clauses, echoing Hittite precedents. China's Zhou Dynasty developed a feudal system after toppling Shang, granting territories to relatives and allies—arguably reminiscent of Bronze Age clan-based governance.

While structures changed, the underlying principle—central authority delegating power to subordinates who pay tribute—remained. In certain Greek city-states, the concept of basileus leading lesser chiefs might reflect Mycenaean traditions carried into the "dark age." In Europe, hillfort chieftains forming alliances or paying respect to a regional strongman can also be traced to the earlier Tumulus or Urnfield cultures.

Thus, the Bronze Age's multi-layered governance, with a hierarchy of loyal local rulers, left an imprint on subsequent political formations. Some direct lines of continuity (like Hittite treaties influencing Neo-Hittite or Aramaean states) are archaeologically and textually documented. Others are more thematic, showing how the idea of controlling large territories through subordinate alliances endured as a practical strategy for forging early empires in the Iron Age.

8. Memory of Great Builders and Engineering

People in later eras marveled at Bronze Age monuments: the Egyptian pyramids, Mesopotamian ziggurats, the "Cyclopean" walls of Mycenae. Iron Age Greeks believed mythical Cyclopes built Mycenaean fortifications because they seemed beyond normal human capability. Egyptians continued to restore or build near older temples, reverently preserving the aura of Old and Middle Kingdom sites. Assyrian kings boasted of restoring ancient sanctuaries, linking themselves to storied Sumerian or Akkadian pasts.

This veneration of old architecture was not purely antiquarian curiosity; it served national or dynastic propaganda. Claiming stewardship over venerable monuments conferred legitimacy. Explorers or conquerors rummaging through old palace ruins might adopt surviving iconography or re-carve inscriptions, reasserting continuity. Greek or biblical sources referencing "ancient walls" or "giant tombs" reflect how Bronze Age feats remained in cultural consciousness as the works of heroic ancestors.

Over time, these monuments inspired engineering breakthroughs—like refined stone cutting or advanced approaches to city planning. The methods for large-scale building discovered in the Bronze Age continued evolving. Even if not all techniques were directly documented, local masons or families of builders passed knowledge generationally. The mystique of monumental building—pyramids, labyrinthine palaces, massive fortresses—shaped Iron Age ambitions, fueling a sense that grand architecture signaled divine or royal might.

9. Artistic Motifs and Decorative Continuity

Artistic motifs—spirals, rosettes, winged creatures, bull iconography—did not vanish at the Bronze Age's end. They reappeared on Iron Age pottery, metalwork, or architectural reliefs. For example, the Phoenicians used Egyptian and Mesopotamian motifs in their ivory carvings, shipping them across the Mediterranean. Mycenaean decorative elements (spirals, waves) influenced the Protogeometric and Geometric phases in early Greek pottery.

In Anatolia, the Neo-Hittite states continued sculpting basalt orthostats with scenes of feasts or hunts, reminiscent of Hittite palace reliefs. The motif of a ruler smiting enemies or clasping a libation cup survived as a sign of authority. Bronzes in China also retained taotie masks well into the Zhou, though with evolving styles. The concept of blending geometric designs with stylized animals carried forward.

These continuities exemplify how artists and craftsmen—despite political collapse—maintained older traditions, adapting them to new patrons or tastes. Over time, cross-cultural influences might shift emphasis (e.g., more figurative scenes, or simpler geometric patterns), but the deep visual vocabulary from Bronze Age cultures remained a creative wellspring. Even in Europe, "Celtic" art from the Iron Age might trace some swirling patterns back to earlier Urnfield or Atlantic Bronze Age motifs.

---

10. Mythic Genealogies in Post-Bronze Age Dynasties

Royal lineages in the Iron Age often claimed Bronze Age heroes or gods as ancestors. In Greece, city-states boasted founders linked to legendary Mycenaean kings or demigods (e.g., Athens linked to Cecrops, Sparta to the Heracleidae). The Neo-Hittite kings might reference the old Hittite imperial line, adopting ancestral cults. Babylonian rulers used genealogies that traced them to ancient Sumerian or Akkadian dynasties, conflating myth and history.

Such genealogical claims bridged the gap between present rule and the "golden age" memory of Bronze Age might. It legitimized new regimes by implying continuity with revered ancestors or divine sponsors. Even if the exact lineages were fictional, they consolidated social trust in monarchy. Over centuries, these genealogies shaped national myths. The Roman tradition of descending from Trojan refugees (Aeneas) is a later Iron Age–classical era example, but it shows how Bronze Age Trojan War lore was retooled to serve new genealogical narratives.

Thus, the Bronze Age's storied elites—like Gilgamesh in Mesopotamia, Minos in Crete, or the Shang ancestors in China—kept inspiring claims to greatness. The power of these genealogies was not just in history but in mythic resonance, conferring cosmic or heroic legitimacy to Iron Age rulers forging fresh polities on old foundations.

---

11. Evolution of Writing Systems and Education

While some Bronze Age scripts vanished (Linear B, Hittite cuneiform, Indus script), the impulse to record governance, trade, and mythic tradition endured. New alphabets emerged—Phoenician, Aramaic, Greek—each simpler to learn than cuneiform or hieroglyphs. This shift from complex signs to phonetic alphabets gradually widened literacy beyond specialized scribes.

Cuneiform itself survived in Mesopotamia, though refined and used by fewer scribes as Aramaic gained traction. Egyptian hieroglyphs continued but were increasingly used in religious texts, while Demotic script (a simplified form) gained popularity for everyday writing. In China, Shang oracle bone characters evolved into Zhou bronzes and later forms, leading eventually to the standardization of Chinese script under the Qin and Han dynasties.

The Bronze Age legacy here is that once literacy took root, societies rarely abandoned it altogether. The conceptual framework—writing used to fix law codes, store myths, coordinate trade—remained. The next wave of scripts built on the principle of record-keeping established in palatial bureaucracies. Over time, literacy spread to new social classes, fueling intellectual leaps in philosophy, science, and literature. The impetus to "write things down" in a systematic way was a Bronze Age gift that flowered in the Iron Age's more diverse educational contexts.

---

12. Comparative Religion and Mythology: Modern Discoveries

Modern scholars only rediscovered many Bronze Age myths in the last two centuries, through excavations of Mesopotamian libraries (like Nineveh), the decipherment of Egyptian hieroglyphs, or the unearthing of Linear B tablets. This has dramatically enhanced our understanding of ancient religious traditions. Gilgamesh's epic, for instance, was unknown in medieval or early modern Europe. Its reintroduction reshaped biblical and classical studies, revealing earlier flood stories and heroic motifs.

The same applies to Hittite archives discovered at Bogazköy (Hattusa) or the Minoan frescoes at Knossos. These findings showed that Greek myth drew heavily on prior Aegean and Near Eastern influences, challenging older notions of an isolated classical heritage. Indus seals perplex modern scholars, hinting at a lost mythic dimension. Chinese oracle bones similarly confirm a sophisticated Bronze Age religious practice with deep mythic underpinnings.

This rediscovery has fueled comparative mythology, revealing cross-cultural parallels in cosmic battles, flood myths, or hero journeys. It highlights the deep unity of human storytelling: Bronze Age societies from distinct language families often shared structural mythic themes. As more tablets, inscriptions, and artifacts surface, our appreciation for the Bronze Age's role as a cradle of mythic imagination grows.

---

13. Political Ideas: Divine Right, Law Codes, and Empire Governance

Another long-lasting legacy is the notion that rulers had a **divine mandate** or cosmic sanction—whether by "Mandate of Heaven" in China, or direct sonship of gods in Mesopotamia and Egypt. The Bronze Age normalized the idea that kings answer to a higher cosmic order, guiding empire-building from the second millennium BCE onward. Even in medieval Europe, the concept of "divine right of kings" has partial analogies to Bronze Age ideologies.

Law codes, such as Hammurabi's, shaped future legal traditions. The idea that laws should be publicly displayed or that crimes had graded punishments according to social status resonates in later ancient civilizations. The memory of a "great lawgiver" or wise king issuing a codified set of rules also appears in Greek tradition (e.g., laws of Lycurgus or Solon) and beyond. Although not a direct unbroken chain, the precedent of systematic law from the Bronze Age influenced how subsequent rulers approached governance and justice.

In empire governance, the practice of installing vassals or governors, collecting tribute, and using official seals or documents to confirm loyalty was standard in Bronze Age polities like the Hittites, Egypt, and Mesopotamia. Iron Age empires, from Assyria to Persia, refined these methods. This continuity in statecraft shows how organizational frameworks from the Bronze Age undergirded future large-scale political systems.

---

14. Artistic and Literary Inspiration in Later Eras

Bronze Age art motifs continued to inspire subsequent ages. Greek sculptors admired Egyptian proportions or derived column designs reminiscent of older palace forms. Renaissance and modern artists eventually rediscovered Minoan frescoes and Mycenaean gold masks, shaping how we interpret "classical roots." Mesopotamian lamassu or Egyptian sphinxes reappeared in neo styles during the 19th-century "Egyptomania" or "Assyrian Revival."

Literary inspiration also abounds. Gilgamesh's quest surfaces in countless modern retellings, influencing fantasy or epic genres. The Trojan War narrative, rooted in Mycenaean conflict, remains a staple of Western literature, from ancient Greek plays to modern novels and films. Contemporary retellings of the Minotaur or Osiris myth reimagine Bronze Age mythic archetypes for new audiences. Even Chinese historical dramas sometimes allude to the mystique of Shang or Zhou legends.

These artistic afterlives show that Bronze Age creativity was not sealed in the past. The timeless allure of labyrinths, bull-leapers, heroic journeys, cosmic floods, and divine kingship continues to captivate. The depth of emotion in epic narratives or the grandeur of colossal temples resonates with universal human questions about identity, mortality, and the quest for meaning—ensuring that Bronze Age motifs remain a wellspring of cross-cultural fascination.

---

15. Lessons on Systemic Vulnerability

Finally, the collapse that ended the Bronze Age stands as a cautionary tale. The interconnected "world system" of trade, diplomacy, and resource dependencies unraveled under cumulative stressors. Modern scholars draw parallels: overreliance on global supply chains, climate-induced agriculture crises, migrations due to conflict or famine. The lesson is that advanced complexity can breed vulnerability if alternative resilience strategies are lacking.

However, the rebuilding that led to the Iron Age also teaches us that creativity and adaptation can arise from devastation. Societies that learned to pivot—adopting iron, forging new alliances, decentralizing power—eventually flourished. So the Bronze Age legacy is twofold: it exemplifies high cultural achievement, vibrant trade, and sophisticated states, but also highlights how fragile these achievements can be under converging pressures.

Modern researchers thus see the Bronze Age both as a success story of early civilization and a reminder of cyclical patterns in history. Its final collapse underscores that no matter how advanced, societies must constantly adjust to environmental, economic, and social shifts. The lasting legacy is a deeper understanding of how human innovation and vulnerability go hand in hand, shaping long-range historical processes.

---

16. Conclusion: An Enduring Foundation for Human Civilization

The Bronze Age ended millennia ago, but its inheritance remains woven into the fabric of later civilizations. Metalworking, urban planning, writing systems, temple religions, heroic myths—these all carried forward, either directly or through transformations in the Iron Age and beyond. Once-lost epics reemerged from clay tablets, bridging ancient voices with modern curiosity. Monuments that once symbolized cosmic order still captivate as archaeological wonders. Religious structures and genealogical claims from Bronze Age polities echo in the mythic genealogies of classical, biblical, or Chinese traditions.

In capturing the Bronze Age's achievements—whether the Ziggurats of Mesopotamia, the Great Pyramids of Egypt, the palaces of Knossos or Mycenae, the Indus urban designs, or the Shang bronzes—we see a remarkable period of creativity and interconnection. Even the catastrophic collapse that followed did not erase these cultural bedrocks. Instead, they persisted or inspired reinvention, underpinning the Iron Age expansions of empire, the dawn of classical Greek culture, and the advanced states in East Asia.

Thus, the Bronze Age stands as a pivotal chapter in humanity's shared story, forging lasting legacies in governance, art, myth, and technology. Its memory lives on in the silent ruins that once bustled with trade and ceremony, in epic tales told through centuries, and in the fundamental tools of civilization—metallurgy, writing, monumental building, religious frameworks—that we continue to use. As we conclude our exploration of this era, we recognize how deeply its legacy extends into all subsequent epochs of ancient history and, in subtle ways, into our present world.

Help Us Share Your Thoughts!

Dear reader,

Thank you for spending your time with this book. We hope it brought you enjoyment and a few new ideas to think about. If there was anything that didn't work for you, or if you have suggestions on how we can improve, please let us know at **kontakt@skriuwer.com**. Your feedback means a lot to us and helps us make our books even better.

If you enjoyed this book, we would be very grateful if you left a review on the site where you purchased it. Your review not only helps other readers find our books, but also encourages us to keep creating more stories and materials that you'll love.

By choosing Skriuwer, you're also supporting **Frisian**—a minority language mainly spoken in the northern Netherlands. Although **Frisian** has a rich history, the number of speakers is shrinking, and it's at risk of dying out. Your purchase helps fund resources to preserve and promote this language, such as educational programs and learning tools. If you'd like to learn more about Frisian or even start learning it yourself, please visit **www.learnfrisian.com**.

Thank you for being part of our community. We look forward to sharing more books with you in the future.

Warm regards,
The Skriuwer Team

www.ingramcontent.com/pod-product-compliance
Lightning Source LLC
LaVergne TN
LVHW012038070526
838202LV00056B/5539